PORTRAIT OF THE ISLES OF SCILLY

OTHER *PORTRAIT* BOOKS

Portrait of the
ISLES OF SCILLY

CLIVE MUMFORD

Foreword by the
Rt. Hon. Harold Wilson, M.P.

ILLUSTRATED
AND WITH MAP

Third Edition

ROBERT HALE · LONDON

First edition August 1967
Second edition May 1968
Third edition June 1970

ISBN 0 7091 1718 3

Robert Hale & Company
63 Old Brompton Road
London SW7

PRINTED IN GREAT BRITAIN
BY EBENEZER BAYLIS AND SON LIMITED
THE TRINITY PRESS, WORCESTER, AND LONDON

CONTENTS

ILLUSTRATIONS

7

Illustrations

The photograph of Hugh Street, St. Mary's was supplied by D. Illingworth. The remaining photographs were taken by F. E. Gibson.

FOREWORD

By the Rt. Hon. Harold Wilson, M.P.

I was very glad when I heard that Mr. Clive Mumford with his great knowledge and unrivalled local contacts had decided to add to the literature of the Isles of Scilly. His *Portrait of the Isles of Scilly* is a testimony to the unremitting hard work he has put into it, authoritatively covering the history, geography and features of the Islands.

His work gains especially from the human touches which illuminate every chapter, drawing on the memories and experiences of families from every island. It is a picture above all of an island people ruled, in Mr. Mumford's words, always by the sea. But equally it is a picture of a community in constant change, and adapting itself without losing its great qualities of character.

Mr. Mumford's book deserves to be read by all who visit the Islands for pleasure or holiday, and by all who want to know more about them, in perspective and in change.

Harold Wilson

10 *Downing Street*
Whitehall

ACKNOWLEDGEMENTS

As a bibliographical source of much material I am indebted to the *Scillonian Magazine*, the lone regular publication within the islands and a voluntarily produced "quarterly" which has faithfully recorded the passage of Scillonian events for many years. Access to one of the few complete sets of volumes was afforded me by my father Tregarthen Mumford. The writings of such contributors as Frank McFarland, J. E. Hooper, Trevellick Moyle, Miss Tiddy, L. Hayward, Glyn Daniel, Geoffrey Fyson, Crosbie Garstin and K. Sisam have proved especially valuable.

My grateful appreciation is also due to the following for advice and assistance: Mr. Rodney Ward, chairman of the Isles of Scilly Steamship Company, and Mrs. Ward; Mr. Sisam, Mr. Frank Gibson and Mr. Norman Jenkins of St. Mary's; Mr. Lewis Hicks of Agnes, who kindly consented to read the proofs; Mr. John Goddard of St. Martin's; Mr. Frank Naylor, head gardener at Tresco Abbey Gardens. Also Mrs. Margaret Smart, the management of Tregarthen's Hotel, St. Mary's—and many others who, unfortunately, cannot be listed here.

In particular my wife and I wish to thank Barneslie and Betty Ward of Normandy, St. Mary's. Their kindness and readiness to help when in a jam will not easily be forgotten.

C.M.

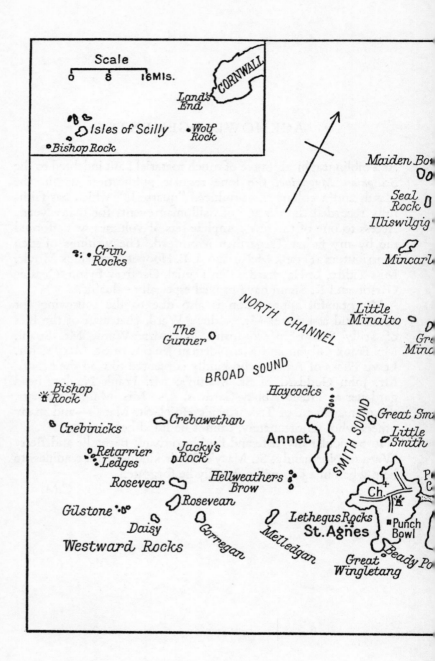

Scale

0   8   16 Mls.

CORNWALL

Land's End

Isles of Scilly
Bishop Rock

Wolf Rock

Maiden Bo

Seal Rock

Illiswilgig

Mincarl

Crim Rocks

Little Minalto

NORTH CHANNEL

Gre Min

The Gunner

BROAD SOUND

Bishop Rock

Haycocks

Great Sm

SMITH SOUND

Crebinicks

Crebawethan

Annet

Little Smith

Retarrier Ledges

Jacky's Rock

P
C

Rosevear

Hellweathers Brow

Ch.

Gilstone

Rosevean

Lethegus Rocks

Punch Bowl

Daisy

Corregan

St. Agnes

Westward Rocks

Melledgan

Great Wingletang

Beady Po

THE ISLES OF SCILLY

Scale

0   1   2 Miles

cilly Rock

Shipman Hᵈ

Men-a-vaur

Round I.

Hell Bay

Lion Rock

al

Cas.'s

Goldⁿ Ball

St. Helen's

White I.

Pool Ch+

Old Grimsby

Northwethel

The Town

Bryher

Towns Hill

TEAN Sᵈ

le

Quay New Grimsby

Tean

St. Martins

er

te I.

Lizard Pt.

Lower Town

St. Martins Bay

Nᵗʰ Hill

Abbey

Pool

Tresco

Middle Town

Murr Rk.

Sand Long Crow

Gdns.

St. Martins Flats

Higher Town

amson

Flats

Skirt Pt.

DAYMARK

ROADSTEAD

Nut Rock

Carn Near

Tobaccoman's Pt.

Quay

160

Crow Rock

Guthers I.

English Is. Pt.

Creeb

Bar Pt.

Ganninicks

Nornour

St. Mary's

Telegraph

Innisidgen

Hanjague Gt. Ganilly

al

Quay

Golf Links

Maypole

Watermill Bay

Arthur I.

Innis- vouls

Castle

St. Mary's Pⁱ.

Holy Vale

Raggᵈ I.

Menawethan

arrison

HUGH TOWN

Moors

Toll's I.

Eastern Isles

Tower

Porth cressa Bay

Heliport

Deep Pt.

CROW SOUND

ᵧ'S SOUND

Old Town Bay

Normandy

h

Peninnis Head

Giant's Castle

Porth Hellick Bay

Pt.

To
DIANE

PREFACE

Time, for centuries, passed the Isles of Scilly by. Ignored and unsung, their inhabitants lived in poverty, their breathtaking beauty, charm and climatic advantages went unappreciated—and unused.

In 1882 the Reverend George Woodley, something of an ecclesiastical clairvoyant based on St. Martin's—one of the Scilly off-islands—wrote:

> Perhaps the time will come in Scilly's better days when it shall have received the numerous improvements of which it is capable when the islands shall be preferred to foreign shores by those who, in quest of health and renovation, have been accustomed to look to a long and expensive voyage to a distant land.

Woodley's dream took a long time to take physical shape; the islands remained very much *terra incognita*; his "better days" mere words. Even in comparatively recent years a phone call to the Scillonia exchange has been known on more than one occasion to wind up with the caller being put through to Sicily, while Scilly was regarded as no more than rocky appendage to the south-western tip of Cornwall (which itself was tucked away in the misty backwaters of the provinces) and rarely merited a dot in the bottom left-hand corner of the television screen to indicate its existence. To the vast majority of Britons Scilly was only familiar in the context of the Shipping Forecast, together with such distant cousins as Viking and Forties.

It was not until post-war Britain, with the improvements in social welfare and the introduction of holidays with pay, that there was any radical change. Now Scilly, for the first time, came within the range of the labourer of the Midlands, the factory worker of the North, the Londoner. A demand had at last been created.

Realization of Woodley's prophecy was assured when four years later the Duchy of Cornwall landlords of Scilly sold Hugh

Preface

Town, the islands' capital. The sitting tenants straight away celebrated their new status of freeholders by interesting themselves in providing for tourists. It was not long before supply swiftly rose to accommodate that demand.

Today Scilly can lay valid claim to being the most celebrated island group in British waters, while its inhabitants have a good, yet unpretentious standard of living which their less fortunate antecedents would not have believed possible. Woodley's "better days" are here.

But the holidaymaking worker, who set the tourist machine in motion, must never be forgotten by Scillonians. He has played a significant part in the unravelling of island history.

I

A LILLIPUTIAN ARCHIPELAGO

We'll rant and we'll roar like true British sailors
We'll rage and we'll roam o'er the salt seas,
Until we strike soundings in the channel of old England
From Ushant to Scilly is thirty-five leagues.

So goes the chorus of a famous old Elizabethan sea shanty sung today by holidaymakers in the bars of St. Mary's as vigorously—and insensitively—as it was nostalgically harmonized by the seamen of times long gone. To the latter the name Scilly spelt England, family and loved ones; it represented a sublime emotional experience—the first glimpse, perhaps in years, of Britain for homebound shipping from the south (the Mediterranean and all points east of the Cape of Good Hope) and west (the Americas, the Horn and beyond). The procedure reversed, it was the edge of England and a memory of home dropping steadily astern.

First and last . . . so must Scilly always remain to the voyaging Briton, but no longer does the islands' import and reputation depend solely on the narrow, transitory associations of the sailor. The two poles nowadays embrace a far greater substance, as signified by Scilly being elected to rub shoulders with the likes of the Lake District and Dartmoor in a Portrait series which includes most of the well-known and standard tracts of the British Isles.

What, then, are these islands which are so often confused with their infinitely larger brethren, the Channel Islands, and which have absolutely no common denominator save that of flower-growing and vague similarity in situation?

The archipelago of Scilly, the vast majority of which is owned by the Duchy of Cornwall, is made up of approximately 145 islands and stumps of granite set in a latitude of 49 degrees

55 minutes N, longitude 6 degrees, 19 minutes W and the nearest part of the "mainland", as England is referred to by Scillonians, are the granite cliffs of Lands End, twenty-eight miles away with Penzance, the nearest town, at a distance of forty miles. "Scilly of the hundred islands, Scilly of the hundred reefs" it has been called and you can probably throw in another hundred for good measure, depending on the state of the tide when you make your census. Some writers put the total as high as three hundred, others even higher. Whatever the number it is important to realize that the smallest rock constitutes an island in the Scillonian context.

Six of the islands, namely St. Mary's, St. Agnes, Gugh, Bryher, Tresco and St. Martin's are inhabited and contain a collective population of 1,940 while the total acreage of these six is a postage stamp 3,573. A small percentage of the remaining pieces of Scilly boast a few tufts of grass and winsdwept sea thrift and have nothing more animate than an itinerant shag[1] or two. This earns them, somewhat dubiously, the status of islets. The great majority are no more than virgin rock, but for all their lack of substance they have an arresting quality which defies description and can only be fully appreciated first hand.

By far the largest and most important island is St. Mary's, which has a vast, for Scilly, acreage of 1,611 and a population of 1,534. Over three-quarters of Scilly's population is packed into St. Mary's. The island is virtually made up of two parts which are tenuously connected by an isthmus just 150 yards wide. The settlement which hugs this narrow neck comprises the "capital" of Scilly, Hugh Town. The part of St. Mary's situated west of Hugh Town is the "Hugh", a headland that was once garrisoned by soldiers and is commonly known in the islands rather as "The Garrison" than by its original name. To the east of the Hugh Town strip lies the main bulk of St. Mary's where the majority of the island's flower farms are found. All roads, or rather seas, lead to Hugh Town. It is the commercial and business centre for all the islands, and the Council of the Isles of Scilly which administers the affairs of this Lilliputian island-world sits here. For the visitor to Scilly St. Mary's is the point of arrival and departure, whether it be by boat or by helicopter. Most holidaymakers tend to make St. Mary's a base from which they make daily sorties to the other

[1] Scilly's most common cormorant.

lesser islands. St. Mary's is the only island with metalled roads and is, in fact, the one island in the group containing suggestions of the mainland.

Two miles out from St. Mary's, over to the east, lies St. Martin's which contains a population of a hundred, is two miles long, three-quarters of a mile wide and is the first piece of Scilly seen by anyone travelling to the islands from the British mainland. St. Martin's, as elongated as St. Mary's is circular, has some of the most beautifully white beaches imaginable, and also contains three "towns"—Higher Town, Middle Town and, naturally, Lower Town—all in the extensive area of 552 acres!

Moving westwards in an anti-clockwise arc, we find Tresco, situated a mile from St. Martin's, the same from St. Mary's. This island of 735 acres is the second largest in Scilly, has a population of 201, and is perhaps the most celebrated of the entire group on account of its world-famous sub-tropical gardens. Tresco is the seat of the well-known Dorrien-Smith family who, until recent and more democratic times, were Lord Proprietors of the islands. The latest of the line, Lieutenant-Commander T. M. Dorrien-Smith, continues the family tradition in leasing the island from the Duchy. Tresco is another island which contains three settlements within its limited confines, New Grimsby the capital, Old Grimsby and the charmingly named Dolphin Town.

Westwards again, but only a quarter of a mile this time, to Bryher island, separated from Tresco by the narrowest of channels. Bryher has been dubbed "The Pearl of Scilly" by one writer, and with a population of forty-nine and an acreage of 317 is the smallest inhabited island yet mentioned. Due south of Bryher lies Samson of the twin humps (that is its total content). Although unpeopled, it deserves a mention, as it is a fairy-tale desert island, 120 acres of bracken, bramble and sand.

Continuing to move anti-clockwise right down to the western side of St. Mary's, we reach the last two inhabited outposts of Scilly, indeed of the British Isles, St. Agnes and Gugh. St. Agnes, which for the purposes of this book will be referred to as plain Agnes—its common name in Scilly—is three-quarters of a mile long, half a mile wide and holds fifty-four people. Gugh, pronounced like Hugh, is the "Siamese twin" of Agnes as the two are joined by a low water sand bar, but on the flood it is an island and is saved from the ignominy of "desert" classification on the strength of a family of two who have chosen it as their home! Gugh and Agnes make up a combined acreage of 358.

So far Samson has been the lone intruder in a list of inhabited Scilly islands, but there are a number of others which, if not quite Samson's size, are bigger than most. These are Tean, pronounced tee-un, St. Helen's, the lighthouse rock Round Island and North-wethal, which comprise a little group lying in the channel between Tresco and St. Martin's. In addition there is the bird sanctuary Annet, on the western flank and a veritable network of ugly, treacherous rocks which infest the sea to the back of Agnes and which guard the westerly approaches to the islands. These are known as the Western rocks and few of them consist of anything more than granite, although every single one of them bears a name.

To the west of Bryher is found yet another group of rocks, called the "Norrads" (Northward rocks), while on the eastern flank of the archipelago between St. Martin's and St. Mary's lie the Eastern Isles. As their name suggests these are vegetated islands rather than bare rocks, even though they are all minute.

Most of the sizeable islands, if that adjective can be used in all good faith in the miniature world of Scilly, have been accounted for—but what of the hundreds of others not yet listed? These are made up of a miscellany of rocks of every shape, size and form, which are strewn at random over the forty-five square sea-miles in which the archipelago is set. Sometimes they can be seen, other times they are submerged: but they are all there, all have names and go to make up the rocky mosaic of the Isles of Scilly. On a very clear day the outlines of the towering cliffs of Lands End can be faintly discerned to the east from certain vantage points in the islands. To the north and south there is nothing, while down to the west behind Agnes there is only an immensity of sky and sea stretching as far as the eye can see. America next stop. Only an occasional ship climbing up over the distant horizon breaks the monotony of the Atlantic wastes.

Seen at a distance at sea level the most striking of Scilly's physical characteristics are its phenomenally low-lying situation; the riot of rocks which litter the land, the shore and jut out of the sea; the jagged, much-indented sea-eaten sides of the islands; and the general treelessness.

Legend tells us that Scilly was the high ground of a land which was once joined to the mainland of Cornwall and which was inundated by a huge flood; hence the low-lying nature of Scilly. Be that as it may the Isles of Scilly are set remarkably, almost disturbingly, low in the water. The highest point above sea level in the entire group is a mere 165 feet, at Telegraph, St. Mary's. There are many places in the islands where the land is more or less at sea level, where the water threatens to (and at times does) encroach. The most outstanding example of sea-level situation in Scilly, is Hugh Town, on St. Mary's. People have been prophesying for centuries that St. Mary's will, one day, be cut into two distinct islands at the low-lying neck that is Hugh Town. But the islands' capital is still there perched defiantly on its narrow strip like Canute defying the waves, although old timers' tales of "punting" down the main street occasionally tend to make one wonder!

Even if Scilly was never joined to the mainland (at least in historic times) the islands in the Scilly group were certainly at one time attached and long ago were probably one land mass. One has only to note the general shallowness of the surrounding waters and the many sandbars which appear at low tide and connect up the various islands, to realize this. Going "up channel" between Bryher and Tresco at low water the bottom of the boat is continually scraping the sea bed and navigation across the waterless flats around the southern parts of St. Martin's can be equally hazardous.

Much has been written about the rocks of Scilly. The whole group, from steepling Hanjague in the Eastern Isles down to the Bishop in the west, is one solid lump of granite, its extent supplemented by much windblown sand, and the joint action of wind and storm over thousands of years has weathered the rock into fantastic and grotesque forms. Here smooth and round, there jagged and rough, they have been chiselled to assume, in places, animal and human features and these are known in the islands by such names as the Tooth Rock, the Nags Head, the Monk's Cowl. In some places the landscape and shores are a chaotic causeway of strewn boulders "stretching away under every diversity of scopulous proportion". Whenever and wherever in Scilly, one is aware of the rocks: but more of this phenomenon when the two granite showpieces of Peninnis Head, St. Mary's and Wingletang Downs, Agnes, come under discussion.

Barring the belts of conifer on Tresco and on the hillsides below Maypole, St. Mary's, stretching from Holy Vale past Longstone, Tremelethen around to Carn Friars, and on the Garrison, Scilly is notably lacking in trees. Gorse, heather and bracken grow in profusion all over the islands, but trees are the exception rather than the rule, probably due to the islands being so exposed to the violent Atlantic winds. In the summer the tree-lessness of Scilly is not unpleasant as one might have expected because a riot of colour is provided by the many other types of vegetation, but in the bad weather of winter the sparsely clad slopes take on a dull, bleak colour and present an often desolate appearance. Scilly has always been short of trees. A late seven-teenth-century manuscript entitled "Some Memorialls towards Natural History of the Sylly Islands" says there were "no trees, no not so much as shrubb, except Brambles, Furzes, Broom and Holly, and these never grew above four foot high. Nor is there in all these islands one Tree. . . ."

The general appearance of Scilly has changed but little over the centuries except for building development. My impression of low-lying, predominantly treeless islands edged by rocky fore-shores which I get whenever I come to Scilly by boat ("torn strips of granite" as Alphonse Esquiros called them)[1] were, I find, also recorded by writers of old Scilly.

In 1822 the Reverend Woodley wrote, possibly uncharitably,

There is nothing engaging in the general aspect of this British archipelago. Rugged ridges, utterly destitute of trees—their sides tinted with a dull, brownish hue of scanty vegetation: their bases streaked by long and broad beaches of white sand or darkened by sombre rocks of every variety of size and form. Such are the prominent features of the Scilly Isles.

The basic parts of this description are just as appropriate today. Obviously more trees have been planted, especially in the garden-island of Tresco, but the rocks are still there and the islands certainly have got no higher in the water.

In 1776 Borlase, a famous Cornish antiquarian and historian, recorded the following impressions in his book *Observations of the Ancient and Present State of the Islands of Scilly and their Importance to the Trade of Great Britain* (1756), which is generally held to be one of the most authoritative works on the islands:

[1] *Cornwall and its Coasts*, 1865.

These islets and rocks edge this Sound in an extremely pretty and different manner from anything I have seen before. The sides of these little islands continue their greenness to the brim of the water, where they are either surrounded by rocks of different shapes which start up here or there as you advance, like so many enchanted castles, or by a verge of sand of the brightest colour. The sea, having eaten away passages between these hillocks, forms several pretty pools and lakes, and the crags which kept their stations, intercepted and so numerous that the whole seemed but one large grotesque rockwork.

Robert Heath, an officer who wrote a book[1] on Scilly during a year's stay as an engineer in the St. Mary's garrison in 1744, also commented upon the group's low-lying, rocky aspect:

Beheld at a distance the islands appear like so many high banks in the water. But the rocks about these islands, especially those to the westward, appear off at sea like old castles and churches.

None of the writers of Old Scilly, however, mention one of the most striking points about the layout of the islands as a whole—and that is balance of situation. For it is, indeed, hard to imagine a more perfect example of an archipelago *per se*. The main, most sizeable island of St. Mary's is fittingly situated as the hub; the smaller islands, or "off islands" as they are locally known, fringe it in an arc stretching from St. Martin's in the east down to Agnes in the west. Rocks guard the eastern approaches, there are rocks to the west ("citadels of Nature" as Heath called them). Contained by the rough semicircle of islands is a deep and good anchorage, the Roadstead, into which vessels can enter via St. Mary's Sound, between Agnes and St. Mary's; Crow Sound, between the Eastern Isles and St. Mary's; Old Grimsby channel, between Tresco and St. Martin's; New Grimsby Channel, between Tresco and Bryher; and the wide mouth of Broad Sound in the west.

In imagining the layout of the Isles of Scilly, try to think of a cartwheel cut in half. Hugh Town, St. Mary's is the centre, the "off islands" are dotted in a semi-circular arc on the rim. The space in between is the Roadstead. The overall impression is one of compactness and homogeneity, despite the sea area the islands cover.

As that noted landscape architect G. A. Jellicoe, wrote recently,[2]

[1] This book has a title of monumental length—131 words—and is commonly known as *A Natural and Historical Account of the Islands of Scilly*. . . .
[2] *A Landscape Charter of the Isles of Scilly*.

"Not even the floating islands of Delos of classical antiquity are set more dramatically in the Aegean than are the Scillies in the sea off the coast of Cornwall."

Helliwell, in trying to give an impression of the layout of Scilly, wrote, "If you collect a large bagful of pieces of granite of different sizes and throw them indiscriminately into a shallow pool of water, you will probably obtain a tolerably correct model of the Isles of Scilly." This description is accurate in as far as it conveys the idea of hundreds of granite rocks set low in the sea at random, but it does not show how the larger pieces have somehow formed themselves into as perfect a group of islands as one would ever wish to come across.

So far we have looked at the physical aspect of Scilly from sea level: what of an aerial view of the islands' topography? Scilly is linked with the mainland by both sea and air. British European Airways run a daily helicopter from Penzance to St. Mary's, while for those who prefer the water the Isles of Scilly Steamship Company maintains two vessels, the *Scillonian* and the *Queen of the Isles*. These also ply daily between Penzance and St. Mary's. The journey in the twenty-six-seater Sikorsky helicopter, over in twenty minutes, is often preferable to sea travel, especially in rough weather when the passage can be as formidable as any round the coast of Britain.

From the air the shallowness of the waters around Scilly can straightaway be appreciated. The sanded bottom shows through continually, and the impression gained at sea level of a chaotic distribution of rocks is, if anything, heightened.

The part of St. Mary's east of Hugh Town shows itself to be a chequer board of box-like flower patches, with their distinctive shelter-belt hedges. Crisscrossed by roads which at best are indifferent, they dominate the landscape even to the extent of creeping down the very sides of the islands close to cliff edge and the sea itself. The other areas, which are not given over to flower-growing, are either open fields, cliffland or heathland marked with the usual Scillonian litter of granite boulders. This landscape pattern is only broken on St. Mary's by the gradually distending built-up area of the Hugh Town isthmus, and by various tiny settlements consisting of a few houses and sheds which are set sporadically all over the island.

The same topographical mixture is in evidence on the "off

islands" of Agnes, Bryher and St. Martin's. The all-important need for shelter from the strong island winds has caused the native populations to build their small hamlets largely on the southern slopes of the islands, and in these areas are found the rows of flower fields. Almost without exception the northern extremities of these three islands are barren and uncultivated, left alone to granite and bracken. Tresco is a spectacular exception to the general rule. True its northern end is as wild and untouched as those of its neighbours, but its southern part is dominated by the lush arboration of the Abbey Gardens, very much out of keeping with Scilly's treeless character. But this section also contains the characteristic flower patches.

An idea of the minute size of the Isles of Scilly can never be gained from the deck of the *Queen* or the *Scillonian*—but it can readily be appreciated from the air. From the Sikorsky helicopter the first-time visitor to Scilly can immediately begin to understand how tiny the individual islands are; indeed, how minute is the collective world of Scilly. And only a true appreciation of this smallness can lead to a real understanding of Scilly, its islanders, their way of life—in fact all matters Scillonian.

There is, of course, no substitute for personal intimacy and physical contact, but if one seeks to win an understanding second hand via the written word, then the idea of Lilliput must always—and I stress always—be in the forefront of the mind. Only then will the reader appreciate why an Ordnance Survey map has to be blown up to a scale of two inches to one statute mile in order to bring out the detail; why the folk of St. Mary's, an island of just a few square miles, live "in the country" if they are not Hugh Townites; why a public garden of a few square yards is called a park; why a hamlet of a few cottages on the "off islands" is called a town, and why phrases suggestive of great area such as "the Plains", "The Moors", "Down to West'ard", and "Over to East'ard" are cheerfully used to cover an area of just a few square miles. He will then also realize why *Portrait of the Isles of Scilly* must necessarily be compounded of what may seem by normal yardsticks trivial, sometimes insignificant and "parish pump" matter. Other books in this Portrait series have dealt with vast agricultural tracts and extensive areas, big industries and sprawling cities, but as these things obviously cannot exist within the tiny confines of Scilly, things which would not merit a mention in a "standard size" work are suddenly relevant, even vitally important. One of the chapters in Harry Scott's excellent account of the vast area of Yorkshire opens "From the top of Mickle Fell to the Scottish border is less than 50 miles . . . !" Stop and consider. The whole of Scilly's land would fit comfortably into a quarter of that area.

Just as the writer on Yorkshire deals above all with large components, so then must the writer on Scilly depend on small detail for his material. If needs be the names of individual persons must be mentioned as such a practice is only being logically consistent with a place where even the smallest of rocks is faithfully given a name by islanders. Yes, in Scilly the minute plays an intrinsic part in the make-up of a not-much-bigger whole, and the archipelago must be treated like a scale model that has turned out to be the real thing. Thus one's thoughts, one's ideas and one's imagination must be pared down accordingly. Dean Swift must have had Scilly in mind when he wrote his *Gulliver's Travels*. Lilliput—Scillyput: what's in a name?

II

ISLES OF CONTRAST

November month in Scilly. For an hour now I have been trying to follow the insidious progress of the fog. Almost imperceptibly it has crept off the sea, over the dank weed which fouls the foreshore of Sharks Pit, St. Mary's, until, suddenly, everything is obliterated. "It's thick as a bag" as islanders so graphically observe. I know there's sea out there, but only because I can hear the desolate tolling of the bell-buoy warning shipping off the dangerous Spanish Ledges in St. Mary's Sound, down at the back of the Garrison. I know, too, that over to the East'ard, across the Roadstead, there are islands, since, by straining, I can just make out the winking red eye of the Round Island light. From the west, struggling through the fog, comes the muffled report of the cotton gun on the Bishop Rock Lighthouse.

To be on St. Mary's on a day such as this is to experience a strange, lonely feeling. The helicopters have been grounded and there is no boat to link the islands with Penzance. Scilly is cut off from the mainland, a marooned half world of swirling sea mists amid an inhospitable Atlantic. It is as if the S.S. *Scilly* has slipped her cables and is drifting, drifting out to sea. True Scillonians, islanders brought up in Scilly who have the place in their blood, do not mind these conditions. Indeed, I believe there is a certain sympathy between them and their environment. Fog and the resultant restriction of communications robs them of their mail, provisions and papers, but also helps to bring them closer to their surroundings; it identifies them with their heritage. But to the uninitiated it is all very strange, especially so if one is on the remoter "off islands", which are not only cut off from the mainland but also from St. Mary's—and each other.

Yet, and peering into the "cotton wool" I can hardly believe it, yesterday, only twenty-four hours earlier, Scilly was bathed in the

27

sort of sunshine for which it is renowned—in November too!—
and topped the national table with hours more sun than anywhere
else in the United Kingdom. The sun blazed down on deep-blue
seas, the islands sweated in the autumn heat and suddenly the
vitality of summer was with us again. It might have been August
in the Mediterranean or the Aegean. Hardly a breath of wind
stirred the surface of St. Mary's Pool and I had my lunch in
shirtsleeves on the veranda.

Tomorrow, if I know this unique part of the world, the wind
will take over, for they are to Scilly what fogs are to Newfoundland and never spare the islands their attention for long. Today's
fog will be blown away and these exposed rocky islands will be
scythed by hurricane gusts that will tear into the hedges of
veronica, escallonia and pittasporum lining the flower fields, and
the surrounding seas, so docile yesterday, will be whipped up into
an ugly, white fury. Boats which have not already been dragged
up the beach following the departure of the late summer tourist,
will huddle for protection in the harbour and Hugh Town will
be the original deserted village as Scillonians leave the islands at
grips with their oldest enemies, the crashing surf and shrieking
winds.

Sun, fog and wind all in the short space of seventy-two hours.
Three such totally contrasting weather conditions on three
successive days are difficult to conceive, and silly to those accustomed to a more settled, conventional weather cycle. Scilly,
indeed, it is! For in few places in the British Isles is weather so
capricious, so variable—and the kind of rapid switches just
described can come about just as easily in spring and summer as
in the months of winter.

Scilly is called, among other things, the "Fortunate Isles" the
"Isles of the Blest", "The Isles of Fowers" and "Sunny Lyonesse",
but it is above all else "The Archipelago of Contrasts". This must
be stressed straight away, so that the fallacious belief that the
islands are permanently bathed in sunshine can be nipped in the
bud. I point this out regretfully and at the risk of incurring the
undying enmity of the local "Hotel and Guest Houses Association"! Only one who lives permanently in these islands, who sees
them in all their many and varying moods, can really appreciate
the contrasting conditions. The tourist spends a summer fortnight
in Scilly and leaves imagining the sunny weather to be prevalent

all the year round. After all, had he not been told, and rightly so, about the mild climate of these islands and that the flowers grow in the open fields in January? The equable conditions, and, more important, the mildness of the winters is one of the most remarkable features of Scilly. But although frost and snow are infrequent visitors that is as far as it goes, for the weather in Scilly is constantly changing, and with bewildering rapidity.

Past writers have contrived to paint an idyllic, but false picture of a 365-days-a-year sun-drenched paradise. Unfortunately this is so inaccurate as to be laughable. It is certainly true that Scilly, when compared with most places on the British mainland, gets more than its fair share of any sunshine that is going (and when the sun shines it is *hot*), but to really know these islands is to know contrast and change; to live with fogs, winds and storm—as well as sun.

I recently asked a Scillonian to give me his idea of a typical Scillonian day when away from the islands. He replied: "Standing on Peninnis Head with the wind whipping me off my feet and the seas like a boiling pot, crashing against the cliffs below." A colleague had a very different picture: "Lying on the sand at Pentle Bay," he said, "with the blue sea gently slapping the shore under a cloudless sky. Everything still and quiet." There you have two completely divergent "ideals". Both men cannot be right, yet both are born Scillonians, who know all there is to know about their island home. The answer, I suspect, lies somewhere in the middle. Both conditions are, in part, typical of Scilly, but both are only facets of the whole picture of contrast. It is perhaps worth relating *en passant* that the tanned faces of most islanders are as much due to a pre-Celtic blood strain and the weathering of wind as to any persistent presence of the sun.

When the winds drop, the fogs have vanished as mysteriously as they appeared, and the sun shines on Scilly, then it is difficult to imagine a more beautiful and blessed spot on the face of this earth. The island sun, which owing to the air's high ozone content is intense and tanning even when masked by cloud, seems to shroud the islands in a pall of lethargy. They seem to sleep and the surrounding seas are strangely passive in sympathy. The waters of the Roadstead become creamy and glassy—like "a pan of milk", completely free from their accustomed movement. A boat coming from Tresco to St. Mary's leaves a visible trail all the way from quay to quay. The circle of islands could be taken up and deposited in the South Seas and no one would know the difference.

The clarity of the unpolluted Scillonian air is heightened in calm and sunshine—both visually and audibly. Every rock on the ring of inhabited islands which enclose the Roadstead, and the reefs beyond them become more defined. From St. Mary's the individual houses on Bryher island can be seen; the lighthouse on Agnes seems close enough to touch from the Garrison; the flag atop Tresco Abbey can be clearly seen, as can the workers in Lower Town, St. Martin's from St. Mary's Bar Point. Individual ships on the horizon can be picked out as clear as a pin. In the calm weather of summer, sounds carry far across the smooth water and reverberate around the theatre of granite islands. From Tresco the bustle and noise of St. Mary's quay when the steamer has just arrived can easily be heard. The sounds and noises of daily living drift lazily across the Roadstead to and from every corner.

Looking across the still waters to the friendly circle of white strands, the islands coated in green bracken, the gorse, the rocks over which lush mesembryanthemum flows like a tide,[1] one gets the feeling of being in an over-idealized, unreal world, and the strange and wonderful shapes of the rocks only serve to intensify that feeling of fantasy. "Time stands still" says the old cliché, and it might have been born in Scilly. One might as well throw one's watch overboard straight away, for there is a timelessness that pervades everyone and everything. There is no sense of urgency, for there are no tubes to catch in Scilly, no trains, no traffic lights, no buses, no time schedules to adhere to—just the bare bones of nature and the spirit of *mañana*. And overhead the sun beating the islands, the islanders and the sea down into a torpor. One of the most remarkable factors about the islands when the sun shines is the utter tranquillity which falls over the archipelago. To the visitor it is startling, and one American woman once said, "I never heard such an appalling silence!"

The sun has a strange effect on Scilly. I really believe that the more romantic among us would not bat an eyelid if Long John Silver limped around one of those rocky carns down to the west of Agnes with his spyglass under his arm. Or should the strains

[1]Gorse and mesembryanthemum (ice plant) are as dominant in the island landscape as are winds in the weather cycle.

of "Yo Ho Ho and a bottle of rum", come over the light summer breezes into a deserted cove on St. Martin's where we were picnicking. Scilly is a place where the imagination can run riot, where even the most sober-minded individual can, for two weeks in the summer sun, become a Caliban, foolish, childlike and fanciful. In summer conditions Scilly becomes a prototype of the fascinating dream isles of literature—a never-never land.

It is almost impossible to describe in black and white the arresting and elusive quality that these islands possess when the sea is still and the sun shines on them, but only the most hardened soul would fail to come under the magic of Scilly. The sea, sand and salt-tanged breezes seem to weave an enchanted spell, and the romantic *mood* of Tennyson's passage in "The Passing of Arthur" comes to be understood when in Scilly, even if the words are today not particularly relevant:

> Where fragments of a forgotten peoples dwelt,
> And the long mountains ended in a coast
> of ever shifting sand and far away the
> phantom circle of a moaning sea.

I have cherished memories of these islands when the sunny face of Scilly smiled. Of picnics on the powdery sand of Pelistry, St. Mary's; of walks among the great boulders of Peninnis with the sea shimmering like glass; of swimming off a boat moored in the transparent waters of New Grimsby Channel with nearby Tresco and Bryher dozing in the afternoon heat-haze; of the peace and beauty of St. Helen's as the shallow waters of Old Grimsby Channel caressed its beach. But perhaps my favourite memory of all, one which will always spring to mind when mention of Scilly in the sun is made, is of sleepy summer afternoons when the St. Mary's Cricket Club used to gather at the quay to embark for Agnes to play cricket; of lolling among the sea pinks on Priglis bank, gazing up into a cloudless blue sky with the sound of bat on ball mingling pleasantly with the swish of the water in the bay; of returning across St. Mary's Sound in the evening, lazily trailing a mackerel line from a punt astern of the motor boat, with the setting sun a ball of fire behind the twin hills of Samson. At times like this the beauty that is Scilly is breathtaking. This is the Scilly which everyone loves, a picture postcard world of colour, beauty and peace. This is an island Eden that draws people from all parts of Britain, and from abroad as well, like a magnet. In these conditions one can really begin to understand the inspiration which moved Swinburne to such poetic heights as "A small sweet world of wave encompassed wonder" and produced such phrases as "a dreamland fairy isles floating in a silver sea" and "The Scilly Isles, those struggling outposts of dear Old England like bits of fairyland—uncut jewels scattered over a silver sea." (F. T. Bullen).

But sadly it does not last. The winds have slept long enough, change is in the air. The glass is falling rapidly, storm cones have been hoisted at Telegraph Tower on St. Mary's—now it is the turn of Scilly to show her other face, one which is as ugly as the other is beautiful. Watching a storm brew is an exciting and rather terrifying sight. Dark clouds roll across the hitherto clear sky, the granite islands take on a stark appearance, the winds build up menacingly as if Aeolus has let them out of his bag one by one. The sea starts running with little flecks of white.

A dramatic transformation is taking place and the so-tranquil scene is soon to be one of rare savagery. The waters of St. Mary's Sound become a heaving, protesting mass, and the lagoon-like surface of the Roadstead a cauldron as huge waves roll in from the west through Broad Sound in an ugly breaking line from Bishop to Mincarlo. All around Scilly the Atlantic builds up to thunder against the granite bulwarks of the islands and funnels into the narrow channels sending spray leaping hundreds of feet upwards. All hell seems let loose. No longer is the sea a friendly, deep blue; now it is a forbidding green and black. The salt flung up on to the cliffs by the breakers is carried into the heart of the islands by the winds and is a constant taste on every lip. Car doors are encrusted by the salt, wind-blown sand scythes blindingly down street and across foreshore, settlements are deserted as Scillonians stay indoors leaving Scilly at the mercy of the contesting elements which contribute a din as deafening as sunny conditions are tranquil.

In these circumstances Scilly is elemental and could not be further removed from the Utopia conception. But it is truly magnificent. It seems incredible that these islands, now so storm-torn, were not so long ago basking in sunshine. Scilly is, indeed, "beautiful in calm" but it is also "terrible in storm", and there are few more unforgettable sights than the huge breakers

Pelistry Bay, St. Mary's: St. Martin's in the background

savaging the crags of Peninnis Head, St. Mary's, or Hell Bay, Bryher.

Set in the rocky northern extremity of Bryher at the mercy of the Atlantic rolling in from the west, Hell Bay in storm is a revelation. The bay is aptly named. The north-westerly winds whip the seas straight into it, transforming everything into a foaming mass of white. One is literally drenched on the cliffs above.

Poor Agnes probably has the worst time of all. The most exposed island of the group it is an easy prey to the wind and sea. During some gales seaweed and flotsam are flung hundreds of yards inland and when islanders inspect the damage chunks of coast are found to be missing, washed away. Once all the land between the bays of Porth Askin and Beady Pool was awash.

The worst gales in recent years were those that ravaged the islands in the March of 1962. All the inhabited islands suffered extensive damage, but St. Mary's was probably worst hit. The entire bank bordering Porthcressa beach was ripped up, granite boulders weighing many, many tons being tossed about like toy-things. The same thing happened to Old Town Beach where violent southerly winds drove seas in over the bank into the flower fields. The job of repair and renovation has cost thousands of pounds. The power of the sea is unbelievable. Boats snap their moorings as if held by straw, are washed clean out of their sheds, and I well remember the 921-ton *Scillonian* warping away from St. Mary's quay after its wrist-thick hawser had parted with the report of a rifle shot.

The lyrical superlatives of the poets are as out of place here as are oilskins in Oxford Street. Perhaps John Wesley put things in their true perspective when he visited Scilly way back in 1743. Wesley managed to get hold of a boat through the auspices of the mayor of St. Ives and with several companions did the crossing to Scilly in, apparently, the dirtiest weather imaginable. The voyage took more than seven hours, Wesley and his disciples kept their spirits up by singing hymns and when they stepped ashore at St. Mary's they were more dead than alive. Wesley only stayed in Scilly long enough to give an address to a small group of curious and unreceptive Scillonians outside what is now the Town Hall, then embarked for the return journey which was, by all accounts, as bad, if not worse, than the first. Wesley's

3

The first Scillonian—*on the Wingletang Ledge*
Old island gig with cargo of flowers

opinion of Scilly was unkind, yet predictable: "a dreary, barren place", he observed.

Weather conditions do not provide for the only contrasts in Scilly. There are physical and topographical ones too. And if a two-weeks' holiday hardly allows the visitor a chance to see the extraordinary caprices of island weather, then just one summer steamer trip to the islands will afford him the opportunity of noting the amazing discrepancies of shape, colour and form. As the *Scillonian*, or it may be the *Queen*, nears the group after little under a three-hour voyage, turns along the southerly shore of St. Mary's and slides through the Sound which separates that island from Agnes, a fine sight is presented. Austere granite outcrops thrust up grotesquely from the cliffs and above the shore, scarred and furrowed into the most weird of weather-beaten shapes. Beneath them, contrastingly beautiful, sleep little sandy bays and beaches edged prettily with gorse, fern and flowers. The green of the bracken, the yellow gorse and the silver sand contrast strongly with the dull granite—and setting off both is the blue, blue sea.

The colour of the waters around Scilly never fail to impress. They are a deep blue, a pleasant surprise from the murky dullness which characterizes mainland waters. One of the reasons for the blueness and the startling clarity which enables one to see the bottom fathoms down, is that island waters are free from plankton and from the effects of silt-laden rivers. The rocky seabed around Scilly also accounts for much of the blueness. Yet even this friendly colour changes to an ugly opaque in this place of contrasts—especially when sunshine is replaced with bad weather —and at all times in the year Scillonian waters are cold. If you hear tales of the Gulf Stream's favourable influence on the temperature of island waters, disregard them; there is, rather, a touch of the Humboldt about Scillonian seas!

The richness of contrasting colour is a notable feature of Scilly. The bright sun allied to the clear air sets off the yellows against the greens, the browns and whites against the blues; a photographer's paradise. The boat passes the entrance to Porthcressa bay from where a view of Hugh Town can be seen. The sea level situation is accentuated by the higher ground flanking it on both sides. Into the Roadstead now where an impressive panoramic view of the "off islands" arcing from Agnes in the west to

St. Martin's in the east is represented to all on board. The lush wooded appearance of Tresco is set off by barren Samson. The blueness of the sea now gives way to intermittent patches of green as the sandy bottom shows through, now to purple when weed-covered rock is passed over. With a blast of her siren that bounces around the ring of granite islands, the *Scillonian* slips into St. Mary's Pool, where Hugh Town nestles snugly into the Garrison hill, and as the newcomer steps ashore he must but reflect on the kaleidoscope of colour, shape and form he has witnessed in such a short space of time.

In subsequent days as he explores the islands and rocks, and gets to know the tiny world of Scilly more intimately, the contrast will become even more apparent. Every isle, however small, he will see to have its distinct and individual characteristics. He will cross St. Mary's Sound to Agnes and note the ruggedness and wildness of Wingletang Downs in the west and the contrasting tranquillity of Porth Conger in the east. He will sense the loneliness of Agnes which no other island possesses. He will compare the often awesome savagery of the dangerous Western Rocks to their peaceful counterparts across the Roadstead—the Eastern Isles. He may take a trip over to Bryher and walk along the western part, battered and torn by a thousand Atlantic gales. Only a few minutes away is the east side of the island, quiet and sheltered. Across the channel is Tresco, again all granite magnificence in the north, sheltered and tree covered in the south. He will make a mental note that the northern and western parts of the archipelago are generally rugged, the south and east more placid. On St. Mary's he will be impressed by the switch from cliff and granite scenery to the seclusion of Holy Vale in the centre of the island where the sea cannot be seen and where one is hardly aware of being on an island.

And so it goes on. Wherever he goes in Scilly, whether it be by boat or on foot, he will see a fresh aspect, a changing face—and if the weather switches from calm to storm during his holiday, a third dimension will enter. Things in the islands take on different shapes and appearances when observed from different spots, and after all one can observe from all points of the compass in Scilly— through 360 degrees. Rocks and islets which at a distance appear to be one will be found on closer inspection to be divided by channels often quite wide. From St. Mary's, Agnes and Gugh look to be a whole, but at high water they are both separate islands. Again from St. Mary's, Bryher and Tresco seem to be one land mass, but they are, of course, not.

The visitor will see how the movements of the tides dramatically alter the face of the islands. At high water, especially big sixteen-foot spring tides, each island "seems to be lying down upon the water like a duck half asleep".[1] The grass and scanty vegetation are virtually lapped by the sea and the islands seem to be on the brink of being swallowed up. One gets a feeling of gross satiety. But when the water retreats there is yet another of those startling transformations so peculiar to Scilly. The sand bars and straggling causeways of seaweed-covered rocks are bared, the water goes right down and to be on a beach then is rather like sitting in a bath when the water has run out, as someone once graphically remarked.

One of the more notable features of Scilly's changeful scene is the regular disappearance and reappearance of countless rocks and reefs with the rise and fall of the tide. The renowned Hard Lewis rock in the Eastern Isles affords a perfect example of this. At low tide it is exposed, but on the flood it is submerged, lurking just below the waterline to rip the bottom out of any boat rash enough not to give it a wide berth. There are hundreds more.

It has often been said that people who live in one environment for any length of time fail to take in things to the same extent as strangers; the scene has been before their eyes for so long that it has become taken for granted. This, I think, is in many cases true of the person born in these islands. When I broached the matter to one he readily admitted that the contrasts within Scilly had not struck him, but, after reflecting, agreed that there was truth in it. As if to substantiate his discovery he pointed out that differences in Scilly were not just confined to weather, shape and colour— but even to the inhabitants themselves.

The St. Mary's person can usually be identified because he nowadays is getting a mainland taint about him. (Native Scillonians tend to be clannish. Although they will not admit it, mainlanders are considered a "race apart" until integration takes place in the course of time.) The long-established family names such as the Banfields, Hicks, Woodcock's, Penders, Mumfords, Gibsons, Phillips and Sherris are, admittedly, still much in

[1] Lady Vyvyan: *The Scilly Isles.*

evidence, but the holiday traffic has brought many new faces to Scilly. The "off islands" being that little bit more inaccessible to the influence of the mainland—and so-called civilization—are, to a large extent, still dominated by names that have been there for centuries. Occasionally a mainlander comes out of the blue to settle, but the off islands are more truly Scillonian than St. Mary's where it seems to be increasingly more difficult to find a native.

On Agnes the predominant family for generations has been that of Hicks and still remains so. Bryher is still largely an island of Jenkins and Stedefords, while St. Martin's is the traditional home of the Christophers and Goddards. Tresco, like St. Mary's, is becoming less Scillonian than its neighbours. In recent years there has been a steady influx of "foreign blood".

Agnes folk can be pinpointed a mile off. Swarthy and dark— "Turks" by nickname—they are somehow just the sort of people you would expect to live on a lonely sea-beaten island "down to the west'ard". On the other hand, "the Ginnicks", the people of St. Martin's, seem to be fairskinned, blue eyed, even redheaded. St. Martin's is the island furthest away from the "hub" of Scilly, and somehow this remoteness has rubbed off on the people themselves. St. Mary's does not see them for months on end, then they suddenly come down to do their shopping and fade away as mysteriously as they appeared. As for Bryher folk, Scilly's traditional fishermen, there is a certain *je ne sais quoi*, a stolid individuality that stamps them as people from "over to Bryher".

In the previous chapter we saw how tiny Scilly was, and now we have noted the great wealth of contrasting detail within that minuteness. The Isles of Scilly is surely as perfect an example as any of *multum in parvo*.

III

SCILLY DOWN THE AGES

Myth and Legend

Just as there is not much geography about the Isles of Scilly, so is there precious little history. Or, to be more accurate, little proven historical data. Little of the knowledge of these islands we possess is substantiated by hard fact and what comes to us today is often confused and distorted, having been merged and jumbled up with snippets of myth here, titbits of legend there. What has happened to Scilly in the past is as much a mystery as are the origins of the very name of this tiny archipelago—and there are gaps. Yawning gaps plugged with a hotchpotch of fact and fiction. Everything seems to be "shrouded in the mists of antiquity" as R. L. Bowley put it in his admirable book *The Fortunate Isles*.

In relatively recent years Heath, Borlase, Troutbeck[1] and Woodley have been the standard guides for the seeker of the truth of Old Scilly. But further back there seems to have been an historical vacuum. The "Itinerary" of Leland, the sixteenth-century antiquarian, is immensely valuable, but even here there are inconsistencies as well as some sketchiness. There is evidence to substantiate the belief that Leland did not, in fact, visit Scilly at all for he appears to have confused St. Mary's with Tresco! It is possible he might have compiled his notes from material at hand at Tavistock and much later, when he sat down to make up his notes into a comprehensive piece there were difficulties which he surmounted with pure conjecture. This is the sort of thing with which the student of Scillonian history has to contend. Much of present day knowledge has been handed down from book to book, embellished and exaggerated—while all along the source

[1] *A Survey of the Ancient and Present State of the Scilly Isles,* 1794.

was probably fictional anyway! Much of the old documents and prints are lost or in private hands—and have never been published.

Accounts of ancient tin islands sought by Pole-star-navigating Phoenicians are the very stuff of legend and romance. So, too, are burial chambers and tales of an Eldorado flooded by seas never to reappear; of pirates and Viking sailors, wreckers and rum-running smugglers. But they are not wholly divorced from authenticity—and what follows is an attempt to differentiate.

Origin of name. There cannot be many people living in Scilly who in their childhood were spared the well-worn mainland jibe of "You come from Scilly, well that explains it" or "You Scilly boy" and like nonsense. But when they have got their heads down to discovering the origins of the somewhat embarrassing name of their home they more often than not draw a blank. Like so many other questions relating to these islands the answer is only provided by the processes of surmise—not fact.

One of the theories, and a very superficial one, is that the group takes its name from Scilly Rock, a towering, cleft granite landmark situated in the sea to the west of the island of Bryher. This is very unlikely as Scilly Rock is rather "the rock of Scilly". We first come across it in Elizabethan times, and it seems to have no significance other than that of being a prominent recognition mark for ships approaching from the north-west.

Invariably a comparison has been drawn between Scilly and Scylla, the fabled rock of the Messina Straits between Sicily and the Italian mainland often mentioned in Greek mythology. Students of the classics will remember that Scylla was the rock on one side of the strait, Charybdis the whirlpool on the other—and sailors in avoiding the latter foundered on the former. In the British context Scilly has been identified with Scylla, the treacherous waters surrounding it with Charybdis. This theory is made more attractive by the fact that Scilly, like Scylla and Sicily, is, in situation, the "football" to the "leg" of the mainland. However, all this is complete conjecture, as are the claims that these islands derived from the Romans' *insulae Solis* (islands of the sun) or *insulae silicis* (*silex* is Latin for rock, *silicis* is its genitive—hence "islands of rock"). Yet another fanciful idea is that Scilly comes from Sellye or Selli which is the old Cornish for conger eel. By far the most plausible and certainly the most erudite commentary on the problem was written by Mr. Kenneth Sisam in the *Scillonian Magazine* (Volume XXXVI, No. 129): the gist of his argument is set out as follows:

The earliest reasonably certain reference to these islands is in A.D. 400 when Sulpicius Severus writes in his Latin Chronicle of "the island of Sylicancis which is off Britain". The "cancis" part is difficult to fathom, but "Syli" fits in. The Vikings who raided Scilly in the period between the tenth and twelfth centuries must also have known these islands as "Sylli" for they called the islands Syllingar. The "ar" marks the plural, while the "ing" can be found in other Scandinavian names of islands or groups. All this leads one to believe that, had there been an English record of the name before the Norman Conquest, it would have been "Sylli".

In the subsequent early English period there arose a difficulty in distinguishing between the sounds "i" and "y". The vowel "i" was pronounced as "pit" while "y" was halfway between the vowels of "pit" and "put" and in many of the words in which it appears the troublesome sound of "y" went different ways. So in early English the "y" in Scilly becomes "u" (Sully) or "e" (Selly) or "i" (Silly). In the south–west "u" dominated and so in this period Scilly is commonly seen as Sullye, Sully, Sulli and Sulley.

Towards the year 1500 the East Midland dialect of London (the one in which the "y" became "i") became recognized as standard English, and from about 1475 the East Midland Silly or Silley (sometimes spelt Sylly or Sylle) is the most common spelling of these islands.

The first example of the "Sc" coming into the name was in Leland's notes. He called them Scylley, the Scylleys and Isles of Scylley. When he composed his "Itinerary" on Scilly there was no fixed spelling in the English language and writers spelt as they felt. However Leland's "Sc" did not see the light of day until the early eighteenth century as his notes lay unpublished, and by that time it had been incorporated in the spelling and Scilly was common.

Dignity, says Mr. Sisam, might have had something to do with the adoption of "Sc" as during the Civil War of the mid seventeenth century a well known joke was "Silly men live in the far west". At last the spelling embarrassment had been overcome, but present day islanders still have a pronunciation similar to the quite unrelated word "silly" to put up with.

The origin of the adjective "Scillonian" is also difficult to explain. "Scillian" and the "Scillians" was used on isolated occasions, but Scillonian became the standard word. Had it been like "Devon-ian" or "Eton-ian" one could have understood the formation—but there appears to be no reason for this strange word "Scillonian". One might also have reasonably expected "Scillonia" for the name of the local steamship (like *Mauretania* or *Lusitania*), but here again "Scillonian" is used. There have been isolated attempts to popularize "Scillonia" to portray a sort of sea-girt Arcadia. Happily this pretentious collective noun has never really caught on.[1]

Megaliths and the "Isles of the Blest". Many thousands of years ago, the writers of ancient Rome and Greece made frequent references to the Isles of the Dead, the Isles of the Blest, or Hesperides to which the inhabitants of the mainland of Britain used to convey their dead heroes and chieftains for burial. There the souls of the departed found immortality amid conditions of plenty and bathed in peace and everlasting tranquillity. The isles were normally untainted by human habitation, and a certain sanctity was always attached to their remoteness and isolation. The Isles of the Dead were an insular Elysian Fields.

Among many other claims, some reasonable, others extravagant, the Isles of Scilly have been identified as these ancient Isles of the Dead and although most chances of determining the authenticity of the claim have been lost in the mists of prehistory, the notion, nevertheless, cannot altogether be discounted. Walk around Scilly today and you will find a quite remarkable number of granite burial chambers—links with the megalithic culture—in which the remains, cremated or otherwise, of Bronze Age man were placed. The concentration of so many graves in such a limited area as Scilly is taken to be certain proof that these islands were singled out as an island graveyard, a sacred cemetery. In the British Isles there are only two other places where the particular Scillonian-type of burial chamber, the "Entrance Grave" can be found—County Waterford in Eire and the Penwith

---

[1] The correct name for the islands is Isles of Scilly, or Scilly, used collectively. Scilly Isles and Scillies are hideous misnomers.

district of West Cornwall. These last-named tracts are quite
extensive yet between them they only boast nine, while Scilly
of just 4,042 acres, has no less than fifty! This tripartite burial
chamber area is therefore known to archaeologists as the "Scilly
Group". The density of burial graves in Scilly is further underlined when it is realized that the whole of England and Wales
contains 250—giving tiny Scilly a massive fifth of the total! This
big number in such a small area settled the argument for some
people. Scilly, they aver, must have been a mausoleum for dead
heroes, a vast temple of the living dead—the Isles of the Dead.
There would be much support for these romantic views if, during
the time in question (Bronze Age, 1900–800 B.C.) Scilly had been
uninhabited. Then the megalithic tombs we see today could have
been erected by those from across the water, for the dead from
across the water. But we now know that Scilly was, in fact, very
much populated and its megaliths were the handiwork of an
indigenous peoples—very probably the first inhabitants of Scilly.
They built the burial chambers for their island dead, although the
possibility that the deceased from across the sea were also brought
there for their last resting place cannot be ruled out.

The number of graves relative to such a small area can easily be
explained away. Scilly, before and at the time of the megalith
builders, was a far more extensive tract. Signs of settlements near
the water's edge prove this. Many of the islands, if not all, were
joined, making one reasonably large land mass at about the ten-
fathom mark, and much of the area now subsided and claimed by
the sea was once fertile land. There is good reason to believe that
the inundated parts between Tresco, St. Martin's, the Eastern
Isles and St. Mary's were the sites of Bronze Age settlements.
Perhaps it was there that the megalith builders existed in their
tiny villages, tending their cattle and farming their plots of land
for the cultivation of corn, wheat and barley? Perhaps it was in
this sea-claimed area that they made pottery, bone and stone tools;
knapped and flaked arrowheads; polished and ground their stone
axes; wove their cloth and worked on wood and metal.

How Scilly came by its first inhabitants probably provides a
clue to the origins of the traditional Celtic link Scilly and Cornwall have with Brittany. For it was from this western corner of
France that the megalith builders are believed to have come,
crossing the Channel to settle in Scilly and, as the entrance graves

have indicated, in Waterford and West Cornwall as well. Marks and legacies of their occupation cannot be missed. One has only to glance at the map of Scilly and note the number of times "Tumuli" is written, to realize it. It is scrawled along almost every shore of almost every island, inhabited or not. High ground and the tops of hills were much favoured by the grave builders, as the twin hills of Samson island bear witness. Also headlands jutting way out into the sea, and lonely cliffs—places removed, aloof, supposedly sacred. Whereas a lot of Scilly and signs of Bronze Age settlements have long since slipped beneath the ever-encroaching waves, the extremities and hill tops have been untouched and so many of the burial chambers still survive.

Scilly's "Entrance Graves" are one of two kinds—the chambered tomb built on to a mound or the plain chamberless barrow, often called cists, kistvaens or stone boxes. The chambers consist of huge granite slabs and were used over a great period of time for communal and collective family burial. The slabs were erected in such a way that they formed the walls, while large granite cap-stones were laid across them transversely for roofing. Sometimes fashioned rock was ignored in favour of living granite which formed the sides and floor of the chamber (as in a chamber on South Hill, Samson).

In the early Bronze Age inhumation was favoured, the bodies being laid in the chambers in a flexed or crouched position, but later cremation was practised with the remains being placed in a rude pot or urn. Sometimes the possessions of the deceased were also placed in the tomb as well—flints, saddle querns for grinding corn, and other articles. Sometimes offerings were placed at the entrance of the chamber. Cremation was most extensively practised by Scilly's tomb builders, although when some cists dating from the Roman period were unearthed in 1960 during preparations for the building of a council housing estate on St. Mary's a complete skeleton was found with knees drawn up to the chin: proof of inhumation.

Over the years much cremated remains, from which experts can in some measure piece together the picture of Bronze Age Scilly, have been irretrievably lost. Chambers and barrows have been destroyed, often unwittingly by people ignorant of their antiquity and archaeological value. Inevitably the sea has swallowed many; often farmers removed the hand-fashioned slabs for use in stone-walling;[1] some cap-stones were used in the construction of the old quay; while, in addition, vandals and treasure seekers have taken their toll. Tombs have been broken open, their urn contents rifled and much valuable information lost for ever. In this way two ancient barrows on Buzza Hill, St. Mary's were destroyed when the tower there was erected, while three were ruined on rocky Round Island when the lighthouse was under construction. However, happily, a number of the islands' most celebrated burial chambers are now protected by the Ministry of Works, notably Porth Hellick Down Burial Chamber, Innisidgen Burial Chamber and Bants Carn Burial Chamber, all on St. Mary's.

For thousands of years Scilly's tombs held their secrets. The antiquarian Borlase was the first to delve into their past, but his work was by no means authoritative or extensive. It was not until as relatively recently as 1901 that any full-scale professional excavations were carried out—by George Bonsor; and one of the first tombs he opened was on Gugh island. Discovered by an Agnes man, Obediah Hicks, it is known to posterity as Obediah's Barrow, and in it Bonsor found an urn containing cremated remains and also a bronze awl. At the time the latter was the only bronze object found with original burials in any burial chamber in the British Isles. Bonsor's visit gave archaeological interest in Scilly a long overdue fillip. Since that day increased interest has been shown in the megaliths and their erstwhile contents, and today, apart from the three St. Mary's chambers, we have a good many more, notably Knacky Boy Carn, Yellow Rock Carn and English Island Carn, all on St. Martin's.

Scilly's relics of the megalithic culture are not confined solely to burial chambers and their smaller brethren cists. There are some standing stones in the islands as well. The most celebrated granite column is on Gugh (near Obediah's Barrow) and is called the Old Man of Gugh. There is another near Harry's Walls, St. Mary's, just a few yards from where I write, while another, after which the St. Mary's area, Longstone, was called, has long been destroyed. A ramble around the headlands of Scilly today will not bring to light as many barrows and chambers as were formerly. Human and natural agents have assisted in their

---

[1] Hedging as it is known in Scilly. In the old days all property boundaries were marked by granite stones taken usually from the beaches.

reduction. But one can still unexpectedly happen upon one of these Bronze Age relics, perhaps partially submerged in a tangle of undergrowth, or exposed on a rocky carn, looking much like any other Scillonian outcrop from a distance. Significantly many of Scilly's rocky headlands are called "carns"—a word which elsewhere in the British Isles means cairn. As Lady Vyvyan rightly says, these relics of a forgotten past have "a strange power of impressing the imagination". They look sinister at first—the lairs of some prehistoric wild beast, but when you find one on a raised hilltop or an exposed cliff fringed by grotesquely weathered granite and with the blue sea all around, the imagination races. The mind flies back 3,000 or 4,000 years to a time when ancient man laboriously fashioned these great granite slabs by hand; levered them painstakingly into place believing the remains would live on in immortality. They are a tangible link with an ancient past—and somehow one feels terribly insignificant when confronted with this example of the infinity of time.

The stone tombs are Scilly's most valuable legacy of Bronze Age man. Although much of their contents have disappeared they have helped to piece together at least some of the jigsaw of Scilly's past. Strangely the megalith builders, the most ancient Scillonians of all, have left more signs of their occupation of these tiny isles than many succeeding peoples, for our knowledge of Scilly in the early years of the Christian era is indeed limited. When the tomb builders left the islands we do not know. Perhaps they survived while their fellows across the water were supplanted by other peoples?

The Cassiterides. For hundreds of years attempts have been made to identify the Isles of Scilly with the ancient Cassiterides—or tin islands—set somewhere in the western seas beyond the Pillars of Hercules (Straits of Gibraltar) from where the Phoenician traders used to obtain their supplies of the precious metal. It has been a favourite wrangle for archaeologists, geologists and historians ever since Camden suggested the identification in his *Britannia* long ago, but nobody has yet come up with the final word. Those set on solving the age-old mystery of the Cassiterides have to a large extent to depend on the works of the writers of ancient Greece and Rome. In the latter's favour is the fact that they were far more contemporary with the period in question than anyone else, but on the debit side is their limited geographical knowledge, their vagueness and inconsistencies. Let us start, however, with what we know for fact and then descend to conjecture.

The first millennium B.C. (or to pinpoint more specifically, the period of pre-Roman Italy) saw the heyday of the Phoenician. From his tiny Eastern Mediterranean strip of Tyre he rose to a position of dominance in the western theatre of that sea through a remarkable aptitude and zest for trade and commerce. He set up colonies in Sicily, North Africa and Spain (Gades) and *c.* 800 B.C. founded the great city of Carthage at a strategic point on the Mediterranean trading routes. In this millennium—or before—the Phoenician colonists of Gades pushed west beyond the bounds of the then known world into the Atlantic and discovered some islands rich in tin. These they naturally called the Cassiterides—the tin islands—and a constant supply of that metal from this source helped to keep them pre-eminent in the Mediterranean for centuries. The Phoenician had little time for anything else but trade. He largely ignored industry and left agriculture to the natives of the colonized areas. But his expertise with commerce has become a by-word—synonymous with the name Phoenician. It brought him the vast bulk of his wealth and made Carthage the richest city in the western Mediterranean. From this point on we have to depend on the often conflicting evidence of writers such as Herodotus, Pliny, Diodorus Siculus, Strabo, Solinus—and our old friend, conjecture.

The Greek historian Herodotus who wrote *c.* 450 B.C. tells us

... of that part of Europe nearest to the west I am not able to speak with decision. I by no means believe that the barbarians give the name of Eridanus to a river which empties itself into the Northern sea; whence, it is said, our amber comes. Neither am I better acquainted with the islands called the Cassiterides from which we are said to have our tin. It is, nevertheless, certain that both our tin and our amber are brought from these extreme regions.

Pliny says "opposite Celtiberia are a number of islands called Cassiterides by the Greeks in consequence of their abounding in tin".

Diodorus Siculus, writing in the first century B.C. mentions three sources of tin:

Tin is found in many parts of Iberia[Spain], not being discovered on
the surface as some have claimed in their histories but dug and
smelted like silver and gold. For beyond the land of the Lusitanians
[Portugal] are many mines of tin in the islands that lie off Iberia in
the Ocean which on this account are called the Cassiterides. And a
great deal is brought from the British island also to that part of
Gaul that lies opposite; and across the midlands of that Celtic country
it is brought to the people of Massilia [Marseilles] and to the town
called Narbona.

Caius Strabo, the great Greek geographer who wrote in the
the first century A.D. says

The Cassiderides, which are opposite to the west parts of Britain,
situate as it were in the same climate with Britain, are ten in number
and lie near each other in the ocean towards the north from the
shore of the Artabri. One of them is desert, but the others are
inhabited by men in black cloaks, clad in smocks reaching to their
feet, girt about the breast and walking with staves. They subsist
chiefly on their cattle and lead a nomadic life. But they also dig up
tin and lead and barter with the merchants for earthenware, salt and
brazen vessels.

Strabo also explains how the Phoenicians kept their secret of
the tin mart from the Romans:

In olden days the Phoenicians had a monopoly of this trade from
Gadeira [Gades] and carefully concealed the passage from everyone
else. On one occasion when the Romans followed in order to learn
the secret of the mart the Phoenician shipmaster jealously guarded
the secret by deliberately running his vessel on a shoal and so leading
his pursuers into a similar disaster. The Phoenician captain escaped
on a piece of wreckage and later was recompensed by the State for
the value of the cargo he had lost. The Romans, nevertheless, persisted with their search and finally discovered the secret mart.

Solinus tells us that the Cassiterides "were cut off from the
coast of the Damnonii by a rough, narrow sea"—and we know
that the Damnonii were the inhabitants of Devon and Cornwall.

From these accounts from the classics those who wish to prove
Scilly as the Cassiterides gain some measure of satisfaction. The
islands certainly lie in the rather vague area described by these
writers. But on delving deeper into the subject there is little else to
substantiate their claims. For, unhappily, there is no evidence

whatsoever that tin was mined to any great extent in these islands—certainly not enough to make it a commercial proposition. A few metalliferous veins and lodes have been found on Agnes, St. Marys, St. Martin's and Northwethel, while some shallow workings remain to this day in the north of Tresco, but none of these could have yielded any considerable quantity of tin. As H. O'Neill Hencken says in an article entitled *Cornwall and Scilly* (in *The County Archeologies*): "It is incredible that such feeble scratchings could have been of any importance in supplying the bronze foundries of the ancient Mediterranean."

One of the favourite theories put forward by those wishing to identify Scilly with the Cassiterides is that there was a great subsidence in the island group, and that any evidence of mining has been submerged by the sea. Others like to claim that the mines were shallow surface workings—which is the reason why there is now no evidence. However, these ideas are surely over fanciful. The truth is probably that the Cassiterides was a name given generally to the Atlantic tin lands which lay west of the Mediterranean, in the strange unknown; that the source of tin was not Scilly at all—but Cornwall, which today, after a dormant period, is producing tin as of old. It is not unlikely that the rich tin areas of north-west Spain and Brittany were all part of this vague tin Klondyke called the Cassiterides.

It has been suggested that if Scilly was not the place where tin was actually mined, then it was an entrepot or trading centre; that the tin, mined in Cornwall, was shipped to Scilly for barter with Phoenician merchants. Here again this seems most unlikely as Ictis (St. Michael's Mount in Mounts Bay near Penzance) has been generally accepted as the main clearing house. The claim of St. Michael's Mount is substantiated by Diodorus Siculus:

The inhabitants of that part of Britain which is called Belerium [Lands End] are very fond of strangers and from their intercourse with foreign merchants are civilized in their manner of life. They prepare the tin, working very carefully the earth in which it is produced. The ground is rocky, but it contains earthy veins, the produce of which is ground down, smelted and purified. They beat the metal into masses . . . and carry it to a certain island off Britain called Ictis. During the ebb of the tide the intervening space is left dry and they carry over into the island the tin in abundance in their wagons. Here then the merchants buy the tin from the natives and

Higher Town, St. Martin's with rows of flower patches

carry it over to Gaul and, after travelling over land for about thirty days they finally bring their loads to the mouth of the Rhone.

It seems that initially the Phoenicians traded for their Cornish tin at Ictis and sailed back to the Atlantic port of Gades. Much later when the Romans exploited the tin trade and had conquered Gaul the tin was shipped from Ictis to Corbilo at the mouth of the Loire in the Bay of Biscay, then taken over land by pack horse to the ports of Massilia and Narbona on the estuary of the Rhône.

Occasionally one comes across accounts of tin being mined in the Isles of Scilly. *Transactions of the Royal Geological Society of Cornwall* mentions a small quantity raised in 1818, while Robert Heath writes that there was tin in Scilly and that overtures were made to Sir Francis Godolphin, the Lord Proprietor, to mine it. However, nothing was done, and this is significant as Godolphin was one of the leading authorities on tin mining of his day. A mineralogist who accumulated a sizeable fortune from mines in the Breage and Godolphin areas of Cornwall, Sir Francis was largely responsible for introducing foreign miners into the county to teach deep-mining techniques and blasting with gunpowder. He served with Sir Francis Bacon on a Commission of Inquiry into mining matters, and had there been the slightest chance of exploiting tin in Scilly he would not have overlooked it. The fact that Sir Francis paid scant attention to a mining concession granted in 1563 to Martin Dare, John Elliott of St. German's and Roger Carew of Antony speaks volumes.

However, although everything points to the conclusion that tin was never mined on any great scale in these islands, the legend of the Cassiterides still lingers on (a famous Scilly-built ship was called *Cassiterides*). When one stands on a headland in Scilly surrounded by huge boulders of granite, a rock which has come to be associated with tin mining, and looks out across the water to Lands End, one remembers the rich Levant mine which is tunnelled miles out under the sea towards Scilly—and one wonders. . . . Periodically finds are made in the islands and the old controversy is resurrected, only to die down once again. To the over-imaginative every hole is an ancient mining adit, every pit a working—sure proof that Scilly was the Cassiterides of old. No matter how much proof is weighted against the identification,

4

Picking flowers at St. Mary's

one cannot help but feel that the story will never die; for if it did then yet another gap in Scilly's already scanty history would appear and Scillonians, like islanders the world over, like to cling on to the few threads of history left to them.

The Lost Land of Lyonesse and Arthurian Romance. Local legend has it that the Isles of Scilly are the remnants of the lost land of Lyonesse, a piece of country which once upon a time joined the islands to Lands End (and included St. Michael's Mount) and which was drowned by a huge flood never to reappear. This catastrophe was supposed to have happened in the sixth century at the time of King Arthur and the Knights of the Round Table. Most legends have a basis of truth, but not this one, as, of course, no such disaster has been recorded in the period *homo sapiens* has been on this earth. Had such an event taken place it would certainly have been noted for posterity.

We are led to believe that Lyonesse was a tract of incomparable fertility and bounty containing rich orchards, 140 villages and churches, where a flourishing population whiled their lives away in absolute peace and contentment. The main settlement was supposed to have been on the site now occupied by the Seven-stones Light, known to fishermen as "the City". The Cornish are notoriously superstitious and even today one comes across people who honestly accept the story of the lost land of Lyonesse. They claim that vegetation has been washed ashore in Mount's Bay—proof of a former land; the original name of St. Michael's Mount—"Hoar rock in the wood"—is further evidence they maintain. They point to Heath's words "at Sennen Church Town, near the extremity of Cornwall, there is a base of an old stone-column belonging to a building which was taken up by some fishermen at the Place of the Seven Stones, about eighteen inches height and three feet diameter at the circular base. Besides which, other pieces of building and glass windows have been taken up at different times in the same place with divers kinds of utensils". There are many, and often ingenious arguments put forward by the disciples of Lyonesse. Scilly has at one time or other suffered from the encroachment of the sea, so why not a land between the islands and Cornwall? They also note that the water between Cornwall and Scilly is inordinately shallow—far more so than the water north and south of the line; also that the seabed is remarkably

level. The similarity in the rock formation of Lands End and
Scilly is a favourite point, and we even get tales about fishermen
hearing bells tolling when hauling pots off Lands End! The
"proof" is never-ending and indeed some of the arguments do
go towards making a fair case for considering the possibility of a
once-joined land mass—when allied to a deal of imagination. But
the fact must remain that if there were a flood or a subsidence
then it happened way back in neolithic age, not as recently as
Arthurian times and it was a gradual process over centuries, rather
than one spectacular disaster. If this is so there can be no connection whatsoever with Arthur and Lyonesse.

A geologist-type argument is out of place here. The subject has
been dealt with exhaustively elsewhere. Indeed whole books have
been soberly devoted to the question whether Scilly and Cornwall
were one land mass. What concerns us is the story of Lyonesse and
King Arthur. The legend was immortalized by Mallory and
Geoffrey de Monmouth and subsequently provided the inspiration for Tennyson's "Morte D'Arthur" and "Passing of Arthur".
Tennyson visited Scilly to set the mood for his work, and one of
St. Mary's hotels bears an inscription to this effect. Perhaps the
best description of the legendary happening, certainly the most
imaginative and graphic, was written by the Reverend H.
Whitfield. The Reverend H. Whitfield came to Scilly by one of
the infrequent packet boats in 1840 for the purpose of studying the
legends of the islands. After freely admitting there were precious
few of them, he proceeded to fill a book with legends! While
much of the content of his *Scilly and its Legends* (pub. 1852) must
therefore be accepted with reserve, his account of King Arthur's
epic battle with the rebel Mordred is eminently readable. The
following account is taken from his book, with some of it being
condensed from a little book on Scilly by J. C. Tonkin and
Prescott Row.

The story is taken up at Tintagel Castle where King Arthur is
holding court together with the Knights of the Round Table.
Sir Bors de Gamis is there, so is Sir Caradoc, and Sir Tristram and
Sir Lancelot of the Lake and many others which made up the
king's peerless retinue. But there is a strange air of gloom in this
company so accustomed to joy and gaiety, for treason has seduced
Prince Mordred from their allegiance. A feeling of evil is in the
air. The following morning news came of Mordred's revolt. Foes

banded together and friends fell off, the bands united swelled
into an army and the army with Mordred at its head endeavoured
to strike a blow for the crown of England. The land of Cornwall,
never too friendly with Arthur, was alive with his foes. They
marched upon Tintagel where Arthur lay grimly, his renowned
knights within the walls. At daybreak one morning the hero king
rode out followed by those who still adhered to him. Hitherto
unconquerable, in proud defiance they went forth to do battle for
God and for their king. Alone at their head rode Arthur to his
last of fields.

Next evening a band of warriors were seen urging their steeds
across the wild heaths of Cornwall. Their course was in the
direction of the Cassiterides and of that fair tract of country
called in the Cornish tongue Lethowsow. They hurried for life
over the waste in their hacked armour and torn surcoats, all that
remained of the chivalry of Britain. Arthur lay dead upon the
plain. The survivors of the dreadful day were fleeing for their
lives and Mordred thundered upon their rear. Looking back,
shields, morions, and lances gleamed fitfully from the brow of a
distant hill. It was the glimmering of the pursuers' arms. Should
they make a stand and die? There was the traitor, the murderer
of his kinsmen and sovereign, should they not await his coming
and strike one blow in revenge?

They paused gloomy and irresolute and there seemed to become
between them a shadowy dimness as of a mountain mist yet
wearing the shape and aspect of humanity and uprising its huge
outline between the spoilers and their prey; it was the awful ghost
of Merlin. It was a gulf between the two parties impassable as that
between the Egyptians and the fleeing Hebrews and it checked
the following host in their headlong speed. Mordred reached a
lofty slope from which he could more clearly see his retiring
enemies. They were already at a considerable distance upon the
winding road that led over the fertile track of country called
"Lethowsow" and in after days "Lyonesse". Around him was
that fair land now so long lost and forgotten where men dug
mineral wealth and upon which were seen no fewer than one
hundred glades, it never looked so grandly glorious as in that hour
of its fate.

"As Mordred pressed on, full of one thought alone, already in
imagination hemming in to slaughter or driving into the waves

his enemies, his attenders and followers began to be sensible of a change in the atmosphere, of a something oppressive and horrible, though he himself perceived it not.

"Huge battlemented clouds, tinged with lurid red hung over the horizon. The air became sultry and choking. A tremulous and wavy motion shook the ground at intervals. A low sound like distant thunder moaned around.

"At last, amid a silence that might be felt, so dreadful was it and so dull—that fearful shade, which had hitherto gone before him, and restrained his madness, suddenly itself stopped. It assumed a definite shape. It was the form of Merlin the Enchanter.

"Right on Mordred's path, face to face, did the avenger stand. They remained for a few seconds, motionless, frowning upon each other. Neither spoke save with the eye. After those few seconds the great wizard raised his arm. Then there ensued a confused muttering, a sound as though the foundations of the great deep were broken up. Soon the voice of the subterranean thunder increased and the firm soil beneath their feet began to welk and wave and fissures appeared upon the surface and the rock swelled like the throes of a labouring sea.

"With a wild cry of agony the band of pursuers became in turn the pursued. They wheeled and turned away in headlong flight. But it was in vain. The earth, rent in a thousand fragments, in the grasp of that earthquake upheaved its surface convulsively, gave one brief and conscious pause, and then at once sank down for ever beneath the level of the deep.

"In a moment a continent was submerged with all its works of art and piety, with all its living tribes, with all its passions, and hopes and fears.

"The soldiers of Mordred were whirled away in the stream created by that sudden gulf, which even now flows so violently over its prey below. Last of all Mordred remained, as it were fascinated and paralysed, gazing at the phantom with a look in which horror struggled with hate and which was stamped with scorn and defiance to the end.

"That morning had dawned upon as bright a scene as ever met the eye. At evening there was nought—from what was then first termed the Lands End to St. Martin's head—but a howling and a boiling wilderness of waves bearing here and there upon its bosom a fragment from the perished world beneath or a corpse tossed upon the billows over which sea birds wheeled and screamed.

"The remnant that was preserved reached in safety Cassiteris, called afterwards Silura and now Scilly. There the wicked ceased to trouble and the weary were at rest. In their island home upon which still the sea encroached daily, they dwelt securely. From St. Martin's height on their arrival they saw the catastrophe that overwhelmed their enemies, and dismounting knelt upon the turf and thanked God for their deliverance. They never more sought the Britain of their hope and fame. It would have been a changed and melancholy home for them. Arthur was in his tomb at Glastonbury. The Round Table was broken and its best Knights perished or dispersed. Their work was done.

"In the Isles of Scilly, miraculously severed from the mainland and as it were set apart from their lives, they lived and there they died. In after days their children raised a stately religious house at Tresco over their bones. But their memory gradually faded away and was forgotten.

"Sometimes on a clear day there may be seen the remains of walls or buildings under the sea. Sometimes fishermen bring up relics of other times and men wonder at them and speculate on their cause and use. Strangers make pilgrimages to Scilly and marvelled whether it ever exceeded its present limits. But the account of its isolation is remembered only as a confused dream; it is a mystery, an old world tale; a fragment of which, like a portion of a wreck, floats about, here and there, in the visions of the past.

"Such is the legend of Lyonesse."

If the story of the inundation is fanciful, then so is everything surrounding the person of King Arthur himself. We know of an obscure man who bore the Roman name of Artorius, but little else about him. And yet it seems this vague figure was to live on until by dint of tales and embellishments he was to reign over the vast realm of medieval romance as King Arthur.

Yet however over-imaginative the story of Lyonesse is—or any tales concerning a subsidence or flood which divided Scilly from the mainland—the legend lives on as strong as ever in these islands. Boats are named *Lyonesse*—one of the most faithful of Scilly's steamers bore the name—so are houses and one of the St. Mary's sports teams, now unhappily extinct, was called after the legendary land. During the last war the Lyonesse Remembrance League was formed to help Scillonian servicemen overseas.

Olaf Tryggvason. The story of Olaf Tryggvason is a "natural" for the cinema screen. The period is the tenth century, perilous days for the inhabitants of Britain. A handsome, fearless Viking pirate-king ravages the coasts of western England, Scotland and France in a protracted cruise of four years; he happens on a peaceful group of islands off the shores of western England where he pauses to rest and careen; he hears of a hermit living on a tiny isle and that he has the gift of prophecy; the Viking king visits his cell—is baptized and converted from his pagan ways to Christianity; he returns to his native Scandinavia a changed man, and turns the might of his sword to the stamping out of the worship of Thor and Odin and to the spreading of the Word. Vintage Hollywood!

The tale of Olaf is not as widely known as those of Lyonesse and the Cassiterides, yet it has more historical fact as its basis than either of the other two. In the Dark Ages the Norsemen were for two or more centuries a constant menace to the shores of Britain with their lightning raids on wealthy settlements, and there is no reason to believe that Scilly was spared their attentions. King Olaf undoubtedly did come to Scilly. But the story of his baptism and conversion is no more than legend, although it is incorporated in Scandinavian history and is recorded by Snorri Sturluson in his *Saga of Olaf Tryggvason.* This is what this thirteenth-century writer has to say of the event, which he dates as 980 and which we are assured helped change the whole course of religion in western Europe.

Thereafter Olaf Tryggvason sailed to England and ravaged wide around this land. He sailed all the way to Northumberland where he plundered and thence to Scotland where he marauded far and wide. Then he went to the Hebrides where he found some battles, and then southward to the Isle of Man where he also fought.

He ravaged far around in Ireland and then steered to Bretland [Wales] which he laid waste with fire and sword, and also the district called Cumberland. He sailed westward from thence to Valland [Northern France] and marauded there. Then he left intending to sail to England to come to the islands called the Isles of Scilly, lying westward from England in the ocean.

Olaf had been four years on this cruise from the time he left Wendland till he came to the Isles of Scilly.

While he lay in the isles he heard of a seer, or soothsayer on the islands who could tell beforehand things not yet done, and what he foretold many believed were really fulfilled. Olaf became curious to try this man's gift of prophecy. He therefore sent one of his men who was the handsomest and the strongest, clothed him magnificently and bade him say he was the king; for Olaf was known in all countries as handsomer, stronger, braver than all others. . . .

Now when the messenger came to the soothsayer and gave himself out for the king he got the answer "Thou art not the king, but I advise thee to be faithful to thy king". And more he would not say to that man. The man returned and told Olaf and his desire to meet the soothsayer was increased; and now he had no doubt of his really being a soothsayer.

Olaf repaired himself to him and, entering into conversation, asked what he foretold about Olaf's future, if he would have kingdoms or other luck. The hermit answered with holy soothsaying.

Thou shalt be a glorious king and bring forth glorious work. Thou shalt bring many men to the Truth and to become Christians. Thereby shalt thou help thyself and many others, and that thou shalt not have doubt about my answer thou canst have this evidence. Near to thy ships wilt thou meet treachery and foes and wilt come to battle; thou wilt lose some of thy men and thou thyself wilt be wounded. From that wound thou shalt near be dead and be born on the shields to thy ship; but from that wound thou wilt be well in seven nights and shortly after wilt thou be baptized.

After that Olaf went down to his ships and there he met foes who would slay him and his men. But the meeting ended as the hermit had told him, so that Olaf was borne wounded out to his ship and likewise was he well after seven nights.

Then it seemed clear to Olaf that this man had told him the truth and that he was a true soothsayer from whom he had this foretelling. Olaf then went again to find the man, spoke much with him and asked carefully whence he had this wisdom by which he had foretold the future.

The hermit said that the God of Christian men let him know all he wished, and then he told Olaf of many great works of God and after all these words Olaf agreed to be baptized; and so it came about that Olaf and all his following were baptized. He stayed there very long and learned the right Faith and took with him from thence priests and other learned men.

On his return to Norway King Olaf forced his heathen subjects to embrace the Faith. Their only alternative was death.

> King Olaf from the doorway spoke
> 'Choose ye between two things my folk
> To be baptized or given up to slaughter!'
>   Longfellow

Tradition has it that the lonely isle where Olaf was baptized was St. Helen's, and the soothsayer was the Welsh hermit St. Elidius, renowned for his sanctity. The isle was named after the hermit, and from St. Elid's isle subsequently became St. Helen's. It is known that at the time of King Olaf's wanderings there were hermits cloistered at Tresco and St. Helen's.

In the Dark Ages the Vikings certainly had many dealings with Scilly, and even today suggestions of these marauders of long ago are given by the fairskinned, fairheaded inhabitants of St. Martin's. It is exciting to speculate that little Scilly might have played so large a part in the spread of Christianity in Western Europe.

History: from piracy and poverty to prosperity

From the time of the megalith builders right through the early Iron Age, the Roman invasion and the subsequent Dark Ages (aptly named from the Scillonian historian's point of view) to the Norman Conquest, precious little is known about Scilly. We come across pieces of information here and there and have to piece them together the best way we can in order to form a hazy picture of these islands. Just about the first recorded event is the banishment to Scilly of the bishops Instantius and Tiberianus by the Emperor Maximus in the late fourth century for heresy. We have reason to believe that the islands were used as a sort of penal colony for offenders, but only sporadic evidence has turned up to allow us to form a picture of Scilly in the days of Roman Britain. There have been "finds"—such as the Roman village of Bants Carn, St. Mary's dating back to the second and third century A.D., the unearthing of a circular Roman hut on St. Martin's (on the shore) with pottery dating back to the third and fourth centuries A.D.; the finding of a Roman bronze brooch in a kistvaen on Old Man near Tean; the discovery of a Roman urn when some cists were disturbed when a Council housing estate was being built on

St. Mary's; coins found on Samson, a Roman altar found on St. Mary's and now at Tresco Abbey. But the most important discovery of all took place as recently as 1962 when following violent gales and storms a hut, dating from the Roman era, was unearthed on the tiny uninhabited Eastern isle of Nornour. This discovery has set archaeologists and islanders thinking afresh about Scilly during the Roman era.

The period between the departure of the Romans and the coming of William the Conqueror is to all intents and purposes blank. King Athelstan is said to have visited Scilly in the tenth century to drive out the Vikings, but there is little substantiating evidence. However, one thing is certain; this period saw the origin of the association of pirates with Scilly and the accompanying tales of lawlessness and misdeeds that have survived to this day. As we have seen, Olaf and the Vikings based themselves on these islands, and there was obviously little form of law and order, a position that was to remain well into the sixteenth century. At this time Scilly probably contained some hermits who owned some land and built small oratories which were the first ecclesiastical buildings in the islands.

In the early twelfth century the monks of Tavistock came to Scilly, and island history proper is recorded for the first time. A charter of Henry I in 1114 granted the chapelries to the Monastery of Tavistock in Devon and they established the Benedictine priory of St. Nicholas on Tresco, which at the time was known as St. Nicholas isle. The monks' role was to be a fairly extensive one for they were to control all spiritual matters and a fair amount of the secular for over four hundred years, until their establishment was broken up and they disappeared with the dissolution of the monasteries in the sixteenth century.

The monks were given all the chapels and oratories in the islands, the tithes and offerings, some of the lesser isles, small plots of land on Aganus or Hagness (Agnes) and on Ennor (St. Mary's) and the right to profit from any wrecks which might occur in their islands. They also engaged in trade on a modest scale, but their overall living was never more than meagre owing to the one evil which continuously blighted Scilly during this period—piracy. It seems that the seeds sown many years before in the days of Olaf and his Viking marauders, had now produced a veritable harvest of lawlessness. Scilly became a favourite base for French,

Spanish, Cornish and Channel freebooters, while robbers, thieves and every kind of outcast of society converged upon the islands—and islanders and monks alike lived in fear and dread of them. The Tavistock Abbey historian, Dr. Finberg, wrote, "In this year [1209] on Ascension Day pirates were beheaded in St. Nicholas Isle [Tresco] in Sully to the number of 112." Tales of Scilly and its pirates lived on for many a day until they gave way to the more sophisticated arts of smuggling and wrecking.

The islands had little form of defence during this period, which is not altogether surprising as the civil authorities frequently consorted with the privateers and derived a percentage of their spoils in return for turning a blind eye. Unprotected, the monastic settlement in Scilly could hardly have expected to flourish; by the mid 1400s the abbey had fallen into a shocking state of disrepair, and when the monks were not sending desperate pleas to their parent abbey in Tavistock for financial aid they were fleeing the islands to seek temporary refuge from the pirates. They even pleaded for a secular clergy to conduct Scillonian affairs!—and in the early 1400s King Edward III made pleas to mariners touching on Scilly to help the priory and its monks. The monks depended almost entirely on the tithe-payers, and as islanders got little protection from the puny twelve-men force which more often than not garrisoned Ennor Castle on St. Mary's, the priory rarely got its dues.

Scilly was such an unattractive place in those days that there is reason to believe the monks were dispatched there to take up their duties as a sort of expiation for sins committed. One thing is certain that when the Tresco Priory was broken up in common with other monastic establishments in 1539 the monks were not sorry to see the back of Scilly. All they had experienced there was a near hand-to-mouth living, barren and singularly unsympathetic soil from a religious point of view, continual friction with the lay authorities who made little effort to establish any order, and, always, ill treatment from the pirates. Bankrupt and with their buildings falling down, the monks of Tavistock probably left Scilly well before the Dissolution. Their stay in the island had been anything but a happy one and with their departure religious records in Scilly grew hazy until well into the seventeenth century.

Let us look at the secular authority in the period up to the dissolution of the monastries. When the monks first settled in Scilly lay control was exercised by the absentee Earls of Cornwall, among whose resident representatives were Drew de Barrantine and Ranulph (or Ralph) de Blanchminster. In the early fourteenth century a second Blanchminster was established in the Norman-built Ennor Castle, which at the time was the only fortification in Scilly, by King Edward I. Ennor Castle, of which there is little trace today, was at Old Town, which was the then capital of St. Mary's. Old records called Old Town Hencastle, or Heyug-castle, from which, perhaps, the name of the present capital Hugh Town derived. Blanchminster was the first of a number of that name who were to administer as Lords of Scilly—or rather mis-administer—in the two centuries leading up to the Dissolution. The Blanchminsters were a celebrated West Country family. Apart from being Lords of Scilly and Constables of Ennor Castle, they possessed other lands, Carhays, Week, St. Mary and Stratton. Sir Ralph is variously recorded under his Latin name of "Sir Ralph de Albo Monasterio"; Norman-French "de Blanch-minster"—and English "Sir Ralph of Whiteminster". Successors of the Blanchminsters included Denvers, Whittington, the Coles-hills and the Arundells—the last-named two both being implicated in piracy. None of the Blanchminsters, it seems, was above profit-ing from the existing lack of order at the expense of the islanders who were reduced to a near subsistence-level living. Most islanders realized the fruitlessness of opposing the lawless, so they swam with the tide and were generally a party to crime.

In 1337 the Duchy of Cornwall[1] was created to endow the Black Prince, and Scilly was included in the estate—but it was not to be a profitable possession. There was no noticeable im-provement in the situation. Scilly continued to deteriorate while the authorities worked in league with the pirates who remained free to carry on their various pursuits of villainy without reproach or restraint. "William le Poer, coroner of Scilly, went to Tresco to inquire into a wreck and to take charge of the salved cargo. He was seized and imprisoned by a mob whose ringleader was prior of St. Nicholas. He bought his freedom and a subsequent inquiry showed men-at-arms and their leader who guarded Ennor Castle were principal offenders!" (*Victoria County History, Cornwall*). Scilly took on a wasted look. Houses and buildings

[1] The Duchy's association with Scilly stretches to the present day.

went to ruin as honest islanders fled the attentions of the lawless; good land went untilled; the "Fortunate Islands" have probably never been at such a low ebb in their whole history. It is recorded that, in 1342, 600 Welsh soldiers, wind bound in Crow Sound on the way to the French wars, ravaged and pillaged throughout Scilly, while the notes of Leland, the antiquarian who is believed to have visited the islands shortly after the Dissolution but may well have not, bear witness to the slump in the fortunes of Scilly: "The houses of St. Mary's," he wrote, "were sore defacid and woren" and "few men were glad to inhabit these islettes for all the plenty for robbers by sea that take their cattle by force. The robbers be Frenchmen or Spaniards."

The official value of the islands also reflects the situation. Ranulph de Blanchminster had only to keep twelve armed men and pay annually 400 puffins or six and eightpence for his post, while when the Duchy assumed control, Scilly's value was, in time of peace forty shillings; in war nothing!

The corruption in high places is further illustrated in the sad affair of Lord Admiral Thomas Seymour, who was one of the last of the succession of administrators. It appears he was involved in the piracy business up to the hilt, and in 1549 was accused to that effect in a bill of Attainder, together with plotting against the monarch and various other contraventions of State affairs. The Bill claimed "he had gotten into his hands the strong and dangerous Scilly Isles where he might have a refuge if anything for his demerits should be attempted against him." He was convicted and beheaded.

The case of Seymour seems to have, at long last, brought Scilly to the attention of the Crown, for in the same year as King Edward VI disposed of the subversive Lord Admiral he sent two Falmouth Killigrews and one Richard Hutton—all building experts—to the islands to supervise Scilly's first-ever scheme of fortifications. A number of blockhouses and installations were set up on Tresco and St. Mary's, but none of them were subsequently to play a very effective role in the defence of Scilly. King Charles Castle on Tresco and Harry's Walls, St. Mary's date from this time, but faulty siting in both cases reduced their effectiveness. The King was succeeded by Queen Elizabeth in 1558, by which time control had been invested in William and later Thomas Godolphin, who became military governors under the Crown.

For the first time royalty were taking an active interest in Scilly.

We now come to one of the major landmarks in the history of these islands. In the year 1571—the thirteenth year of the Tudor queen's reign—Francis Godolphin was given the lease of Scilly for a term of thirty-seven years (to 1608) in return for an annual payment of £20 (£10 "new rent", £10 "old rent"). The coming of Sir Francis—he was knighted in 1580—brings to an end this awful period for Scilly (until fortunes lapsed again in the mid eighteenth century) and marks the start of a long association which Scilly was to have with this famous old Cornish family. For the first time Scilly had an administrator of undoubted worth, and, barring the years of the Interregnum, descendants of Sir Francis were to hold Scilly for the Crown from this date through to 1775 when the male line became extinct and the islands passed to Thomas Osborne, fourth Duke of Leeds who had married the only daughter of the previous Godolphin Lord Proprietor, Earl Sydney. The Godolphin-Osbornes continued in Scilly until 1831 when the lease was not renewed and their 260-year tenure was at an end. But I am getting ahead of my story.

Straightaway on taking up the lease Francis Godolphin set about the mammoth task of renovation. He inherited nothing but disorganization but out of it he managed to restore some semblance of order. Land was divided up into plots and allotted to tenants; people began to come to the islands; employment was found; gradually a measure of well-being was attained; but there was still one need which had yet to be met, and that need was protection. Ennor Castle in Old Town had long fallen into disuse and disrepair due to the negligence of the wayward Lords of Scilly, and the islands were still an easy prey for channel pirates. Godolphin wrote at the time: "Scilly is a bushment of briers and a refuge for all the pirates that range," and Queen Elizabeth, too, realized the urgent need for some form of fortified protection, but for a different reason. The Tudor queen feared the attentions of Spain. The Armada had been vanquished in 1588 but the two countries were still at war and Spaniards were making sporadic raids on English coastal settlements.[1] The Queen anticipated that they might seize Scilly as their base and, with this uppermost in her mind, she instructed Godolphin to build a fortification on St. Mary's.

[1] The sack of Mousehole and Penzance in 1595.

The Governor, disregarding the abandoned Harry's Walls, chose the high ground of the Hugh as the site for the building, an ideal spot for it commanded the Roadstead and the entrance to St. Mary's harbour. Work began in the summer of 1593 under the direction of Robert Adams, an engineer from the garrison at Plymouth, and so industrious were those engaged on the construction that eighteen months later it was finished. They called it Stella Mariae (Star of Mary)—or Star Castle—owing to its taking the form of an eight-pointed star. Surrounded by a moat, it was a fortress within outer walls and its ramparts contained ninety-six loopholes. Star Castle is standing in its dominant position today, but since 1933, as a hotel, has been given to more peaceful pursuits. Robert Adams' creation is a plain building. It did not presume to be anything else. Its job was purely functional —to provide the islands with protection in a way that was quickest and cheapest. The Queen allowed Godolphin only £400 and the whole operation cost less than £1,000, Godolphin providing the balance himself. He was later reimbursed. Star Castle is believed the cheapest-built of all Britain's castles. Despite the parsimony, the granite-walled fort has withstood a siege in the mid seventeenth century and the passing of time far better than many a more elaborate and costly edifice—a remarkable tribute to the characteristic Tudor ability to produce much out of little. Islanders welcomed the new fortification by uprooting themselves from the old capital of Old Town where the decaying Ennor Castle was demolished and settling on the narrow isthmus below the Hugh under the Star Castle guns. When Godolphin built the first quay in St. Mary's Pool in 1601, Hugh Town's destiny as the main settlement in Scilly was assured. It has, of course, remained the hub of Scilly ever since. Godolphin also set about fortifying the hitherto unprotected Hugh promontory by building a curtain wall of bastions across the isthmus from the Pool to Porthcressa.

The effects of Star Castle were to warn off both Spaniards and would-be pirates alike—for until the Civil War not a single shot was fired against it in anger—and Scilly now settled down to what islanders hoped would be something like normal life.

As well as doing much towards giving Scilly protection and order, the first Godolphin also brought about something of a social change. Before his lease the islands were, in almost every way, Celtic. Scillonians were Cornish speaking, their name-prefixes bore a Cornish stamp ("by Tre and Pol and Pen, you can tell the Cornish men"), and the rocks, isles and places had Celtic names. The only "outside" blood was provided by the Vikings in the early days, then by pirates and adventurers who settled continuously over the centuries and gave Scilly its basically mongrel population which it still has to this day. Scilly was an introverted community, totally cut off from mainland influence. However, Sir Francis and his train brought a breath of the mainland with them. In short, they "anglicized" Scilly. Many people living in the islands today can trace their family tree back to the days of the first Godolphin and to marriage with men and women who followed him here from England and settled.[1]

Nothing untoward is recorded in Scilly in the early seventeenth century, barring the imprisonment of Dr. Bastwick (sans ears) in Star Castle at the order of Star Chamber following his sturdy denunciation of Episcopacy. But hardly had the memory of war with Spain begun to fade than the effects of a new, and more unpleasant conflict were to be felt in the islands—the Civil War.

Scilly throughout was staunchly royalist and stayed that way long after the mainland of Britain had capitulated to Parliament. By 1646 the outlook was bleak for King Charles. Cromwell's general Fairfax had carried all before him in Cornwall (which, like Scilly, sided largely with their king) and Pendennis Castle was the royalists' sole remaining stronghold on the mainland. With Parliamentarian pressure becoming intense the Prince of Wales, who, on the Restoration in 1660 was to become Charles II, fled Pendennis to the refuge of Star Castle in Scilly. The Prince stayed for six weeks and then narrowly escaped the attentions of the Parliamentarian fleet in fleeing to Jersey in the Channel Islands. We have a graphic and unintentionally rather humorous account of the Prince's stay in Scilly in the memoirs of one Lady Fanshawe, who was in the Prince's retinue. Following a description of a disastrous voyage in a ship called the *Phoenix* from Lands End—during which, among other things, they were robbed

---

[1] Today the "anglicization" has run amok. The Celtic names are rapidly being submerged by immigrant Anglo-Saxon, although Scilly still has its Trenears, Trezises, Tregears, Trenearys, Trewhellas, Trenwiths, and Penders.

Augustus Smith

by the crew whose mutinous intent was subsequently only quelled by her husband's money—she wrote:

The next day, after being pillaged and extremely sick and big with child, I was set on shore almost dead in the Island of Scilly. When we had got to our quarters near the Castle where the Prince lay, I went immediately to bed, which was so vile that my footman ever lay in a better, and we but three in the whole house, which consisted of four rooms or rather, partitions, two low rooms and two little lofts with a ladder to go up; in one of these they kept dried fish, which was their trade, and in this my husband's two clerks lay. One there was for my sister, and one for myself, and one amongst the rest of the servants; but when I washed in the morning I was so cold I knew not what to do, but the daylight discovered that my bed was near swimming in the sea, which the owner told us it never did but at spring tide. With this we were destitute of clothes; and meat and fuel for half the Court to serve them a month was not to be had in the whole island, and truly we begged our daily bread of God; for we thought every meal our last. The Council sent for provisions to France, which served us, but they were bad and little of them; then after three weeks and odd bad days, we set sail for the Isle of Jersey, where we safely arrived, praise be God, beyond the belief of the beholders from that Island, for the pilot, not knowing the way into the harbour, sailed over the rocks, but being spring tide. . . .

Shortly after the privations of the unfortunate Lady Fanshawe, Scilly was occupied by the Roundheads, who remained until the end of 1648. But as soon as they had departed Scilly declared itself boldly for the king, and until 1651, long after the cessation of mainland hostilities, Sir John Grenville and his cavaliers carried on a successful guerrilla-type campaign against Parliamentarian shipping. Grenville, a member of the famous West Country family, had been appointed to the Governorship when the tide was running strongly against the Royalists. It seems that after the departure of the Roundheads the Star Castle fortress became hard-pressed to obtain ammunition and provisions, so Sir John fitted out a fleet of ships to obtain supplies from France, which knew Scilly as "Les Sorlingues", and also adopted the simple, if some-what piratical, expedient of satisfying his wants from channel shipping, regardless of flag flown.

The Dutch and Van Tromp of broom-to-the-masthead fame made an appearance at this juncture. Following some action against a Dutch merchantman by Sir John's men, Van Tromp

5

St. Mary's Pool, with Samson across the Roadstead
Golf links, St. Mary's Pool and Hugh Town

appeared off the islands with a fleet of twelve ships demanding redress. Van Tromp tried to persuade Grenville to hand over the islands under the pretence of holding them until such times as Prince Charles was placed on the throne.[1] However, Sir John, a loyal Englishman, even if he was at war with his countrymen, turned down this dubious proposal, and with the Dutch fleet still cruising menacingly around Scillonian waters awaiting its Government's instructions, Parliament came to hear of events and were moved to action. It was decided that the situation on Scilly had been allowed to drag on long enough, and steps were promptly taken to eliminate the "Scilly pirates" who had harassed their shipping for so long. At Plymouth a fleet was being fitted out for an expedition to the West Indies under the joint command of Admiral Blake and Sir George Ascue, and this was redirected by Parliament to Scilly. A supporting land force was provided by Colonel Clarke, bringing the invading strength to about 2,000 men. Their instructions were to investigate the Dutch threat as well as to reduce Scilly.

Some history books claim that after Sir John Grenville had refused to treat with Van Tromp, the Dutch admiral laid off Scilly in order to offer assistance to the Parliamentary fleet—and actually declared war on tiny Scilly. The truth of these confused days we shall probably never know, but one thing is certain: Parliament would have no part of Van Tromp, and when the Dutch realized little of benefit was to be gained from the situation, they sailed out of Cornish waters, leaving the intriguing problem in their wake—are Holland and Scilly officially at war?

The Dutch menace out of the way, Parliament set about the reduction of Scilly, which, not surprisingly, was a short-lived affair—it took just over five weeks. However, the deciding factor was not weight of numbers, as has often been supposed. Since the fall of Charles, a continuous build-up of royalists wishing to strike a blow for their king had gone on in Scilly; large numbers of troops had been brought by Prince Rupert from Ireland in 1649, and when the imposing Parliamentarian force of no less than twenty ships and nine companies of Foot sailed against the islands in 1651 they found themselves by no means

[1]There is also reason to believe that in 1650 Prince Charles, in financial trouble, offered Scilly to a group of Dutch merchants as security for a loan of £50,000.

overwhelmingly superior in numbers. Indeed, in Star Castle there were said to be enough officers to head an army. Lack of supplies from France, water and munitions, contributed more than anything else to the downfall of Sir John Grenville. For a long time the royalist fort had been in straitened circumstances owing to the Parliamentary blockade, and was in no position to repulse a fully-equipped enemy. However, the "pirates of Scilly" gave a good account of themselves. The invaders made no less than two abortive attempts to carry Tresco, an island which had to be subdued before a full attack could be mounted against St. Mary's, while St. Mary's itself stubbornly resisted before bowing to the inevitable. The sea and land actions of those eventful weeks—especially those in the Old Grimsby Channel area of Tresco—have been recorded for posterity by one Jos Lereck, an officer in Colonel Clarke's land force, in his *A True Accompt of the late Reducement of the Isles of Scilly, Published in regard to the many false and Scandalous reports touching that Service*, a valuable document in the hands of the Council:

After we of the Parliamentary forces had laid at sea from Saturday April 12 till Thursday 17th, in the morning betimes (each officer having received orders overnight) we boated our soldiers, intending to gain a landing place upon Triscoe. . . . But the quicknesse of the Tyde had set our Boats so much to the Eastwards out of the way, and the fearful Pilots directing another course among the Rocks, we were necessitated to set all forward toward Old Grimsby Harbour. . . . Our boats, being all of them exceedingly cramd with men and many of them very slenderly accomplished for such a service, rowed exceedingly heavily and could not by any means be brought to row close one with another, and some were set fast upon the rocks for want of water.

Whereupon Orders were given that the Boates should stop under a Rock until they came up altogether that we might joyntly set upon the work.

But in the progress the Pilots and many of the Rowers (who were taken up in the West Country, very backward to the Service) misguided our headmost Boats to a little island called Northworthal, standing in the entrance to Old Grimsby Harbour and within half-a-musket shot of Triscoe, divided by the water and so situate as none save those who were acquainted could know whether it were part of Triscow or not. To this place the timerous or treacherous Pilots directed, affirming once and again that it was Triscoe, and when Major Bawden replyed he was doubtful of it (in regard he discovered none of the Enemy coming down to oppose the landing), one Nants (accounted the most knowing Pilot of and for the place) affirmed resolutely (upon his life) that it was Triscoe, whereupon three Companies presently landed, but the mistake prevented the landing of many more, yet not without some disorder pon our business. Not withstanding which and that the Tyde and opportunity might not be lost, orders were given that the rest of the Boats should row on into the Bay where we intended to land; but our foremost boats were again misguided and unadvisedly made for that part of the Island nearest to hand, occasioned the rather, I suppose, for that the Enemy had there drawn down a Body of Muskateers and fired much upon our Boats, with whom our men desired to be doing, but the place proved craggy and inaccessible, so that we could not land.

Here was hot firing between our men and the Enemy (the Rocky shore being the only Interponent). They had a sufficient advantage against us, having the Rocks for their shelter, and our men so thick crowded in their open boats as many of them could not make use of their arms. Indeed it was a miracle of mercy that we lost not many men there. If any of our Boats had been foundered, all the men must needs have been lost, for every boat was so exceedingly full. . . .

Now to be plain, where the Boats drew somewhere near and the great, small and case shot flew about to some purpose, and the danger must be looked in the face (for I believe we endured about 70 great shot besides muskets in abundance), many of the Boats, instead of rowing forward into the Bay, turned the helm and rowed backward and aside from the Business. And not withstanding Lt-Col Clark struggle all he could to draw them on, earnestly calling to one and commanding another to follow him with their Boats, yet would neither commands nor threats persuade them to observance, but do what he could they rowed off.

Capt Dover may please to remember that he, among others, was called to—yea, and commanded to upon pain of death—to follow on with his Boat. What his answer was and how carefully observed cannot be unknown to himself, nor yet to others, for I am sure his boat rowed off and came no nearer.

After some time spent, I think neer half an hour, in this perilous yet successless manner, we withdrew to Northworthal, the little island where our Boats were first misguided.

Three Companies were left upon Northworthal to keep the Enemy busy, and the rest were landed on an adjacent island called Tean, from whence we had a better discovery of the Enemy's shore. The place yielded but little fresh water, which through the number of our men was soon troubled and made unfit to drink, which, together with the want of provisions and the raw constitution of our men, newly come on shore, made this cold night's ladging the more irksome and comfortless.

The next day, April 18th, the Enemy spent some great shot at us which fell among some of our tents and brake them, but did no further harm.

We laboured to get some provisions ashore (which could not be suddenly done, our ships riding at that distance), for want of which our men were indeed distressed, and some whereupon murmured even to discontent, repining at the condition of the service thay were to undergo upon such faint terms. But through a supply of victual and careful regard of Lt-Col Clark all were put into an exact posture in order to make a second attempt.

To which end Capt. Hatsel and Capt. Smith were sent aboard Admiral Blake to desire that the Boats and Rowers who would stick more resolutely to their oars, might be sent to us, which he did.

And that we might be the better besteaded in our landing, he moreover appointed 150 or 200 seamen (who were better acquainted with Marine Affairs) to attempt with us under the conduct of Capt. Morrice.

Upon consultation we resolved (it being judged best) to storm the Enemy by night, and to that end had in this daytime carefully observed how to direct our course to the place we intended for landing (which was about three-quarters of a mile and interrupted with many rocks in the way). For now we became our own Pilots.

We boated our men (having drawn off those three companies from Northworthal) in the dark of the evening and left there only some 80 men to Alarum and Arouse the Enemy in that quarter while we fell on and between 11 and 12 of the Clock at Night set forward (the Seamen's Boats being head-most) at which time it pleased God it was very calm, so that the Enemy's Frigates, whom we doubted might injure us in our passage (being thereto designed) and do most prejudice, could not come up to do us any harm, though they spent some great shot at us.

We made fires on Tean as if we had continued there, the smoke thereof was blown towards the enemy which somewhat obscured our passage. Yet the Enemy discovered us when we came about half way over and took an Alarum and ere we attained the shore fired many Ordnance upon us which did no hurt.

The Boats came up for the most part roundly together, and put to the Shore where the enemy disputed our landing with stout resistance insomuch that the Seamen were forced back into the water, yet our men charged them resolutely, even to club-musket, and through the Blessing of God worsted them, killed upon the place one Captain and some 12 or 14 others took prisoners 167 and 4 Captains, the rest fled and none had escaped had we been better acquainted with the Island.

And now what reason is for some to write and report that the Seamen did all the work. That they alone gained the landing place. That they did the main work undervaluing and declaring the service of the Soldiery let all men judge. . . .

A sense of humour is vital to the understanding of Scilly. This cannot be overstressed. Without it one would be totally unable to appreciate how the most serious island matters can degenerate into farce at the drop of a hat, even in the twentieth century. Judging from Jos Lereck's account the situation was much the same in the mid seventeenth century.

Consider the Comedy of Errors that was the Roundhead assault of Tresco. Boatloads of land-lubbing soldiers hard and fast on the rocks of Old Grimsby Channel at low water, so hopelessly overcrowded that they could not bring their arms to bear; a disorderly retreat from the firing line when matters became too hot, led, ingloriously, by one of the officers against whom the self-satisfied author slyly directs his indignation; wholesale chaos when Nance, a local Cavalier-inclined pilot, misguides them on to tiny Northwethel (how that island could be confused with Tresco, the second largest in the group, is difficult to understand); a vigorous defence of the part the soldiery played in the attack, and an equally vehement denunciation of the navy who it seems had claimed most of the credit. It could only have happened in Scilly!

When Tresco capitulated many of the defenders fell back on St. Mary's leaving the way open for Admiral Blake to set up a battery on the Carn Near point of Tresco. The guns commanded Broad and Crow Sounds, thus preventing much-needed provisions from reaching the beseiged Royalists on St. Mary's. It was then only a matter of time before Sir John was forced to surrender owing to lack of supplies. Blake's terms were surprisingly generous, taking into account the five-year run-around Grenville and the royalist privateers had given the Parliamentarian forces.

After Sir John had gained assurance that no reprisals would be taken against islanders, also that the Godolphins should continue to administer the islands, the Star Castle company was allowed to leave free men "marching out together with their arms and horses, with beat of drums, sound of trumpets, colours displayed and matches lighted at both ends".[1] Many of them found refuge in Ireland; some stayed on in Scilly to await better times and so more mainland blood was fused to that of the early Godolphin settlers. The courageous Grenville, who had never faltered in his allegiance to the Cause, was allowed to "serve on the continent in the service of any foreign prince, so that such service was not prejudicial to the Commonwealth". However, he joined his exiled king in the latter's travels in France and the Low Countries and his steadfastness was rewarded on the Restoration in 1660 when he was created Earl of Bath and High Steward of the Duchy of Cornwall, among numerous other titles.

Following this action-packed interlude, Scilly was left in peace, never again to experience the stirring events of those days of Stuart strife. The Roundheads departed, leaving as a legacy of their occupation a nasty taste in the mouths of most Scillonians and Cromwell's Castle on the rocky western shore of Tresco guarding the channel between that island and Bryher. The Protector's distrust of the Dutch was probably the main reason for the erection of this circular fortress which is today of great interest to visitors.

Before civil conflict and its ramifications in Scilly we had noted a slight improvement in the state of the islands. The stand of Grenville and the ravages of war, however, set them back severely, and little help was forthcoming from Cromwell, to whom Scilly, now that its nuisance value had been obliterated, was of little interest. In 1658 a commentary on the lapsed state of Scilly was given in a petition to Cromwell by Lieutenant-Colonel Joseph Hunkin, who held the reins of administration at this time, in

[1] The document of surrender read: "Articles agreed on this XXIII day of May 1651 by and between Admirall Blake and Colonell Clerke, commanders in chief of all the forces by sea or land, in and about the Islands of Triscoe and Briar of the one part, and Sir John Grenvile, Knight, Governor of the Islands of St. Marye's and Agnes in Scilly, on the behalfe of his Matie., on the other part, touching the rendition of the said Isles of St. Marye's and Agnes together with all the Castles, forts, fortresses, sconces, and fortifications unto them belonging, to the use and behoof of the Parliament of England as followeth."

spite of Grenville's plea for a continuation of Godolphin control:

> The stores of ammunition in the garrison are decayed; there are only
> 77 barrels of powder left here by the enemy at the surrender of the
> islands, which is now unfit for service. There is also a great want of
> Saker and minion shot, there being only two shots apiece for all
> these guns on the islands. Begs 200 barrels of powder and three tons
> of shot so that he may be able to defend the islands in case of any
> vicissitudes of affairs.

Came 1660 and the Restoration of the Monarchy. The Godolphins resumed as lessees in the person of Sir Francis, grandson
of the builder of Star Castle, but islanders still subsisted rather
than lived, while on the off-islands conditions were particularly
grim. Considering the unswerving loyalty to the Royalist cause,
shown by islanders during the dark days of the Interregnum, it
has always seemed puzzling to Scillonians that the restored
Monarch should have paid so little attention to Scilly's economic
plight. The islands were virtually ignored. From this point for
over a hundred and fifty years, until 1831 when Augustus Smith
brought fresh energy and new ideas, there was to be no real
improvement. One of the reasons for the generally lapsed state of
the seventeenth and eighteenth centuries in Scilly, was the corrupting practice of absentee landlordism often favoured by the
Godolphins and later the Osbornes. The Godolphin family had
risen in status since Tudor times and many of them held important State posts. Consequently they found their duties too pressing
to allow them to personally administer so distant and valueless a
property as the Isles of Scilly. Also the Scilly of those days was
hardly an ideal spot for the sophisticated or those accustomed to
living in the grand manner. (As Lady Fanshawe would doubtless
have testified!) Unable, and often unwilling to be in Scilly, the
Lord Proprietors were in the habit of leaving affairs in the hands
of a Court of Twelve, appointed by them *in absentia*, headed by a
hireling steward and locally called the "Twelve Men". Unfortunately these local administrators were not as principled as the
men they represented, and as the powers invested in them were all-
embracing it is not surprising that circumstances in Scilly did not
improve.

> The good old rule, the simple plan
> That they should take who have the power
> And they shall keep who can.

One Council was disbanded by Sir Francis Godolphin in 1783 "on account of their not duly administering Justice according to their Oath, and punishing all offenders without Partiality, and for encouraging Vice instead of preventing it".

Short leases were one of the main obstacles to progress. Tenants experienced a feeling of insecurity and rootlessness. As a consequence this lack of stability provided no incentive to better their property as they were never certain of remaining tenants. Lack of housing was another factor and with the population being greater than the land could support, the situation began to look serious. There were, in fact, more people in Scilly then than today.

The 1700s were generally dismal for islanders for whom it was one long struggle to make ends meet. About the only notable event in the whole century was an extensive scheme of fortifications around the Hugh peninsula between 1715 and 1742. Undertaken at the time of the French Wars a wall was thrown completely around the headland from the Pool to Porthcressa with batteries inserted at intervals all around the perimeter. With these fortifications the whole character of the Hugh was changed. With Star Castle on top of the hill, walls and batteries garrisoned by men below, this area of high ground west of Hugh Town became known as "The Garrison", as it remains to this day.

The mainstays of livelihood in Scilly at the time were the cultivation of the small strips of land, fishing and piloting. Rye, barley, wheat and potatoes were the chief crops, while some sheep, cattle and pigs were also reared. Kelp-making, the burning of seaweed for use in the manufacture of glass and soap, was another pursuit. Fish was also dried for export, while a limited trade was done in limpets and shrimps. None of these pursuits, however, afforded more than a menial living, and it was these sort of depressed conditions that gave birth to smuggling.

During the latter years of the eighteenth century and the subsequent period of the Napoleonic Wars, Scilly's plight grew grave. The islands were hit badly by the economic restrictions of wartime and further hardship was occasioned by the introduction of a highly efficient Preventive Service in the early years of the nineteenth century to curb smuggling which was rampant in the islands and which Scillonians had become increasingly used to rely upon to eke out their miserable livings. Kelp-making had died out and at this time the combined harvests of sea and soil were barely allowing islanders to subsist, and often famine was dangerously near. Farming was proving particularly uneconomic. For many years a system had existed whereby on a tenant's death his few acres were parcelled up and divided to any of the family who wanted a share. When there was no heir the ground was auctioned off to the highest bidder and in this way plots were scattered all over the islands and hopelessly difficult to run.

A succession of appeals and petitions were now made for mainland help, such as that sent to the Rt. Hon. Robert Peel, M.P. for Oxford University in 1818. At the time the Duke of Leeds held the lease of Scilly, and in his absence an agent conducted local affairs. The appeal said

> We, the undersigned, inhabitants of one of the Scilly Isles, humbly beg permission, once more, to lay before you, Sir, a statement of our distress praying that you will be pleased to use your influence on behalf of ourselves and starving families. In reply to your kind inquiry "What can be done for you" permit us to say that we are in want of everything; and if some assistance is not afforded, hunger will soon remove us to a situation where human help can be of no avail. Do not leave us to perish for lack of bread.

As a result of this and other pleas, an inquiry was made by two philanthropic Penzance men. A sum of £9,000 was raised, food and clothes sent over and distributed by boats to the various needy islands and two years later a fish cellar was built at Tresco for the curing and storage of pilchards at the cost of several, thousands of pounds. Mainland and government relief also extended to the purchase of two fourteen-ton fishing boats while six island vessels were repaired. To set the industry on a firm footing large numbers of mackerel and pilchard nets were obtained, as well as lines, leads, trammels, mullet nets and a few small boats. However, after only a few years of curing, packing in hogsheads and exporting, the whole venture fell through for lack of funds to meet expenses.

It had been hoped that the pilchard industry would go some way towards alleviating islanders' distress, but with its failure they once again fell back on hard times which, in many ways were reminiscent of the plight of their predecessors of medieval days. To add to the dismal state of affairs, a drought in 1825 hit island crops; and in 1831 the Duke of Leeds decided against renewing his lease of the islands and thus a 260-year-old link between

Scilly and the Godolphin-Osborne family was severed. For the next few years the islands reverted to the Duchy and like a rudderless boat yawned on the very brink of economic disaster.

An indication as to the state of Scilly at this time was given by James Silk Buckingham, who was M.P. for Sheffield in 1823-37, and who visited Scilly in a Revenue cutter:

> Nothing could be conceived more primitive than the state of society among which we were now thrown. The town of St. Mary's had a Governor, two clergymen, three doctors, two lawyers, several merchants, who were all smuggling: the rest were mere tradesmen, shopkeepers and boatmen, who lived partly by fishing, still more by smuggling, and worst of all, it was said, by visiting wrecked vessels and helping themselves freely to whatever could be saved from destruction.

The Duchy now sent George Neale Driver to the islands to inquire into the general state of affairs, and he must have found the same sort of chaos which confronted the Killigrews back in 1551. Owing to the bad administration of the Duke of Leeds' stewards, rents were in most cases irrecoverably in arrears, and houses had been erected anywhere regardless of proper building agreements. To put matters right Driver had to ruthlessly levy high rents which caused a resentment of the Duchy which lasted for many years, and letters to be sent to the king. However, the doughty Driver persisted in his efforts, but when he turned to the "off islands" he found matters even worse—and the great number of tenants all bearing the same names only confused things! On Tresco, for example, there were sixteen Jenkinses, ten Nichollses, seven Penders and nine Ellises. In order to differentiate, he had to use the person's nickname, as well as his proper name, in his report, and one can imagine the amazement of the senior Duchy officials in London when faced with such picturesque soubriquets as Billy Chad, Treacle Breeches, Aunt Polly Cunder, Long Tom, Nancy Dango, Cap'n Jack, Tailor Isaac, Long John, Rachel Mungy, Sammy Dagger and Dreamer.

With the failure of the Duke of Leeds to renew his lease the Twelve Men, or to give the body its official name "His Grace's Council", slipped into the pages of history, to the relief of most islanders. However, there was now no machinery to administer local affairs, so in 1832 a public meeting was held at the Council

House on St. Mary's, to appoint Overseers for the Poor, and to set up a Select Vestry, a parish administrative body. The first Vestry consisted of thirty-four persons, and its responsibilities were to include the welfare of roads, health, sanitation, local discipline and other more mundane matters. The "off islands" had all, by now, become independent of St. Mary's, separate parishes, and they too received their own vestries. The Scillonian Select Vestry, born at the lowest ebb of island affairs, was to last no fewer than ninety-eight years before bowing out as recently as 1930. But back to the "interregnum" years following the Duke of Leeds' surrender of the lease.

We have now reached the year 1834, a red-letter one in Scilly's chequered history, and, as it turned out, an even more momentous year than 1571 when Sir Francis Godolphin arrived to pick the islands up off their knees. For there now came to Scilly a new Lord Proprietor. His name was commonplace—Smith—but he was far from being an ordinary man. In a matter of a few years he was to work a near miracle by stamping out the terrible conditions of hardship and setting Scilly on the road to a state approaching, unbelievably, prosperity.

Augustus John Smith, B.A., J.P., was a Hertfordshire landowner from Ashlyns Hall and he took up the lease from the Duchy on the basis of three lives. Later the terms of the lease were altered to ninety-nine years. Like the Augustus of the early Roman Empire, he was far-sighted and visionary, and he foresaw great things for his own special mini-empire, Scilly. Like the Roman Augustus he introduced a veritable fusillade of reform, but unlike his namesake he did not eschew the powers of absolute despotism. The word of Augustus Smith was law. Islanders addressed him with deference as "My Lord" and referred to him as "the Governor", "the General"—even "the Emperor". Bachelor Augustus' very appearance and bearing was autocratic and demanding of respect. Tall and well built, he wore the mutton-chop whiskers much in the vogue at the time, and the sight of him dressed in reefer jacket, with telescope under arm, sitting menacingly in the stern of his rowing gig manned by a well-drilled, uniformed crew, was enough to strike fear into the heart of the stoutest islander. But for all that it can truly be said that people in Scilly today who enjoy any level of prosperity, to a large degree owe it to Augustus Smith.

Radical change was the only way out of the depressed state of the early 1800s, and Augustus knew it. Straightaway he made it clear that the practice of absentee landlordism was a thing of the past by choosing Tresco as the site for building a residence, Tresco Abbey, and islanders were immediately approving. No more would they have to suffer the rigours of absenteeism and the consequent abuses of unscrupulous stewards and agents. Now they would be administered by an "on-the-spot" authority, a landlord among his tenants: their troubles would be appreciated first hand. Augustus considered building his home at Holy Vale, St. Mary's, but decided on Tresco because its situation was ideal for the purpose of administering the surrounding inhabited islands. The "off islands" would now get a fair deal and would no longer be St. Mary's poor relations.

After regular tours of inspection and a look in every corner of his island empire, it was not long before the energetic new Governor plumbed the root cause of Scilly's deterioration—the chaotic system of land tenure. The practice of sub-dividing land was brought to an end and a programme of rearrangement in time brought about a compactness, a homogeneity. No longer did a tenant find he had a plot on the Garrison, and another acre or so on the eastern end of St. Mary's. The basis of economic farming had been laid. Tenants were also told that only one son could succeed to the property, the other children having to find employment elsewhere. This was the very essence of autocratic rule, and not surprisingly many islanders reacted bitterly against it. Further despotic acts included the "persuasion" of the population of Samson (five families) to quit their island for good because of their breadline existence; the removal to the mainland of those for whom there was no work available; the deportation of paupers. Also, if a family objected to the new land reform, Augustus had no compunction about forcing every member to abandon the islands and take up the reins of life away from Scilly.

Although on face value these measures may appear extreme, Augustus, in his far-sightedness, realized harsh action had to be adopted if Scilly was to prosper. He was looking to future generations and in his programme of reform the present were bound to suffer. As a consequence a grudge against the man from Tresco Abbey was born. The Abbey, to many islanders, became to be a symbol of despotism and highhandedness. In their eyes it was the old, old situation of "the rich man in his castle, the poor man at his gate". Nowadays, benevolent despot is a favourite way of describing Augustus, but from a contemporary islander's point of view there was nothing benevolent about being evicted from his home to further Augustus Smith's far-sighted policy. The problem of making a living was as much as he could cope with; ideals of a future prosperity were beyond him. The resentment, in some cases akin to hate, occasioned by Augustus' reforms, is deeply ingrained in Scilly, and it was one of the less savoury legacies to the Dorrien-Smiths who came after him. Happily today, as a new generation supplants the old, it is rapidly dying out.

One of the many problems with which Augustus had to contend was that of unemployment caused by the surplus population, so he found jobs in a scheme of physical improvement, such as building roads, many of which exist to this day. Other labour was found in the building of miles of granite-walled boundaries on St. Mary's, and Tresco, in the blasting of sea-bed rock between Tresco and Bryher to widen New Grimsby Channel, and in the clearing and tidying up of tenants' lands. Many of these improvements were supervised personally. Augustus, with a number of retainers, used to take over a building near where the work was progressing—a far cry from the days of the absentee Godolphins. At Tresco, the Abbey and its surrounds were under construction near the old Benedictine Priory. Much demolition work had to be done, but with the excess of labour available an overgrown hillside was cleared and the basis of his world famous botanical gardens was laid. Being a landowner, Augustus was passionately interested in farming and brought his extensive knowledge in this field to bear in Scilly. He set up a herd of Guernsey cattle, and fostered the potato-growing business. One of the stipulations of his lease was that he should undertake the construction of a new quay and church at St. Mary's. Both had been started in the years immediately preceding Augustus' arrival in Scilly, but he supervised their completion.

Augustus is probably best remembered for his reforms in the field of education. When he took over the lease the schools in Scilly, which had been set up by the Godolphins and the Society for the Promoting of Christian Knowledge, were old and outdated. For a great many years the S.P.C.K.'s Scilly mission had done much good in education and other spheres, but when he came to the islands he replaced their buildings with his own and enlisted the support of all educated islanders to help in instruction. Augustus himself took night classes, and his particular delight was in teaching children the arts of navigation. In the 1850s the radical Lord Proprietor decided that education should be compulsory in the islands, no less than thirty years before the Foster Act ruled to this effect on the mainland. Augustus ensured his schools were well attended by charging a tenant a penny a week for the instruction of each child and twopence if they stayed away!

At about this time a local ship-building trade which had been flickering since before the turn of the century, gained rapidly in momentum, and although Augustus did not support the venture financially he lent his full enthusiasm to it, as he did to any pursuit which was in the best interest of islanders. The ship-building enterprise could not have started under more favourable circumstances, for this was the period of free trade following the Reform Bill of 1832, and Britain's foreign trade received a great boost. The boats built in Scilly were manned by Scillonian seamen, who, as a result of Augustus' educational drive, were nearly all fitted for the role of officers; Scillonians before the mast were a rarity.

To few men falls the distinction of becoming a legend in a lifetime. It did to Augustus Smith, for visibly a change had come over the face of Scilly. An era of a state approaching prosperity had come to the islands, and Augustus Smith was its supreme architect. On the land, order had emerged from chaos; farming was booming; waste ground had been harnessed for cultivation; farmhouses and cottages had been improved and given sanitation; a surplus population had been drastically reduced; paupers had disappeared; unemployment was a thing of the past; ship-building yards were springing up in Hugh Town, St. Mary's; a post office service had been introduced and fire insurance made compulsory; smuggling had been ruthlessly suppressed, and an efficient administrative "tool" for Augustus—the Select Vestry—had replaced the corrupt Court of Twelve.

Augustus Smith's interests were not by any means confined to Scilly alone. A strong Liberal, even if he was the supreme autocrat in the islands, he became Member for Truro in 1857, and held his seat until 1865. Other outside honours which fell on him were the presidency of the Royal Geological Society of Cornwall, while in 1863 he became the Provincial Grandmaster of the Freemasons of Cornwall.

In the July of 1872 this man of energy and enterprise who moulded the framework of modern Scilly, died in a Plymouth hotel where he had been taken following an attack of illness at a Masonic function in St. Austell. He was sixty-eight. How splendidly he had lived up to the family motto, carved in the granite wall of Tresco Abbey: "Thus you do not work for yourselves." As the Reverend Whitfield wrote in his *Scilly and its Legends*, his epitaph may well have read *"Lateritiam inveni, marmoream relinquo"* ("I found it brick, I leave it marble"). Augustus was buried at St. Buryan in Cornwall, and many Scillonians travelled to his funeral. A simple stone monument stands to his memory at Tresco, while at Old Town Churchyard, St. Mary's the inscription on a massive column reads: "In memory of Augustus John Smith, for 38 years Lord Proprietor of the Isles of Scilly, this monument is erected by the inhabitants to preserve among them the recollection of a name hence forth inseparably connected with the isles."

Augustus was succeeded by his nephew Lieutenant Thomas Algernon Smith-Dorrien, to whom he bequeathed his interests in Scilly by will. The terms of the latter stated he should take the name of Smith-Dorrien Smith, but this somewhat unwieldy name was altered to Dorrien-Smith by the process of reversal and lopping off the initial Smith. The new proprietor carried on the good work of his uncle. If these islands have a debt to Augustus for their general welfare, then they owe to his successor much for the drive which furthered the flower-growing business on which so much of today's Scillonians depend for their livelihood. When Augustus was sowing his gorse and planting his trees he discovered that even the most un-British of plants flourished in the Scillonian climate when protected from the winds. Lieutenant Dorrien-Smith followed up this discovery. He introduced protective hedges of pittasporum, enonymus, veronica and escallonia and played a large part in devising the layout of flower fields with their rectangular appearance which characterize the Scillonian landscape today. The flower business was under way. The new Lord Proprietor, although not as adept a horticulturist as his uncle, devoted much of his time and energy to the furtherance of his new industry for he rightly anticipated its great economic value

Sunrise over Peninnis

to Scillonians. Today the business of sending cut flowers to mainland markets is, hand-in-hand with the tourist trade, the mainstay of livelihood in the islands.

Lieutenant Dorrien-Smith died in 1918 after a progressive "reign" during which the Garrison was once again fortified and much consolidation of Augustus' reforms had gone on. He was buried on Tresco, which during the Great War sustained a seaplane base, as did St. Mary's have a Naval Sub-base, and although he handed over to his successor Major Arthur Algernon Dorrien-Smith, D.S.O., a thriving estate, he also left as a legacy to his line, a drastically reduced administrative power. In March 1891 democracy had shown its face in Scilly for the first time, in the shape of a council to conduct the affairs of the islands. Following the Local Government Act of 1888 islanders feared Scilly might be incorporated into Cornwall, and petitioned Parliament. An inquiry by L.G.B. representatives resulted in the Provisional Order (or the Isles of Scilly Order as it was known) of 1890. The council consisted of a Dorrien-Smith, as hereditary chairman, four aldermen, twenty councillors made up of twelve from St. Mary's, three from Tresco, two each from St. Martin's and Agnes and one from Bryher. Lieutenant Dorrien-Smith himself had much to do with this innovation (an act which could hardly have been credited of Augustus), and with the council's inauguration the hitherto all-embracing powers of the Dorrien-Smith Lord Proprietors had taken a body blow.

In 1920 the terms of the original Augustus Smith lease (three lives) were revised so that the Duchy could undertake extensive improvements to their property, and new terms saw Major Dorrien-Smith retaining Tresco and the uninhabited "off islands" while St. Mary's and the other inhabited islands came directly under the Duchy. The situation remains the same today.

"The Major", as he was known widely in the islands, was an acknowledged expert in botany and horticulture (he held the Victoria Medal of Horticulture), and during his ascendancy the flower trade, nurtured so carefully by his two predecessors, really came into its own. Millions of blooms were exported annually and a level of prosperity, never before enjoyed by islanders, was attained and has remained ever since.

The third Smith went a long way towards breaking down the reserve with which islanders, since the days of Augustus, were

6

Hugh Town, St. Mary's with lifeboat slip
Hugh Street, St. Mary's

wont to hold the Abbey. A bluff, redfaced man, "the Major" was universally liked within the islands.

Throughout these years the Select Vestry was still functioning in its modest way, although the creation of the Isles of Scilly Council in 1891 had robbed it of many of its former powers. For example, the Council had taken over health and road responsibility in all the islands. Now no longer were the "off islands" the butts of an isolationist policy; no longer were they languishing in their watertight compartments. There was a general trend towards centralization, with the affairs of each and every island coming under one authority—the Council of the Isles of Scilly. This was a distinct improvement on the former situation where misunderstandings continually arose between "off island" vestries and the St. Mary's Select Vestry. In 1930, two years short of its hundredth birthday, the Select Vestry disappeared from the Scillonian scene for ever, leaving the way clear for the Council.

The Second World War came, and once more Scilly was fortified and contained much Service personnel. Many islanders saw action in the Merchant Navy, and indeed it was said that Scilly sent more Servicemen to war than any other place of comparable size in Britain. Apart from suffering the odd misdirected bomb and the effects of continuous anti-U-boat activities, Scilly itself experienced little physical hurt in these years.

After the war—in 1949—the Duchy of Cornwall sold the freehold of Hugh Town to the sitting tenants; as a direct result tourism began to boom spectacularly and with flower farming at its peak Scilly continued on the upgrade. A group of islands, which for centuries had known nothing but lawlessness and terrible poverty, was now well and truly launched on an era of well being.

"The Major" died in 1955, aged seventy-nine. He was cremated at Plymouth and following a service on board the *Scillonian* his ashes were scattered in the sea beyond the Bishop Rock Lighthouse. I well remember that day. Many islanders sailed down to the West'ard to pay their last respects to "the Major", hundreds of beautiful wreaths were thrown overboard and the Bishop fired a maroon in final salute. That farewell shot was, in effect, to sound the demise of the Dorrien-Smiths' traditional administrative powers in the islands, for not long after his son Lieutenant-Commander Thomas Mervyn Dorrien-Smith had succeeded him at the Abbey, the family's time-honoured right of hereditary chairmanship of the Isles of Scilly Council ended with the election of Alderman "Georgie" Woodcock, the first democratically elected figurehead in Scillonian history.

Today the administrative role of the current Dorrien-Smith in Scilly has been whittled down to that of Tresco representative (one of three) on the Islands' Council. Lieutenant-Commander Dorrien-Smith, of course, is the lessee of Tresco as were his predecessors, but no longer does the "Man at the Abbey" hold sway over greater Scilly. However, such is progress—although islanders can never, and must never, forget the great formative role the family played in the islands during the spectacular transformation from widespread poverty to economic stability.

IV

ALWAYS THE SEA RULES US

Man's way of life and livelihood is largely conditioned by his environment. For the Scillonian of by-gone days, however, the qualification was superfluous—his life was wholly conditioned by his surroundings—the sea. In the centuries of poverty he made kelp, worked in the ship-building yard, he piloted, he smuggled, he fished or he wrecked. Later, if his life did not happen to be directly connected with the water, he most probably grew potatoes or small produce which depended heavily on the then infrequent sea-link with the mainland for a market. More often than not the farmer was equally at home in a boat as on the land, a fact well illustrated by one islander's famous boast:

> I can plough, and sow, reap and mow,
> And sail a ship with any man.

The modern-day inhabitant of Scilly and his relationship with his environment has changed but little. He may not be as directly connected with the sea as his predecessors, but it still dictates his welfare. He now grows flowers which, like the produce of his antecedents the potato growers, depend on the sea passage to win a ready market. He gains his living from running a pleasure boat. If he maintains a guest house or hotel he depends on the attraction to mainland visitors of island seas. If he is a shopkeeper then that forty-mile strip of water to Penzance has to be harnessed if he is to receive his stock.

Always the sea. It has been a dominant factor in the life of Scilly for a thousand years and will dictate for many a day yet. As a former editor of the islands' lone publication, the quarterly *Scillonian Magazine*, once wrote, "Always the sea rules us. We are born into its sound; its voice is forever in our ears."

Kelp-making. A survey of the industries which Scillonians eked from the sea is an absorbing one. Let us begin with kelp-making, perhaps the most fascinating of the varied pursuits indulged in by the islanders of old.

Kelp, as was explained briefly in an earlier chapter, was the alkaline product of burned seaweed which was used for bleaching and making glass, alum, hard soaps, and later iodine, which was needed for munitions. The principal types of weed used in its manufacture were bladder wrack and knobbed wrack—broad-leaved, ribbon weed—both of which abound on the rocks and in low water channels of Scilly. After burning, the resultant impure soda gave a bluish-greenish tinge which is a distinctive characteristic of Bristol and Waterford glass and largely responsible for making seventeenth- and eighteenth-century glass so valuable today. Kelp-making was first introduced to these islands in 1684 by a Mr. Nance, and for over 150 years it was to be a favourite pursuit in the islands. Borlase tells us in a manuscript journal that Mr. Nance was a sergeant of the guard at Pendennis Castle. A ship put into Falmouth harbour one day, and after it had been cleared the Master and Mr. Nance struck up a conversation. The former asked him if he knew of any oreweed (seaweed) to make kelp in the vicinity as that was the reason for his voyage—to supply kelp to some alum works. Mr. Nance learned the trade with this man at Falmouth for many years, and then was approached by some merchants from Marazion and Falmouth about a proposal to start the industry in the Isles of Scilly. In 1684 Nance and his family visited Scilly, leased Tean island from the Duke of Leeds and lived there until he died—"and has the honour of having first instructed the islanders to turn their superfluous oreweed to so good advantage." Kelping was not, of course, peculiar to Scilly. It was also indulged in, and on a far wider scale, on the shores of Western Scotland and Ireland—also the Hebrides and other islands off the coast of Britain. As Lady Vyvyan says, "It is always associated with open boats and waves, with rocks and sandy foreshores, with the glow of steady fires, palls of smoke and the loneliness of island lives."

The new industry came to Scilly at an opportune time and was welcomed gladly by islanders. Leading purely self-supporting lives they were only too pleased to clutch at a new means of balancing their slender budgets, and although never a lucrative business, kelp-making was widely pursued in the islands during the seventeenth and early eighteenth centuries. It nearly always found a home in poor communities of straitened circumstances, and its disappearance in Scilly in the 1830s was symbolic of the transformation from subsistence to near-prosperity brought about so dramatically by Augustus Smith.

The strange processes of kelp-making have been described exhaustively in many a book. Perhaps the widest-known and certainly the best account came from the pen of John Millington Synge, who captured superbly the poignancy of this lonely seashore industry as followed by the peasants of the Aran Isles. However, for the purposes of this book it is appropriate to carry an account of the industry as practised in Scilly and written by a Scillonian, Robert Maybee, who incidentally calls kelp "kilp".[1]

At that time, by making kilp in the summer season a man could get very good wages providing it was dry weather. The first kilp I can remember was worth £5 a ton, and almost every person was working on it that summer. They would begin to make kilp in March all around the island, as soon as they could get any of the late drift-weed in. They commonly used to go two families together; there were but three or four horses and carts on the island at that time, and the seaweed used to be brought up in baskets by men, women and children, and every party had its own piece of ground to dry it on. The weed was spread, and, if the weather was dry, in a day or two it was turned over, and when it was properly dry it was all made up in cocks, just like hay, above high water mark, where the sea could not come to it. After it had been in cocks for some time, and the weather being fine for burning it they would have pits dug in the sand in the shape of a pan, quite small at the bottom and paved with small stones to a height of about two or three feet. The women would burn most of the kilp and the children would bring the weed to them while they were doing it, so that the men could do other work between times. All through the kilping season they would light up the kilp between 12 and 1 o'clock and keep it burning till about 8 or 9 o'clock in the evening, putting on the weed in handfuls as fast as it could consume. After the kilp was burnt, six or eight men would come with kilp-rakes to strike the kiln, that is, to work the kiln up, and when it was worked up it was like so much hot lead. They might have to work up as many as eight kilns, so they would have to run from one to another till they had completed all of them.

[1] *Sixty-eight Years' Experience on the Scilly Islands.*

There might be forty or fifty kilns burning around St. Mary's in one day, so that each party would have to do its own work. The next morning a man would go down with a bar and raise the kilp up out of the pit; it would come out in a hard lump of about three cwt; it was then broken up into handy lumps and put under the cliff, and the pit was cleaned out for burning again the next day; and so they would continue their work till August month, getting as much seaweed as they possibly could. Everyone knew his own ground for drying the seaweed, just the same as going in his fields to work. In the summer days kilp was being made on the six islands, and some days there would be as many as 100 kilns burning on the different islands. The smoke would come from the kilns as thick as it would from a steamer when new coals were put in; and on a calm day the smoke would go up straight, a thin smoke, almost white in colour. The work was finished in the middle of August, and the kilp was then all shipped off to Bristol to make glass and soap. The last kilp was made in 1835.

Many writers—the matter-of-fact Maybee excepted—get the descriptive bit between their teeth when dealing with kelping. Under their over-romantic pens the lonely beaches and foreshores of the burners spring to life as a fantastic backcloth of dancing kiln flames; of weird reflections on face and water, of moonlight and shadows. The kelp burners are painted as semi-barbarians, sweating half-naked and blackened of face over the kiln to fall panting on the cool sand after the crescendo of the "strike" had been made. The whole image is made more unreal by accounts of children joining hands in pagan dance around the pit; of strange songs chanted on the eerie island beaches on Midsummer's Night.

Thus we are led to believe that there was something colourful, even romantic about the calling of the kelp burner. Far from it. It was a drab, miserable life involving a vast amount of back-breaking labour for negligible returns. The initial task of gathering weed on the local beaches and shores was taxing enough. There was no such thing as mechanical aid in those far-off days, so the entire family, men, women and children, had to collect the weed, carry it by basket, pannier or donkey (if they were lucky enough to have one) to the top of the beaches and there stack it. And that was by no means the end of the gathering process. The men now embarked in their tiny punts and pulled miles to the outer islands, the rocks and ledges where at low water they cut the weed and

loaded it aboard their boats. After this exhausting task they had
to pull their over-laden vessels back to shore, unload and set
off to repeat the dismal procedure again. Some families even
camped out on the desolate rocks until the precious weed had been
collected. Romantic? Hardly.

The industry only lasted five months in the year—from March
to August. A prolonged spell of wet weather spelt disaster, the
absentee proprietor's steward and the merchants' agents took a
crippling cut, and the stench caused by the many kelp kilns was
suffocating. It polluted clothes, skin and cloaked the whole island
group in a sort of "smog". Moreover, kelp fetched an abysmally
low price in the islands, the common return being about three to
five pounds a ton. Sometimes it was even lower. At the time of
the Napoleonic Wars the industry did receive a momentary
fillip when, owing to trade embargoes, it soared to an unprecedented nine pounds a ton, but thereafter it dropped away again.
The discovery of synthetic iodine put an end to kelping in Scilly
and it was only fetching thirty shillings a ton in 1835 when the
industry died out.

Kelp has long had its day in the islands. All that now remains
of those hard times are a few stone-lined depressions on a number
of the islands, the old kelp pits. The heady scent of flowers has
now replaced the stench of burning ore-weed, far more pleasant
in itself and as remunerative as the former was not.

Ship-building. Most of the last kelp made in Scilly, as well as local-
grown potatoes, was shipped to the markets of Bristol, Gloucester
and Waterford by Scillonian-constructed cutters, schooners and
sloops, for at that time one of the most remarkable of all island
sea industries was gaining ground fast. Ship-building had been
indulged in for a number of years, in the late eighteenth century,
but only on a small scale, as to produce fishing vessels and small
craft. About the time of the Napoleonic Wars the flickering
industry was given a boost by the growing demand for merchant
vessels, and ship-building proper for trading purposes dates from
this time. By the 1830s, when kelp-burning was in its death throes,
ship-building was really beginning to prosper and continued to
do so in the favourable and forward-looking conditions created
by Augustus Smith, until killed in the 1870s by the coming of
iron vessels and steam.

The heyday of the industry was in the 1850s and '60s, when there were no less than four yards operating on the tiny St. Mary's isthmus of Hugh Town. It is almost unbelievable that so small an island and so limited an area as Hugh Town could have contained so much driving activity. But it did. There were two yards on the Porthcressa side of Hugh Town, on the eastern and western ends of the bank where nowadays visitors bask in deckchairs, and two on the other flank overlooking the Pool—and the ships that came off their stocks became known the world over.

In the early days of the industry sizes were limited and ships rarely exceeded sixty tons register. The old Navigation Acts were responsible for this as the dues on large vessels were crippling. Therefore a tonnage restriction was perforce observed. However, this did not prevent the small island schooners and sloops building up a fine reputation in the fruiter trade to the Mediterranean, Azores and Portugal and in the coastal trade. The Scilly fifty-niners, as they were called, were widely admired. In 1825 there were eleven registered; in 1839 the number had jumped to twenty. The need to keep inside the sixty-ton mark disappeared with the general boom in British shipping and now the customary twenty-ton island sloop of domestic waters gave way to world trading brigs, brigantines, barques and schooners which were often in the 300-ton plus bracket.

Scilly's ships plied their various trades the world over and many of the men who manned and skippered them were true-born Scillonians. The educational drive of Augustus Smith and the emphasis he put on navigation had paid dividends, for few islanders found themselves ill-equipped for world trading. In the boom years of shipping Scilly could boast no less than 135 master mariners—a remarkable achievement.

It was common for womenfolk to voyage alongside their sailor husbands, and take their turn at the wheel. One such lady could never distinguish "port" from "starboard". Her husband tied a bucket to one side, a broom to the other, and subsequently steering instructions were simple orders such as, "Hard a'bucket" or "Hard a'broom".

The ship-building era of St. Mary's was as exciting and colourful as the preceding period of kelp-burning was miserable and drab. Little Hugh Town was a hive of activity with nearly everyone being engaged in some degree or other in the industry.

Shipwrights, joiners and sailmakers worked alongside coopers, riggers and rope makers, while the ring of the caulking mallet and the clank of the forge anvils echoed the day long around St. Mary's Pool. Timber yards above Town Beach (in which the children used to play hide and seek), saw pits and storage sheds for pitch, tar and oakum, cluttered the limited isthmus, along with more formal offices where the business between builder and owner was transacted.

The timber, of course, had to be imported. Special timber ships brought their cargoes to St. Mary's where they were either allowed to float in the water of the Pool to prevent splitting until needed, or buried in the sand of Town Beach or Porthcressa, as were the woods used for making spars and masts.

The steady flow of ships from Hugh Town's stocks and their subsequent world-wide travels which resulted in emigrant Scillonians being scattered all over the globe to this day, soon gained Scilly a name in the general shipping business. Vessels called frequently, either looking for shelter from storms or for general repairs to rigging or hull. During the Franco-Prussian war hundreds of German ships harboured in different parts of Scilly. This sort of shipping brought business to the islands. Hotels, shops and inns flourished, while even the farmer benefited. Many was the time a monotonous diet of ship's biscuit and salt pork was helped out by island produce. In these busy days the sight of strange-looking seamen speaking foreign tongues and swaggering Tortuga-style through the narrow streets of Hugh Town (one was called Blood Alley), was commonplace. There were two shipping agents on St. Mary's, one representing Lloyds, to cope with the throbbing demand, and they handled the requirements of every vessel which put in to the islands—and there were many of them.

By the 1870s the horizon looked bright for Scillonians. The ship-building industry was at its peak; most of the vessels were island-owned with Scillonians holding shares, and after a prosperous voyage dividends were high. The industry's complementary trades were booming, too. Sailmaker's lofts, blacksmith's forges and ropewalks (notably one at Porthloo) provided well-paid employment for all and the general well-being of the islanders looked assured for many a year to come.

Sadly, however, the activity was to cease. The inexorable march of progress had produced vessels of iron and steel, powered by steam, and with the increase of these the days of the wooden sailor were numbered. As steam took over fewer ships were built in Scilly, and by 1880 the relatively short-lived industry was all but dead. I have a picture of the *David Anterson* on the Porthcressa stocks in 1870, the last vessel to be constructed on the southern flank of Hugh Town. The Town Beach yards went out of business with the building of the *Gleaner* and *Rosevear* in 1878, the last of a long line of Scillonian deep-watermen. There was a late burst of activity in the early '80s, when the smacks *Fortuna* and *Queen of the Isles* were built for the east coast trade, but they were the last convulsions of a dying industry.

On the eclipse of the sailing ship, the shipping agents of St. Mary's moved with the times. They turned their attentions to steam coal. They rightly anticipated that homebound steamers short of fuel would put into Scilly for bunker. For this purpose large depots were established at St. Mary's from which the coal was shipped to the steamer by lugger. Later the coal was kept in a hulk anchored in the Roadstead, which was regularly recharged by coasters. Although this new line in the shipping business lasted for a while, it was only moderately remunerative as St. Mary's was never recognized as an ideal coaling station. Gradually it followed ship-building into extinction and Hugh Town was left to peace and quiet, a strange transformation after the years of bustle and excitement.

Today there are few signs of the once flourishing era of ship-building. The face of Hugh Town is greatly altered, and rows of houses and shops now stand on the site of the old yards. Occasionally a tool is unearthed and once in a while an old photograph of a ship on the stocks comes to light, but few of the mainland people who are flocking to St. Mary's to live are even aware that Scilly once had a fine ship-building industry.

Piloting. The exciting shipping days should not be dismissed without a mention being made of piloting, that most Scillonian of sea industries which for centuries provided islanders with an income. The geographical position of Scilly at the apex of the Bristol Channel and the English Channel was ideal for the practice of pilotage, since transatlantic vessels had to pass close to the treacherous rocks of the archipelago. Many was the time the skipper of a homeward-bound ship was relieved to receive the attentions of an island pilot when a big sea was running, easterly winds blowing, or all about him was blanketed by fog. Then he would hand over the helm to the pilot who threaded his way through the tangle of reefs into the shelter of the islands. An easterly wind was regarded as an economic God-send by Scillonians. When the wind was in this quarter there were few shipmasters foolhardy enough to ride it out in the open sea rather than putting into Scilly. And vessels at anchor meant business ashore.

The boats which used to land the pilots on the vessel were pilot cutters, trim, decked craft with tall masts, long bowsprit and thirty foot in length. These sailing craft, which spent long periods at sea waiting for piloting jobs, played a major role in the lives of Scillonians, but they were not so important to the island way of life as the smaller pilot gig which often attended them. The gig was pulled by six oars, although it could, like the cutter, be sailed, and when business was brisk was also manned by pilots. The gig was an all-purpose vessel. It was also used for wrecking, salvage work, carrying flowers, fish and general produce, and even weekend family picnickers used it for transport. The pilot gig even moved in mainland waters. Often it was rowed and sailed to places like Cardiff laden with fish, to return with a cargo of coal. In the heyday of smuggling this versatile vessel made many a trip to France for merchandise. The off-island gigs were run by more-or-less set crews who had plots of land to cultivate when winds were wrong for shipping. But on St. Mary's it was largely a case of first come, first served. When a ship was sighted approaching off Gugh island, the cry went up "a jack",[1] and the first on the spot crewed, and shared in the subsequent financial proceeds. The crew often took on a motley appearance, farmer and labourer pulling alongside shipwright and fisherman. But then everyone in Scilly knew how to handle a boat.

In the early days of pilotage the living was meagre as not enough shipping touched the islands. So the men went through appalling hazards for a mere pittance. Few callings could have been as demanding as that of the pilot. He was "on call" at all times of the day and night, and in all weathers. The farmer might have to drop his hoe at a minute's notice to take his place in the gig crew, while many an island woman was left worrying in

[1] A flag showing a pilot's services were needed.

the dead of night while her husband was at sea. It was hard, too. The oars used in the gigs were heavy, unwieldy implements—twice the weight and length of their dinghy counterparts. Imagine the backbreaking effort which went into pulling these craft miles out to sea with mountainous waves being shipped and progress being cut by a contrary wind. The hardships did not end on the arrival in the shipping lanes. Sometimes they had to wait for the vessel to come up, and lopping in the trough of house-high waves often resulted in the vessel being capsized and her crew being dashed to pieces on the rocks or drowned. The Pilots' Widows' Fund was a well patronized charity.

But the Scilly pilots were equal to their task. Islanders all, they had been brought up to the ways of wind and tide. Knowledge of local waters was handed down from father to son, and the exact position of every rock was known, whether it was above water or submerged, charted or uncharted.

Island pilots received a serious setback in the early years of the nineteenth century. A body of men called Branch Pilots were established. These men monopolized pilotage, steam-rolling lesser island men out of their heritage. One of the complaints made by off islanders in the distress year of 1818 was that local seamen could not get piloting jobs and that the monopoly of the Branch men was killing their livelihood.

The lean years of pilotage, however, went with the general boom of shipping in the mid nineteenth century. Now, despite the objectionable presence of the Branch Pilot, there was work for all and Scillonians embarked on a prosperous era. Good money was picked up by the senior members of the cutter, while the fourpence an outing earned by the shipwrights and labourers who made up the crew was a useful extra on top of their basic wages. Gig crews did well, too. Money was also made by barter-ing (often dangerously akin to smuggling) with an inbound vessel, island eggs, butter and potatoes being exchanged for tobacco, sugar and tea. Shipping agents and Masters had to be ferried to and fro; more business. Much piloting transactions were done in the "Little Western", an Agnes inn.

As more business came to Scilly a great rivalry sprang up between gig crews. When a ship signalled its need for a pilot there was a rush to get the conveniently housed boats into the water. Then a race between rival gigs developed, eagerly watched and wagered upon by islanders from various hilltop vantage points on St. Mary's, Bryher and Agnes. Some pilot gigs contrived to steal a march on their fellows, by cruising beyond the islands awaiting the approach of a ship with her "jack" up at the main masthead, as was the practice of the cutters. Despite this advantage a gig, swiftly launched and manned by a double bank of oars, often caught up and then a neck-and-neck tussle would ensue with the boats coming up on opposite sides of the vessel and sometimes with their respective pilots clambering hand over hand over the gunwale, and arriving simultaneously on the bridge, much to the bewilderment of the Master! Then the gig crew would call for the traditional bottle of rum.

Rarely did a day pass without a ship needing the aid of a pilot, and on one famous occasion when a cutter really "got among" the shipping to the west of the islands, all the crew save one were set on homeward-bound vessels. One man was left to sail the cutter sixty miles back to St. Mary's singlehanded. However, like his colleagues, he received his share of the gross takings.

By tradition, Agnes is the "pilot's island", having all the advantages over its neighbours. It was that all-important bit "westward" and therefore closer to the busy shipping lanes. The Agnes names of Hicks and Legg figure prominently in the story of Scillonian pilotage. So ideally situated was Agnes that mainland pilots often settled there expressly to ply their trade.

Like ship-building, the thriving business of piloting came to a sudden end with the coming of steampower. Gone was the need for ships to shelter from contrary winds, and the cutters became obsolete. They were pulled up on the banks, gradually to deteriorate—a sad sight—or were broken up to build sheds. The smaller gigs stayed on, however, and besides being used for the occasional pilotage job or when steamers called to bunker, it served as an all-purpose boat. It even got into the wedding picture. The bridal gig, dressed overall, was a traditional feature of the off islands.

The occasions a gig was used for its true purpose became fewer and fewer until we see it being manned for salvage work as in the celebrated affair of the German barque *Excelsior* which dragged her anchor in the Roadstead at the end of the nineteenth century. Gigs from Bryher and St. Mary's raced to the spot with thoughts of salvage money uppermost in their minds, but it became a total wreck—largely through the negligence of the skipper who was discovered aft, incapably drunk!

Let me pilot this account into the more sober waters of the 1930s, when just about the last incidence of the exciting old profession of piloting took place. By this date the calling had slipped so much that there were only three pilots in Scilly, but when it was heard that the cruise steamer *Killarney* would be touching Scilly, the old-time rivalry was revived and all three worthies set out to secure the job. However they were handicapped by not knowing which course the visitor was to take. One pilot steered for the Bishop and waited; another plumbed for the region of the Wolf and Sevenstones. The last, and wisest, as it transpired, bided his time at Round Island—and sure enough there she was steaming towards St. Mary's Sound. He intercepted her and brought his prize to safe anchorage in the Roadstead. It was worth recording that the successful pilot was Mr. Jack Hicks from Agnes. His many forebears in the trade would have nodded their heads in vigorous approval.

In 1961 Mr. Hicks retired, and competitive pilotage died. Today only one man holds a pilot's licence and his services are rarely required. However the gigs, which stayed on until the motor boat came on the scene, have made a spectacular comeback. Throughout the summer they now take part in regular races across the Roadstead from Nut Rock off Samson, to the quay head, St. Mary's. Thousands of visitors flock to pier and beach to watch the finely-lined craft, young islanders straining at the oars. So popular have the old gigs become that a body has been established to foster racing in the islands and occasionally contests are staged between island and Newquay crews, both at home and away.

Smuggling. Any discussions of gigs must include smuggling, for much of the latter could not have taken place had it not been for these vessels: much of the "running" was done in them.

Circumstances in Scilly could not have been more favourable for the flourishing of smuggling—and for centuries islanders relied on the proceeds to bring extra luxuries into their lives when the vagaries of nature had adversely affected the harvests of sea and soil, as so often happened. Consider these factors. The islands, as was noted elsewhere, were situated right in the middle of the trading routes, and it was natural that Scillonians should slip out in their gigs under the cover of darkness to "barter" with a passing East Indiaman or the like. In that way tea, sugar, fancy goods (which the luxury-starved islanders delighted in) were brought in free of duty, and it is said that a bucket of island potatoes was worth, in return, a bucket of best tobacco (or "bacca" as Scillonians called it). And transactions with a passing "Frenchy" would result in a windfall of cognac for just a few pence a litre. Small wonder that a weather eye was kept open for passing shipping! Scilly was also situated well within reach of the French coastline and the Brittany ports, and it was nothing for the intrepid gigmen to row and sail 120-odd miles for their duty-free cargoes in their exercise of the "Fair Trade" as it was called.

In addition the arm of mainland law did not effectively stretch as far as the islands (or at least not until the nineteenth century) and the smugglers' sole enemy was the resident exciseman. The latter had a miserable task. He had much ground to cover, received little or no help from the public and a round-the-clock watch on every cove on every island was impossible. He seems to have put up no more than a token resistance, often turning a blind eye and sometimes participating with the "runners". I suspect that Scillonians would have smuggled anyway—even if their situation and economic condition had been against the business taking root. It was in their blood, and outwitting the exciseman was on a par with fooling one's teacher. As Lady Vyvyan said, smuggling has never really been regarded as a criminal thing. The sporting character of the Briton tends to make him sympathize with the smuggler. The latter knew the consequences, but was prepared to take the risk—and we love him for it. Robbing the national exchequer never seemed blatantly illegitimate anyway, and in Scilly (and in Cornwall and other coastal areas) just about everyone was involved up to the neck. The Reverend J. Troutbeck is said to have had to leave the islands following his complicity in a smuggling ring, and yet the hypocritical churchman wrote earlier: "of late years spiritous liquers are so cheap that the poorest persons can purchase them to the injury of their health, the promotion of idleness and the loss of the public revenue!"

In rambles around the islands one sometimes comes across a cove where rusty eye and ring bolts, imbedded in the high water

The "Loaded Camel" at Porth Hellick Bay, St. Mary's

granite, bear witness to the nefarious activities of the smuggler. It does not take much imagination to conjure up the oft-repeated scene of long ago. A lengthy row from Roscoff on the French coast has brought the smugglers within sight of Scilly, and their narrow, open gig wallows low in the water on account of its cargo of tobacco, silk, spirits, ankers of brandy and kegs of rum. The men must lay off the islands and wait, for to attempt to land in broad daylight would be inviting disaster. Tired, but ever watchful, they settle down at their oars to watch the fading light. At last darkness falls. There is no moon (smugglers are true professionals) and an easterly wind has conveniently risen to drown the creek of oar in thole-pin (a gig rowlock) as the gig creeps shorewards. Eyes are strained through the darkness to pick out the all-clear signals from colleagues ashore. The flashes come, like tiny pinpricks, and they go in thankfully handing their cargo through a chain of men up the cliff, or anchoring it to the seabed of the cove attached to a marker float. The tenseness of the last hours disappears; another successful "run" has been completed.

The heyday of the Scillonian smuggler was the last half of the eighteenth century when the islands became a veritable clearing house for contraband goods. It is said that much of the illicit merchandise was cellared beneath the cottages of Old Grimsby, Tresco—some of which still stand to this day. The gigs, incidentally, were ideal craft for smuggling in island waters. Their shallow draught was perfectly suited to local channels through which the revenue men found it difficult to venture.

But the Golden Age of the Scilly Smuggler was not to last long. The drain of the nation's money, not only in Scilly but all over the country, had not passed unnoticed, and Government measures were soon forthcoming to impose a clamp-down. A more efficient Preventive Service was built up, and Revenue boats patrolled island waters, and when, in desperation, smugglers resorted to the West Cornwall coasts to land their cargoes, they found the Customs men in close attendance there too. The methods to stamp out illicit traffic in Scilly were simply to break up islanders' gigs, to outlaw the practice of bartering with passing ships, while the business received a crushing blow when an order was passed forbidding more than four men to crew a gig. Now long trips to the French coast could not be undertaken, and Scilly's livelihood which had depended for so long on the proceeds

7

Carn Leh, St. Mary's

of duty dodging, took a hard knock. Indeed, islanders baldly admitted that the suppression of smuggling was one of the premier reasons for the distress of the early nineteenth century. Notwithstanding that stern action had to be taken by the Customs men, the four-men-in-a-boat restriction does seem harsh as it seriously limited the scale of their fishing and salvaging activities.

The biggest asset of the smuggler, however, was his resourcefulness, and he still managed to find a way through with his contraband despite the restrictions. In due course it died a natural death—but there are people in Scilly even today who remember their fathers' talking of the last of the smuggling gigs—*The Hope* —which ran the "blockade" successfully.

Amusing tales of clashes between Customs officer and smuggler are legion in Scilly. They spring naturally from a situation where the revenue man is on Christian-name terms with everyone, and the lawbreaker rubs shoulders pleasantly with the law representative. One of the best I have heard took place back in 1870 when smuggling was nearly finished, and concerns a certain barque *Florie* which was skippered by an islander who put into Scilly to land his wife before continuing to his port, Liverpool. The good lady was duly put ashore, and a punt-load of islanders rowed the skipper back to his ship. As the barque prepared to get under way, a twenty-eight-pound box of ship's "bacca" was furtively lowered over the side into the punt. Unfortunately this was noted by some vigilant Customs officials who had their spyglass trained on the *Florie* from St. Mary's shore. When the punt reached Porth Cressa, out jumped one man—straight into the arms of a revenue man. The boat quickly shoved off, one of the crew loudly but lamely remarking that by landing there they would get their feet wet! They next tried Morning Point on the Garrison, where the whole procedure was repeated. A man stepped ashore, the persistent official was waiting, the boat sheared off. It was now decided to leave the tobacco in a friend's boat moored across St. Mary's Sound in Porth Conger Bay, Agnes. When they returned to St. Mary's they were searched, but there was no incriminating evidence. However, their equilibrium was shattered the next day when they saw their friend's boat in the hands of the Agnes Coastguard: he had borrowed it as his own boat was being painted. The smugglers did not dare say a word, but eventually they managed to inform their friend, who found the "bacca" where they had put it, and after duly taking his cut, returned it to the relieved smugglers!

Fishing. In former days island waters, which were apparently far warmer than today and were ideal breeding grounds, abounded with every variety of flat, round and shellfish. However, in their many years of economic depression islanders disregarded the commercial possibilities, their main concern being to find sufficient food to keep themselves; anyway, transport was sporadic and markets inaccessible. Surrounded by water, fish became their natural and predominant diet. Everyone, farmer, labourer, shopkeeper, did a "bit of fishing" and the traditional dishes of the time were "scads and taters all the week and conger pie on Sundays". Ling was also caught by long line and salted away for winter use.

When the economic situation in Scilly was at its lowest ebb in the distress years of the early nineteenth century, efforts were made to establish a fishery on commercial lines. Equipment was provided for pilchards and mackerel fishing, a Fishery Company established and cellars were set up on Tresco for the storing and curing of the latter. Despite a remission on the duty of salt used for curing, the venture, as we saw in an earlier chapter, failed. Later, another attempt to turn Scilly's fish-laden waters into hard cash was made in the proprietorship of T. A. Dorrien-Smith. Pilchard driving was embarked upon and the man from the Abbey benevolently provided tanks on the quay for curing purposes. A Mevagissey merchant undertook to deal with the fish which, at the end of each season, were packed in barrels and exported to Italy.

The enterprise, like its predecessor, soon died out, this time because of a series of misunderstandings between fishermen and merchants. However, despite this double failure, seine fishing for scads, pilchards and conger was widely practised in Scilly throughout the nineteenth century. Competition between islanders to haul the seines, which were given names like Habnab and Friendship, was keen, and the Lord Proprietor often had to intervene. A number of beaches round Scilly were favourite spots, but perhaps the most productive place was the Cove at St. Agnes. The seines were hauled there at night and the catch was either loaded into gigs, put aboard a steamer and taken to the mainland, or shipped across the Sound to Porth Cressa St. Mary's where a vigorous auction was conducted on the bank.

Shrimps and limpets were also exported in the late nineteenth century, but the returns were negligible as largely were those of the shellfish men. The latter's crayfish and lobsters were either sold to a Southampton merchant whose smack collected them at Scilly or conveyed straight to Billingsgate. Later a limited continental trade developed. French and Belgian merchants put agents in Scilly who brought the fish direct from the potters, or potting dandies as their craft was called, stored them in carbs and waited for a smack to ship them to the continent. Local fishermen found competition brisk as Sennen and West Cornwall boats came over as well.

The busiest years for island fishermen were in the mid and late 1800s when Scilly was made a rendezvous for the mackerel fishery. Brown-sailed Mounts Bay and Newlyn luggers in their hundreds were a common sight from May to June, filling St. Mary's Pool, and it was sometimes possible to walk along town beach from the Old Quay to the Lifeboat slip on the decks of the fishing craft moored alongside one another. When these boats brought in their catches a Billingsgate-style auction would take place in the early morning. St. Mary's quay was a scene of great bustle with auctioneers bells ringing, and sellers, buyers and packers scurrying here and there.

Sometimes fishermen from the East Coast would join the West Countrymen in the fishery and when they did a great rivalry would spring up. On one occasion a riot developed between rival factions in a St. Mary's inn, which resulted in the local magistrates having to deal out harsh punishment. The reason for the fight was, apparently, the disapproval of the church-minded West Countrymen of their rivals' practice of fishing on Sunday. However, friction was the exception rather than the rule and Sunday nights would see the Cornish sailors gathering devoutly in the Parade to sing the old Methodist hymns with rich and moving harmony. "Let's 'ave 'em soft then give 'em lip", was the inimitable encouragement given by one fisherman conductor!

Despite the activity of this period commercial fishing was never a truly lucrative pursuit, and like kelp-burning, ship-building and piloting, had an ephemeral life. Today it is kept flickering by three "potters" who sell their crabs, crayfish and lobsters to local hotels and guesthouses and ship them to Newlyn. There are a number of St. Mary's men and off islanders who indulge in part-time potting, but it is not their main means of livelihood. "Going to pots" is a hard and dangerous life. In 1953 two island fishermen went down to the westward to haul their pots. It was so rough that they should not have been out—but both their livelihoods were at stake. They were as good seamen as any in Scilly, yet neither was ever seen again. As the fisherman's whole income is bound up in his pots he has to go out in all weathers to haul, bait and shoot— and these days catches are poor. It is not uncommon for a fisher- man to haul a whole string without catching anything more notable than a conger eel, a dog fish or a few tiny crabs. Most of the boats now have capstans to haul in the many fathoms of rope, but it is still a long and arduous job. After pulling a string the fisherman has to move to a new ground and shoot them, and the process is repeated many times over. They go out most days between 6 and 8 o'clock in the morning and are seldom back before mid afternoon. Each man has his own recognized grounds. One may fish off Watermill Bay, St. Mary's and the Eastern Islands; another may lay his pots out through Broad Sound; another off Agnes and the Western Rocks—or off Peninnis Head.

Many theories are offered for the scarcity of fish in Scillonian waters. Some say the grounds are fished out; others blame water temperature and the movement of the warm, plankton-carrying Gulf Stream; "old salts" put it down simply to the invention of the internal—or infernal—combustion engine. Whatever the reason, the fish are just not to be had, and it seems possible that the small trio of full-time fishermen may get even smaller. Occasionally a Spanish trawler puts into St. Mary's for shelter, and it has been noted on more than one occasion that the bad weather which the fishermen always give as the reason invariably comes on a Saturday, and coincides with the Saturday night "hop" at St. Mary's Town Hall!

From a visitor's point of view, Scilly caters inadequately for line fishing. Few boats can be hired as local owners are loathe to trust their craft to the hands of inexperienced visitors. One's only chance of going mackereling or pollocking is either to have a friend with a boat or to make it worthwhile for a boatman to take a crowd out in his vessel in the evening after his day's work is done. These trips are great fun, there being, unlike the unfortunate potters, no shortage of either fish. Feathering generally gets the best results. The motor is cut off, a line of many hooks is put overboard and if a shoal of mackerel is met, then the boat is soon literally jumping with fish. As many as six coming up at a time on one line! It is not unusual to return to St. Mary's after only an hour or so with a 200-plus catch of mackerel and pollock. The mackerel, although considered the biggest scavenger of all, is also the tastiest of fish, but best eaten fresh from the sea. Many a barbecue has followed an evening fishing trip, the delicious mackerel being cooked over an open fire on a cliff or headland.

Wrecking. When a stranger is asked what he knows about Scilly's association with the sea, any mention by him of kelp-making, ship-building, piloting and the like is a rarity. It never takes very long, however, for the accusing word "wreckers" to crop up. We people tucked vaguely away in the West Country are always "wreckers" to those "up the line".

It must straightaway be admitted that the islands have an incredible history of shipwreck. Few coasts in the world have witnessed such wholesale shipping slaughter. The seas of Scilly have been a veritable graveyard for every kind of vessel, whether under sail or steam and there is hardly a rock, ledge or isle in the group not linked with the foundering of a ship, many of which bear the names of the vessel they claimed. The maze of reefs in the savage waters to the west of the islands are the arch culprits. They have taken a heavy toll and the seabed must be littered with wreckage. The rocks of Scilly were feared by mariners the world over. Without the modern-day guidance of navigational instruments they were at the mercy of the strong indraughts and tides. Many a time a shipmaster thought he had given the islands a wide berth, only to find out too late that he had underestimated the drag of the currents. Three wrecks a year was by no means uncommon, and a list of shipwrecks stretches to the formidable dimensions of well over 200 in 150 years. Between 1878 and 1927 there were no less than 74 wrecks!

But the word "wreckers" is misleading. It implies the positive action of deliberate sabotage; as if hoards of grinning islanders were in the habit of lying in wait for an unfortunate vessel in order to swim out with knives between their teeth; as if lanterns were hung on the horns and lights to the tails of cattle to trap ships on the rocks; as if, even more fantastically, lights on light-houses were permitted to go out in dirty weather! Heath wrote of the Agnes light: "Before the coming of the present keeper I've known it scarcely perceivable in the night at the island of St. Mary's where it now shines like a comet; and some are of the opinion that, in the time of the former lightkeeper it has been suffered to go out or sometimes not lighted." All this is, of course, so much fanciful nonsense, for Scilly has a noble and proud record of life-saving to its eternal credit, and countless deeds of bravery have been enacted when vessels have struck upon the rocks of Scilly.

The many deeds of self-sacrifice give the lie to tales of "wreckers". If "wrecking" means the planned luring of ships to destruction then it is ill-used in the Scillonian context. Scillonians were not a bunch of cut-throat Sirens. Believe, if you will, the old Cornish wrecking proverb "From Praa Sands and Breage hands, good Lord deliver us" but do not associate its sentiments with Scilly. However, if what the accusers mean by "wrecking" is the grateful acceptance of the produce of wrecks, then Scillonians are guilty. "Hunting for wreck" was a Scillonian pastime. In their many years of poverty islanders came to look on shipwrecks as the providence of heaven thrown up on their shores by the Almighty to ease their economic hardship. Wrecks belonged to them. What the sea cast up was theirs, and it was their inalien-able right to profit from them. This attitude was born out by the twelfth-century charter of Tavistock Abbey which stated categorically that all wrecks should be "enjoyed" by their monks!

An eighteenth-century clergyman—possibly the one mixed up in the smuggling scandal mentioned earlier, was wont to com-municate thus with the Almighty in church: "We pray thee, Lord not that wrecks should happen, but if they do thou will guide them to the Scilly Isles for the benefit of the poor inhabitants," while another infamous tale centres around the little Agnes church at Priglis Bay. The parson entered the church one Sunday, mounted the pulpit and said: "Brethren, before I open the service I have a sad duty to perform. There has been a wreck"—and before he could complete his message, the church had emptied. A few months later, wrecks being the rule rather than the exception, the parson entered the church and spoke from the door: "Brethren, it is my sad duty to inform you of a wreck, but this time (stripping off his cassock) we all start fair"—and was in the vanguard of the subsequent rush to the beach!

Wrecks are now infrequent, thanks to progress made in navigation and coastal warning apparatus, but there is evidence of past horrors in Scilly even today. Throughout the islands churchyard gravestones bear witness to the cruelty of the sea; the church at Agnes was built largely on the proceeds of salvage; the school bell at St. Mary's came from the wreck *Erik Rickmer*'s; the roof is wreck wood, and a certain section of Hugh Town's Church Street is said to owe its origins to ship-wrecked "greenbacks" washed ashore on Town Beach. Awards for gallantry in saving life hang on many an island wall, while in addition there are a number of old Scillonian families who still bear the scars of shipwreck at sea—here a son lost in salvaging—there a father drowned when a vessel foundered with all hands. Leland tells us that one island (Agnes) was completely depopulated when a boat returning from a St. Mary's wedding went down with all hands.

In attempting to tell the story of Scilly's shipwrecks one is faced with an unenviable task. All of them deserve to be told, either on account of the magnitude of the disaster or because of the gallantry of subsequent efforts to save life. Therefore I have to omit many which well merit a mention, and to start my tale I turn the clock back over 250 years to the twenty-second day of October, 1707.

The scene is the sea to the west of Scilly. The British twenty-one vessel fleet, commander Admiral Sir Cloudesley Shovel, is feeling its way back home after the siege of Toulon in the South of France. Sir Cloudesley is concerned about the position of the fleet. A council of ships captains is called to determine the latitude, and all save one pinpoint the position as off the Ushant. The lone dissenter, however, puts them in close to the dreaded Isles of Scilly. Although the latter's belief is backed up by an ordinary seaman, Sir Cloudesley bows to weight of opinion and keeps on his course. It is dark. Suddenly they are surrounded by rocks. Guns boom out their warning, but too late they strike the Western Rocks. Sir Cloudesley's flagship *Association* breaks up in minutes, as do the seventy-gun *Eagle*, which foundered on the nearby Gunner, and the fifty-gun *Romney* and the fireship *Firebrand*. More than

1,400 men, including Sir Cloudesley, are lost, there being one survivor who floats on some timber to Hellweathers where he is later picked up.[1]

Thus, briefly, is the tragedy of Admiral Sir Cloudesley Shovel. A contemporary, perhaps under-playing the weather conditions, wrote: "One can only be amazed how 'twas possible men of so much experience could be mistaken in their reckoning after they had had ye advantage of a great deal of fair weather beforehand, and no bad weather when they were lost."

The *Association* affair ranks as one of the blackest events in the whole of British maritime history, yet surprisingly little is known of the disaster outside the Isles of Scilly. In 1707 journalism had a limited influence on the public and communications were poor. Consequently the event did not get the publicity it deserved, and only sketchy records of the disaster survive. If today the British fleet were wrecked and a celebrated admiral and 1,400 men were drowned the news would be flashed around a stunned world. Thus the magnitude of this early eighteenth-century disaster is put in its true perspective.

The body of the British admiral was washed up at Porth Hellick Bay, St. Mary's, together with his sea chest and stern board of the barge of his flagship *Association*. (That same stern board was presented to Penzance Corporation in thanks for help received during the "famine" years of 1818–19, and lies in Penzance Town Hall. Many islanders would like to see it back in Scilly, its rightful resting place.) Sir Cloudesley was discovered by some island women, and later buried on the bank bordering the beach on the orders of the Godolphin Lord Proprietor. Later the body was exhumed and identified by the purser of one of the fleet's ships, a close friend of the dead man. Wounds received in action established beyond all doubt that the body was the admiral's. The corpse had been stripped of its clothes and a valuable ring was missing from his finger. Sir Cloudesley was then taken to Plymouth where he was embalmed and subsequently he was buried in Westminster Abbey with the honours which

[1] During 1967, 1968 and 1969, teams of divers searching for Sir Cloudesley's wrecked fleet came up from the Gilstone with bronze cannon and a quantity of coin among other things. Much was made of this by the national Press, and it was eventually proved that the site of the 260-year-old disaster had been at long last located.

befitted his rank. Lady Shovel made great efforts to recover the lost ring, but with no success.

Such is the true story of the unfortunate Sir Cloudesley Shovel and the wreck of the *Association*. I stress "true" because, as if the events just described are not in themselves dramatic enough, writers have tried to enlarge. One popular fable is that the ship-wrecked survivor, the quarter-master of the ill-fated *Romney* and a Hull butcher by trade, told of the following events which took place on the flagship *Association* during the period of time leading up to the disaster. When the ordinary seaman expressed his opinion that they were steering a course for the Scilly rocks, Sir Cloudesley became incensed. This was tantamount to insub-ordination, and he ordered the poor man to be hanged, allowing him the favour of singing the 109th psalm before execution was carried out. Hardly had the wretch finished kicking at the end of the yardarm than they struck the rocks. There is, of course, little evidence of this happening, but the fable has survived to add spice to the affair. Robert Maybee, the nineteenth-century island poet, used this story in his verses on the wreck:

Dark on the Gilston's rocky shore
The mist came lowering down,
And night with all her deepening gloom
Put on her sable crown.

From sea a wailing sound is heard,
And the seamew's shrilly cry,
And booming surge and shrieking birds
Proclaim strange danger nigh.

Wrong you steer Sir Cloudesley, sure;
The rocks of Scilly shun;
Northern move, or no sailor here
Will see tomorrow's sun.

Hold wretch! Dare tell your Admiral
What dangers to evade?
I'll hang you up on yon yardarm
Before your prayers are said.

Oh, Admiral, before I die
Let someone read aloud

The one hundred and ninth dread psalm
To all this sailor crowd.

Let it be done, cursed mutineer;
As if I know not how
To steer my *Association* clear
Of every danger now.

The psalm was read, the wretch was hung
Drear darkness stalked around;
Whilst aloft the dead man swung,
Three ships had struck the ground.

How sad and awful was the sight,
How black and dark the shore.
Two thousand souls went down that night,
And ne'er saw daylight more.

One man alone of that brave crew
Was saved to tell the tale.
How swift and sure God's vengeance came;
He can alone prevail.

All dead and torn they came ashore
Down on Porth Hellick sand
Sir Cloudesley by his ring was known
That glistened on his hand.

A soldier's wife did find him there
All stiff and stark and dead
She gazed with awe on the body fair
She took the ring and fled.

They buried him in the greensward there
This day the place is seen
For the grass has n'er grown o'er the grave
Upon Porth Hellick green.

So, be not my friends too quick to judge
With pride not to relate
Be cautious, and bear well in mind
Poor Sir Cloudesley Shovel's fate.

Another elaboration concerns the ring. We are led to believe that Sir Cloudesley was still breathing when cast ashore, and that a local woman murdered him for the ring. Later, on her deathbed, she repented of her crime and returned the ring to a clergyman. Again this is not very credible, as the admiral would have had to have been particularly resilient to have survived a seven-mile sea drift from the Gilstone to Porth Hellick! However, there is no doubt the ring was stolen, for on being exhumed at Porth Hellick the impression was still on his finger. A stone monument on the bank at Porth Hellick commemorates the tragedy.

If Porth Hellick bay is connected with the greatest sea disaster in the annals of Scilly's history in the wreck of the *Association*, then it is also concerned with the strangest—the affair of the French brig *Nerina* in 1840.

On passage from Dunkirk to Marseilles with a cargo of oil and canvas and a crew of seven, she turned bottom up in a gale off Scilly, and for three whole days and nights drifted with what remained of her crew cramped between some barrels in the hold and the keelson. Eventually during the night she drifted in on Porth Hellick beach and the next morning island farmers collecting seaweed to manure their land came across the upturned hulk. They heard voices. A hole was immediately cut in the planking and, as the report from the French Consular agent in Penzance said at the time, "the poor fellows were liberated from a floating sepulchre".

A remarkable story—perhaps made more so by the fact that the men had earlier come within an ace of rescue. An island pilot cutter had come on the floating vessel and had attempted to tow her to St. Mary's. High winds and adverse currents forced the attempt to be abandoned—the Scillonians little knowing the hulk's content!

Almost on a par with the *Association* is the affair of the *Schiller* in 1875. She was a celebrated steamship, one of the largest of her day, and was in passage from New York to Plymouth when she struck the Retarrier Ledges (one of the western reefs, inevitably) and foundered. No less than 311 crew members and passengers lost their lives. Although the *Schiller* was a German ship and carried few British passengers, the whole country was shocked, especially when the details of the disaster were made known. Apparently, in dense fog, the lead (sounding) was neglected and the master of the ship, like so many before and after him, had no idea he was close in to Scilly.

When she struck a social function was in progress and many

of the women passengers were dressed in their finery. As can be imagined, the confusion and terror was awful, there being a mad scramble to the boats. The captain tried to restore some semblance of order by firing a pistol above the heads of the frantic mob, but to no effect. Only three of the eight boats were launched, one being smashed when the funnel fell on it, and many were then drowned. However, the vessel held together for quite a time, although when day dawned the slaughter was complete. Only a handful of men who had clambered to the rigging were still alive.

For the next few days bodies were washed up throughout the islands. Old Town churchyard, St. Mary's, has never seen such a funeral. The sad procession, containing twenty carts each carrying two bodies, stretched the length of Hugh Street. It is said that the Kaiser was so appreciative of the attention Scillonians gave to the shipwrecked Germans that he forbade any German ships to harm steamers plying between the islands and Penzance during the Great War. Not once were the vessels attacked by German U-boats. My own family has a violin off the *Schiller* washed up in its case on Town Beach, St. Mary's.

If the *Association* and *Schiller* were the biggest wrecks on Scilly's rocks, and the *Nerina* the strangest, then the *Deleware* deserves a special mention, for islanders surpassed themselves in their gallantry while attempting to save life. The *Deleware* was a big-screw steamer which got into difficulties off Scilly in 1871. She did not hit a rock but was capsized by three huge seas which followed one on top of the other. That gives one some idea of the great waves which pound the islands. They descended directly on the ship, stoving in her nine bulkheads, like matchwork, and smashing her to pieces. The captain broke a leg at the first shock and was subsequently swept overboard and drowned. Fifty sailors were either drowned or dashed to pieces on the rocks, with the mate and the third mate, more by luck than design, managing to clamber into a ship's lifeboat. They were eventually thrown up on White Island, more dead than alive.

Now the Scillonians—Bryher islanders to be precise—took a hand. Obviously there was no chance at all of saving the men in the raging seas, but might not the two wretches high and dry on White Island be rescued? The seas were mountainous and would have daunted many lesser individuals. In shocking conditions they dragged and carried one of their gigs from one side of the island to the other—from Par Beach to Rushy Bay—and rowed across to Samson, for the latter was nearer to the scene of the disaster.

On arriving at Samson they shipped oars and embarked on the herculean task of dragging the heavy gig across the narrow waist of that island. With the wind whipping sand into their faces they struggled over the rocks and shingle with their heavy load. This was bravery at its height. There was no reward for them at the end save, possibly, death. They pressed on, however, and exhausted reached the other side of Samson. Now the gig had to be re-launched. Savage breakers drove them back time after time, but they persisted, perhaps spurred to greater efforts by the pathetic sight of the two men clinging to their sea-lashed rock. They succeeded in getting the boat afloat. Through the churning waters and floating corpses they rowed and eventually reached White Island. Landing was a treacherous business, for if they holed their craft in the terrific seas all hope for them and the wrecked mariners would be gone.

Now comes what is to me one of the most incredible incidents in Scillonian sea history. The wrecked men had gathered stones in their hands and their arms were drawn back to hurl them at the gig men; the islanders of Scilly were, they believed, savages who preyed off shipwrecked sailors—and they feared for their lives!

However they soon realized that these men meant to help, not destroy. Their bruised and bloody bodies, hideously gashed by the granite reefs, were tended by the gig men and they embarked for the return trip. Samson was safely reached where the survivors (one now being unconscious) were covered in some ferns for warmth. A signal was sent back to Bryher for help, a second gig was launched—and the epic story of the *Deleware* was over.

She foundered near the Roaring Ledge, and afterwards islanders renamed the rock the "Deleware Ledge". There are many tales of bravery in life-saving but the efforts of the men of Bryher on this occasion can never be surpassed.

So far we have only seen the tragic aspects of shipwreck at sea. Wrecks, amazingly, do have their lighter sides, especially in the Scillonian context; and most of these are centred around the serious business of salvaging.

Take the case of the *Friar Tuck* in 1863. A 662-ton tea clipper, she dragged anchor and was driven ashore at Porthloo, St. Mary's. Frightful chaos now ensued when tea was washed up on the various beaches. The customs and excise men did what they could, breaking open the chests and burning the tea, but islanders were not to be denied. The local schoolmaster sent his pupils down Carn Thomas hill to gather the tea which, when dried, was excellent, and it is said that the commodity was not bought in Scilly for many a long day.

Then there was the wreck of the *Borodino*, remembered for the words used by a wrecking islander. Not appreciating the value of cocoa, he was recorded as saying: "Don't mind about the cuckoo Zachary, save the sugar!"

The wreck of the *Minnehaha* in 1910 is still well remembered in Scilly. Much of its cargo found a way to St. Mary's beaches and homes, and the common answer at that time to an inquiry after one's health was simply "Ha-Ha!" The first time Bryher islanders had any intimation that there had been a wreck was when a huddle of survivors with blankets around their shoulders emblazoned "Atlantic Transport Company" were seen sheltering forlornly on the beach. Scillonians will not forget the "Minnie" for many years. It was a "good" wreck. Because of an outbreak of fire in the docks at New York she was carrying the mongrel cargoes of her crippled sister ships—ranging from pencils to tobacco, from pianos and typewriters to hats. Islanders smoked themselves ill on "Old Judge" cigarettes, chewed plug tobacco; salved cattle put ashore on Samson became mixed up with Lieutenant Dorrien-Smith's herd and were unwittingly "evacuated" by drovers, and one young wrecker (the late Trevellick Moyle) remembered to his dying day the impression on his childish mind given by one survivor who had gold fillings in his teeth. "Every time he smiled, a gold mine looked at you."

"Another Minnehaha, that's what we want," was often heard subsequently.

The wreck of the *Castleford*, or the beef wreck, was another extraordinary affair. Her cargo of bullocks was saved and put on Annet the bird sanctuary. Hay and fodder was brought from St. Mary's and eventually the animals were shipped away to the mainland. There was the *Sussex* which grounded near Seal Rock in 1885, and caused the islands to be covered in her cargo of flour; the *Sado* in 1870 which provided islanders with a windfall of oranges; and the *Parame*, the coconut wreck. The *Horsa* is another unforgettable wreck. Skippered by a James Magellan, she ran aground in Bread and Cheese Cove at the back of St. Martins, and an islander born on the very day of the wreck was christened, naturally, Horsa Magellan Legg. To his dying day he was known as "Horsa" throughout Scilly.

The *Mando*, which went aground on the Golden Ball Ledge in 1955, caused some eyebrows to be raised. The St. Mary's soccer team were to be at home to St. Martin's on the day following the wreck, but the latter informed them that tide would not permit them to come down for the match. Tide, however, did not prevent a number of them being seen in the vicinity of the wreck. Suffice it to say that when the captain returned to the vessel to collect his papers (he had been persuaded to leave his ship), he found she had been stripped bare down to the paint locker. Even some of his clothes were missing and it is said that one St. Mary's man, never before noted for his horticultural interests, was seen to be digging a vast hole in an overgrown patch alongside his house . . . ! A certain Penzance restaurant currently sports much *Mando* brick-à-brac, while one St. Mary's wrecker delights in telling a story against himself of how, after the ship had been declared a wreck, he spent half an hour eagerly hacking his way through a heavily locked oak door, only to find that it was the skipper's private lavatory! However, the affair of the *Mando* has an official side. Salved goods which did not disappear into private hands were later sold by public auction in St. Mary's Town Hall!

While dealing with extraordinary happenings, the unique experience of a certain Italian sea cook must not be overlooked. He was on the S.S. *Isabo* in 1926 when she struck Scilly Rock and sank with the loss of six lives. In 1955, twenty-nine years later, the *Mando* was wrecked—and aboard was the very same cook—to be rescued by the very same lifeboat coxswain!

More notable wrecks include the other *Minnehaha* (1874), whose survivors clambered up the cliffs of Peninnis to be met in the lane by the late Mr. Israel Pender going to milk his cows in the early morning and the *Lady Charlotte*, the first intimation of disaster being when the occupants of Normandy farm were knocked up in the middle of the night by a party of sodden survivors; and lastly, the "vessel unknown", carrying a cargo of rum, indigo and coffee and which sank off the Steval with all hands— and dismissed in the islands' wrecking records by the terse, explanatory words "Crew drunk on said rum!"

The Scillonian *passing Woolpack Point*

But enough of these amusing slants. Shipwreck is generally a nasty business, with tragedy never far away, as will be seen in my last wreck story which concerns the S.S. *Plympton* which went down off the Lethegus Rocks (or "Thickeses" as they are locally known) in 1909.

The morning of that ill-fated day dawned quiet and peaceful, conditions which so often go with fog in Scillonian waters. Never has there been a thicker blanket around Scilly as on that August day. Even the gulls could not find the islands, their mewing being heard clearly through the mist.

The first indication of the *Plympton*'s arrival off Scilly was her blowing; she was sounding her siren continuously and soon the blows turned to distress signals. A rush was made for Porth Cressa bank by islanders to launch the old gig *Dolly Varden*, and soon the St. Mary's men were afloat and inching westward in the direction of the siren. The fog was "thick as a bag" and the crew could hardly see past the end of the gig. However, they reached Dropnose off the Gugh and turned to skirt the Agnes shore where they came up to the stricken vessel. The *Plympton*, carrying Indian corn for a Bristol Channel port was hard and fast on the rocks.

After the Agnes lifeboat had taken off the crew islanders set about their task of salvage, everything of value being stripped off her, compasses, ropes, blocks, paints, et cetera. A break was called for lunch, but the islanders were soon back, the weather still foggy. While the salvaging was going on the tide was flowing and gradually lifting the vessel off the rocks. As if warning the salvagers of impending danger, small spurts of steam were coming from the vessel's funnel, but no one took any notice; the wrecking fever of their ancestors had gripped them.

Suddenly she went; as quickly as that; and islanders were left swimming about in the water, many clutching salved goods. They were taken aboard the boats, but two of their colleagues were not so fortunate. One, an Agnes Hicks, was seen running aft when the ship keeled over, but was never seen again. He must have been dragged down to the bowels of the ship. The other islander, a St. Mary's man, was down in the captain's cabin and was trapped by the rush of water. He, too, was never seen again. A visitor, who was "wrecking" alongside the islanders, had an amazing escape. He was near a porthole when the water rushed in. He was projected to the surface—still clutching

8

Bishop Rock lighthouse from Crebawethan

the steward's dinner bell which he had picked up! Subsequently the shock of his narrow escape turned his sandy hair pure white.

The wreck of the *Plympton* was a tragic business; two islanders drowned—for nothing—because when the salvage of the wreck was sold later by auction on Rat Island, St. Mary's, the returns were not worthy of the gigmen's efforts. There have been many more momentous wrecks than the S.S. *Plympton*, but few as poignantly sad for Scillonians. I make no excuse for recording it; one of those islanders who were drowned was my grandfather....

Lighthouses. One of the main reasons for the shocking carnage on the rocks to the west of the islands was the lack of an efficient warning light. There was just an open coal burner on the Agnes tower, which itself is only fifty feet above sea level, and even in good weather it was far from satisfactory. In foul, the mass of smoke and flames was particularly ineffectual. The main trouble was that the Agnes light was situated *inside* the danger area—the vicious rocks lying to the west of the island. The range of its "beam" was limited—and in poor weather was no more than three miles—useless to shipping groping for a mark coming up the western approaches. Nevertheless Benjamin Franklin, the great eighteenth-century American statesman and inventor, was impressed with the Agnes light. In 1757 a ship in which he was voyaging nearly foundered on the western rocks, and was warned off in time by the Agnes light. Franklin resolved to encourage the building of more lighthouses on his return to America. However, little was done to improve the situation until the pleas of mariners and the continuous destruction of ships forced Trinity House in 1847 to make a move. They decided to build a tower on the most south-westerly rock, the Bishop.

The story of the erection of this world-famous lighthouse deserves a book in itself, for not only was it a superlative engineering feat, involving incredibly hard work, but also the workmen engaged on its construction were plagued throughout with bad luck. The original intention was to erect an iron tower on the rock, but the structure was hardly half completed when it was washed away during the night by a gale. When the workmen returned next morning all they found was the original rock with which they had started.

The famed lighthouse builder Mr. N. Douglas, who was supervising the construction, now decided to build a granite tower. Work was restarted in 1851, and the difficulties faced can be judged by the fact that it took a whole year to lay the base! Building the Bishop was not like erecting a land lighthouse. All work had to be done from boats which were always at the mercy of the Atlantic swell. The blocks had to be shipped out by boat, then winched up. The neighbouring islet of Rosevear was used as a base. Progress was painfully slow, as no construction was undertaken in winter-time.

By 1858 the lighthouse was finished, but now further difficulties were encountered. The tower was so exposed to the Atlantic breakers that the entire construction shook and things inside were thrown all over the place. On one occasion a huge, heavy fog bell was torn from aloft a hundred feet up by a big sea and washed away. Despite strengthening the tower in 1874, the lighthouse was considered still far from safe and in the 1880s Trinity House made further alterations. The height was extended from 110 feet to 167, and the beam made effective from sixteen to eighteen miles—a great improvement on the limited Agnes light. All the work done in this final stage of strengthening was based on a yard at Rat Island, St. Mary's. The granite blocks, shipped from Cornwall, were cut there and transported down to the Bishop by steamer. The job was concluded in 1887. An outer casing of dovetailing masonry had been added to the tower, and a new powerful light and signal put in.

At long last the savage-sounding rocks of the west, Crim, Crebinicks, Gunner, Retarrier, Zantman, Gorregan, Dogs of Scilly and their granite cousins, were, to a large extent, harnessed. While the Bishop was undergoing its protracted construction the Wolf Rock lighthouse was built (1869) and the light on Round Island was also erected (1887). When, in 1911, Peninnis lighthouse succeeded the 231-year-old Agnes light, the safeguarding process was complete. Scilly was circled by a ring of light, strengthened further by the Long Ships, and many a mariner approaching from the west must have blessed the 600,000 candle-power, double-flashing Bishop beam or the red eye of Round Island.

The rocks of the north, which did not lag far behind those of the west in the business of destruction, were now also effectively bridled. Ships kept their distance from the fearsome, but inappropriately pretty-sounding rocks of Maiden Bower, Illiswilgig, Castle Bryher, Scilly Rock, Mincarlo and Golden Ball. Today from St. Mary's no less than eight lighthouse beams can be seen: those of the Bishop, Peninnis, Sevenstones, Pendeen, Lizard, Round Island, Wolf and Longships.

The comforting, shielded feeling which Scillonians get in fog from the ring of lighthouses is perhaps best explained in Crosbie Garstin's poem:

THE SEA LIGHTS[1]

from "The Ballad of the Royal Ann".

Flashed Lizard to Bishop
"They're rounding the fish up
Close under my cliffs where the cormorants nest,
The lugger lamps glitter
In hundreds and litter
The sea-flow like spangles. What news from the West?"

Flashed he of the mitre
"The night's growing brighter,
There's mist over Annet, but all's clear at sea
Lit up like a city,
Her band playing pretty,
A big liner's passing. Aye, all's well with me."

Flashed Wolf to Round Island,
"Oh you upon dry land,
With wild rabbits cropping the pinks at your base,
You lubber, you oughter
Stand watch in salt water,
With tides tearing at you and spray in your face."

The gun of the Longships
Boomed out like a gong—"Ships
Are bleating around me like sheep gone astray
There's fog in my channel
As thick as grey flannel—
Boom—rumble!—I'm busy. Excuse me, I pray."

[1] Reprinted by permission of Mrs. Garstin.

They winked at each other,
As brother to brother
Those red lights and white lights, the summer
  night through
And steered the stray tramps out,
Till dawn snuffed their lamps out,
And stained the sea meadows all purple and blue.

Despite these man-made protections, islanders remained for ever on the alert, and none deserve greater praise than the life-boatmen of Scilly. Each island had its boat, even if it were a gig, and valiant work was done. A succession of lifeboats have served St. Mary's, the sailing and rowing vessel *Henry Dundas*, *Elsie*, *Cunard*, and the present vessel *Guy and Clare Hunter*. Lifeboat service seems to run in families, and none figure more prominently for St. Mary's than the Lethbridge family.

The present coxswain is Matt Lethbridge and during the writing of this book figured with his crew in the headline-snatching drama of the wreck of the 61,000-ton *Torrey Canyon* on the Sevenstones. This Liberian colossus, carrying 120,000 tons of crude oil, hit the Pollard Rock of the "Stones" at a sprinting 16 knots. St. Mary's lifeboat was first there and logged thirty-two and a half hours continuous service before returning to her station with some of the crew—a local record.

The world eyed Scilly during this hectic Easter of 1967 for, in time, 80,000 tons of oil gushed into the sea and presented unprecedented pollution problems. Vessels by the score sprayed detergent, troops were called in to scour beaches, and, after an explosion had killed a salvage man and the tanker herself had broken her back beyond all hopes of reprieve, the Government decided aircraft should remove the oil menace by bombing the *Torrey Canyon* open and burning the oil held in the intact tanks. Crowds gathered at Bants Carn, St. Mary's to see the helpless ship being strafed with rockets and napalm and wonder at the mushroom of flame and smoke which blackened the sky for miles. Eventually, however, the oil threat was checked—and the Fortunate Isles, thanks to favourable westerlies, escaped pollution completely.

Vessels old and new. Wrecks on a large scale may be a thing of the past, as are pilot boats, gigs and all the glamour of sailing craft. Nevertheless islanders still retain their interest in the sea and boats, and one vessel in particular takes pride of place, the *Scillonian*, which maintains the all-important link between Penzance and St. Mary's. Scilly has, of course, got an airlink, but it is the *Scillonian*, "old faithful", which keeps the mainland open in all weathers. Fog, and flying ceases, but the *Scillonian* sails on and island life continues.

The high spot of an island day, even in this age of moon travel and incredible technical achievement, is the arrival of the steamer from Penzance (although powered by diesel the *Scillonian* and her colleague *The Queen* are still affectionately referred to as if ships under steam). When she blows on entering the Roadstead through St. Mary's Sound, or at high water, Crow Sound, clocks are set by her and there is an immediate drift towards the quay. "Four o'clock," islanders remark, when she blows before the return trip in the afternoon. Her arrival is of vital interest, and attendance is almost a way of life.

The story of the boats that have served the islands over the centuries is a fascinating one, but one which can only be briefly touched upon here. Up to the mid nineteenth century the Penzance run was slogged-out by a succession of sailing vessels such as the *Lord Wellington* which brought Augustus Smith to Scilly to take up his lease. Only a few trips were done a month, and many of the earlier vessels were at sea for anything up to ten hours before sighting the islands.

In the 1850s the fifty-two ton cutter, the *Ariadne* was serving the islands, but in 1858 steam came in the shape of the *Scotia*. The following year one of the most celebrated vessels in Scillonian history came into service—the *Little Western* and was skippered by Captain Frank Tregarthen who, we are told, insisted all his passengers should stay at the well-known St. Mary's hotel, which even today bears his surname! The frequency of trips made to the mainland depended wholly on the speed with which Captain Tregarthen got through provisions at his hotel. Food exhausted, he would assay a voyage to Penzance!

In 1872 the islands were hit by a double tragedy, the *Little Western* and the Clyde-built *Earl of Arran* which had acted as auxiliary vessel, being both wrecked. The former went aground off Southard Wells and was lost. At the time it was rumoured that

Captain Tregarthen had deliberately wrecked his ship because he had been frustrated by a salvage job. The *Earl of Arran* ran on Nornour in the Eastern Islands group and until comparatively recently her boiler could be seen on the sand bar.

After the paddle steamers *Guide* and *Queen of the Bay* had kept the service going until 1875, a new boat took up the run—the *Lady of the Isles*. The *Lady* kept the islands in touch with Penzance for thirty years, until 1905 when she was bought by a company to be used for cable and salvage work. In 1889 the screw steamer *Lyonnesse* had come on the scene and carried on in conjunction with the *Lady* until just before the Great War. During the early years of the twentieth century as odd an assortment as ever put to sea butted across the forty-mile strip. There was the *Sir Walter Raleigh*, a tender to liners at Plymouth; the Clyde-built *Aquila*, designed originally for the Hawick-Hook run; the *Melmore*, a yacht once belonging to the Earl of Leitrim; the paddle steamer *Gael* and the *Stormcock* which transported island potatoes and dried fish to the mainland markets; the screw steamer *Deerhound*; the drifters *Ratapiko* and *Deleraine*; two Falmouth tugs *Triton* and *Victor*; the coaster *Artificer* encrusted in coal dust fore and aft. Although this motley selection of craft did great service it can be imagined they were responsible for many an agonizing hell of seasickness.

In 1919 the Isles of Scilly Steamship Company, which owns the two vessels running today, was formed and the S.S. *Lapwing* was chartered to do the run. A few years later, however, the Ministry of Shipping gave the company six months' notice that they were ending the charter and winding up the service—and so there was only one course of action open to the directors—to own a vessel. After many inquiries they plumped for an Admiralty-owned fishery protection vessel, the *Argus*, and set about raising the £10,000 needed for her purchase. Painstaking door-to-door collections throughout the islands provided the initial impetus to a gallant £7,000 sum, but another £3,000 was still required. Loans were sought of the Duchy of Cornwall and the then Great Western Railway, both unsuccessfully, and just when the situation began to look hopeless, a relative of the chairman of the board of directors stepped into the breach in a most original way. An Admiralty man, he put forward the plight of the unfortunate islanders so eloquently to the Naval Board that the latter were

almost reduced to tears. The extra £3,000 was waived! Scilly at
last had its own boat which they redesigned and gave the appropriately Scillonian name of *Peninnis*.

By this time islanders were nearly all engaged in their new
business of flowers, and notwithstanding the natural elation
Scillonians felt in owning their own boat, it was soon plain that a
newer, faster vessel was needed to further the industry. The year
1926, an unforgettable one for strike-crippled Britain, was
equally memorable for Scilly, for in that year the first *Scillonian*,
built at the Ailsa Shipyard, Troon, came into service, taking over
from the *Peninnis* which was renamed S.S. *Riduna* and still did
the occasional relief run.

The *Scillonian*, 170 feet long, with a 28-foot beam and drawing
10½ feet of water, had an adventurous maiden voyage from Troon.
So much went wrong that the superstitious seamen of Scilly
might have taken it as an ill omen. The *Scillonian* had hardly left
port when she ran into bad weather and an oil shortage forced her
to put into Belfast. Still punching into huge seas she was again
forced to put into port—this time Kingston, because her lubricat-
ing pump was out of order. After other minor vicissitudes she
finally made Scilly to a welcome of flashing lights and bonfires,
but not before time, as everyone, from the bridge to the engine
room was nearly dying of thirst; the fresh water had run out and
tea had to be brewed from the condenser's water! The chairman of
the company Mr. Fred Ward, whose son Mr. Rodney Ward
occupies a similar position today, decided against the voyage from
Troon and travelled to Penzance by train!

Despite her somewhat shaky start the *Scillonian* was to serve the
island nobly for nearly thirty years. In 1931 the best-loved of all
Scillonian sea skippers took over—Captain Joe Reseigh—and continued in the high tradition of former famous island mariners,
Captains Tregarthen, Tiddy and McAlister, Ashford, Hooper and
Mumford, until his untimely death in 1953. The company has
never had a more faithful servant. The islands' debt to Captain
Reseigh is immense. Throughout the Second World War he
maintained a regular link with Penzance, hardly ever missing a
trip. He voyaged 6,722 times as master, and brought about 40,000
troops to the islands, plus supplies and equipment. Captain
Reseigh ensured that the flower consignments got through to the
mainland markets, and on one occasion carried no less than

13,000 boxes. For his outstanding services this Mousehole-born man was awarded the O.B.E.

As the holiday trade began to have its effect on Scilly the company realized there was a need for a bigger vessel. The *Scillonian* had been a wonderful servant, but she was now incapable of coping with the increased demand. A contract was, therefore, signed with Thornycrofts of Southampton for the building of a twin-screw diesel vessel of 921 tons. Launched by the Duchess of Gloucester, the second *Scillonian* came into service in 1956 and is, of course, in commission today. In 1965, she was joined by the *Queen of the Isles* a twin-screw passenger-cargo vessel which was built by Messrs. Charles Hill and Sons at Bristol.

The company's decision to take a second vessel was influenced by the great boom in the holiday traffic. The *Scillonian* was hard pressed to accommodate the thousands of people who visit Scilly weekly, either to stay or for a day trip, and a new boat, it was thought, would ease her cargo and passenger burden. In the peak of summer the boats run an efficient shuttle service, meeting all the demands of an expanding visitor trade, while in winter it is now possible to keep the service going while one of the boats is undergoing refit. Unfortunately, however, the *Queen's* association with Scilly opened under something of a cloud as, owing to financial restrictions, she had to be "laid up" for a spell early on.

Over the years it has become almost traditional to criticize the various *Scillonians*. People prefer to attribute seasickness to the unseaworthiness of the boat rather than to the treacherous passage of water or their weak stomachs. The last voyages of the old *Scillonian* were, it is true, miserable and often hair-raising experiences, but she did not deserve the scorn poured upon her. Because of the tidal nature of St. Mary's and Penzance harbours and the fact that the latter was far too open in a south-easterly gale, she could only draw a negligible depth of water, and consequently in rough weather sat on the top of the sea, a prey to the wind. The new vessels, both diesel powered, are great improvements, but they, too, do not possess sufficient draught to get down in the water. However, stabilizers have lessened the effects of a bad crossing.

The stretch of water between Lands End and Scilly is feared the world over. Many years ago someone described Scilly as "a paradise only attained, unfortunately, after passing through purgatory". I wonder how many people have been of the same opinion since? One of the worst spots is just beyond Lands End. There, off the Runnelstone Rock, the currents of the English Channel clash with the swell of the broad Atlantic, and it is at this point that many a protesting stomach rebels.

Respect for the crossing is universal. On one occasion two elderly ladies muffled up between decks asked me, "Have we passed the Runnelstone yet?" How could I tell her that the see-saw motion was due to the water in Penzance Harbour and that, in fact, we had not even cast off from the Albert Pier!

Nowadays the sailing time has been reduced to two and a half to three hours, and in calm weather the voyage can hardly be surpassed. It opens with a pleasant cruise in the lee of the West Cornwall shore, past Newlyn, Mousehole, Lamorna, Porthcurno and Porthgwarra, then the Tater Du Light and soon the magnificent granite mass of Lands End towers into sight. Off Pol Pedn cliffs the dreaded Runnelstone is reached and even on a calm day there is a "run" in the water which rolls the boat. From this point, save for the Wolf Rock lighthouse and the occasional coaster and fishing craft, there is nothing but a vast expanse of sea until the islands hove into sight, the merest of smudges on the horizon. Soon they can be identified individually—Hanjague Rock, St. Martin's and it is not long before St. Mary's is reached.

The *Scillonian* and *Queen* are vital lifelines for Scilly. If anything were to happen to them it would be a shattering blow to the islands' economy. There is not a single person in Scilly whose welfare is not bound up in the two vessels. Happily the managing director, chairman and colleagues who, until recently, were unpaid, only too well realize the importance of the service to Scilly and have wisely attempted to follow a policy of keeping shares within the islands. The Isles of Scilly Steamship Company is a Scillonian concern—an island enterprise—and should men without the true interests of Scilly at heart gain control, then disastrous results could follow.

The *Scillonian* and the *Queen of the Isles*, as befitting their importance, take pride of place in Scilly, but the islands can also boast as fine a fleet of pleasure craft as anywhere in Britain. The men who run these boats are Scilly's latest "livers off the sea". Not so very long ago there were only a few such craft and the demand for an inter-island service was small. So rapidly has tourism hit the islands that, seemingly overnight, a veritable flotilla of launches, mostly operating in a Boatmen's Association, has appeared. In the summer they leave St. Mary's at 10.15 in the morning, returning at lunchtime. Out they go again in the afternoon and back in the evening.

Apart from visits to the main islands the boatmen, whose devil-may-care, buccaneering attitude has captured many a lady's heart, also go to the uninhabited isles and run trips to the western rocks to show visitors the puffins and seals. The boatmen, many of them bearded, have a rakish quality about them and the sight of them, seaman's cap or sock hat at jaunty angle and with the name of their respective boats on their blue jerseys, appears like a scene out of *Treasure Island*, to the conventional city dweller. Occasionally the visitor is afforded a special thrill by being taken down to the Bishop Rock lighthouse to see mail and provisions being handed up to the keeper. He might be lucky enough to see the actual relief of the lighthouse, the old keeper being taken off, the new one taking over. Sometimes trips are made past the Bishop to the shipping lanes, so that visitors can see, at close hand, large Atlantic liners.

With the departure of the last visitor in October the boatman's work is done for another year. His craft is dragged up the beach and installed in the boathouse to await the coming of another season. In the meantime the inter-island link is kept by launch, the running cost of which, it was decided in 1967, should be borne largely by the Islands' Council. The boatmen, following the practice of their maritime predecessors through the ages, now turn their hand to the land and many work on the flower farms. This shore pursuit provides ample employment until the new year comes, the trickle of visitors becomes a flood and the land labourer is back in business on the sea.

V

THE FLOWER INDUSTRY

Nature has blessed Scilly with an extraordinarily mild (by British standards) and generally frost-free winter climate which for centuries virtually pleaded to be harnessed to the pursuit of commercial agriculture. Incredibly islanders failed to recognize the splendid potentialities latent in their temperate circumstances (or if they did they were too poor to do anything about it). Notwithstanding the cultivation for many years in the nineteenth century of early potatoes on an admittedly quite extensive scale for export to the British mainland, and even as far afield as the Mediterranean, they largely followed the sea for their livelihoods at the expense of the soil, as was seen in the last chapter. Corn and other small produce were grown it is true, but there were only domestic ends in view and they only went towards bolstering a sagging, near-subsistence level economy. Exploitation of island land on a commercial scale was unknown to Scillonians. The sea ruled, as it had always done.

The momentous date when islanders at long last rumbled to the possibilities that lay in their natural advantage of climate and hit upon a way of putting it to profitable use; when seamen threw up the oar and took to the hoe; when the basic Scillonian economy passed from "town" to "country"; when, in fact, the widely celebrated Isles of Scilly Flower Industry was born—was in the latter half of the nineteenth century. And the prime mover of Scilly's agrarian revolution was Mr. William Trevellick, a farmer of Rocky Hill, St. Mary's. At the time, and for many years before, narcissus and daffodils growing wild in hedgerow and field were a common sight in the islands. In true Wordsworthian style they grew "along the margin of the bay"—every bay on every island. They might have remained like that to this day had not Mr. Trevellick conceived the idea of picking a few at random, packing them into a long old-fashioned hat-box and sending them to Covent Garden Market. It added up to nothing more than an off-the-cuff experiment. Public demand for cut flowers was not yet developed and the marketing of blooms was little practised. Anyway, who would have ever thought of sailor-minded Scillonians turning land-lubbing flower growers?

The outcome of Mr. Trevellick's action, however, was startling. He received a handsome 7s. 6d. for his casual dispatch. Encouraged he repeated the move—and this time netted £1. Further successes followed and it did not take very long for the nimble brain of the Rocky Hill man to assimilate the potential. He sensed something big was about to happen—indeed was happening: something far bigger than Scilly had hitherto ever experienced. Could it be that the islands were on the threshold of a new industry, an era of unprecedented economic prosperity? Mr. Trevellick discreetly informed his farming neighbours, Mr. William Barnes of Normandy and Mr. Richard Mumford of Holy Vale, and together this trio explored every angle of starting a winter occupation of growing flowers for early export to mainland markets.

The industry, in the hands of just a few bold visionaries, started in a humble way and gave little indication of future success, but when the considerable monetary and philanthropic support of the Lord Proprietor, Lieutenant T. A. Dorrien-Smith, was brought to bear, flower farming in Scilly could be said to have got fairly off the ground. The assistance of the landlords, the Duchy of Cornwall, in exploiting their land was also readily given—and the industry never looked back; it has, in fact, become as much part and parcel of the islands as wind and weather and has had an uninterrupted run right through to the present day.

Very few of the blooms that went to make up the contents of the historic, pioneering "Aunt Ellen's hatbox" were indigenous. They originated from France and the Mediterranean and came to be growing in the islands as a direct result of the old island practice of bartering with foreign vessels, the pursuit so frowned upon and eventually outlawed by the revenue men. French fishermen would exchange bulbs for corn, vegetables and miscellaneous island foodstuffs, and these bulbs which were at first planted haphazardly around the islands were to play a major role in the later development of the industry. One of the first bulbs was the yellow Soleil D'Or ("Sol"), a heavily scented variety with several flowers on its stem. It has always been a great favourite in Scilly and is of vital importance to the industry even today.

The exact date of the dispatch of Aunt Ellen's hatbox is uncertain: it is variously put as 1867, 1870 and 1881. It makes no odds. Recording the fact that it happened is all that matters.

The brand new and so novel (for seamen) industry could not have flowered at a more appropriate moment. It reached the bud stage when the potato market had been captured by the Channel Islands and during the latter declining years of the islands' shipbuilding industry; and when the advent of steam and iron broke up the Hugh Town stocks the flower industry had survived its birth pangs to be sufficiently established as Scilly's number one source of income.

The circumstances of the change-over from building boats to cultivating flowers were unique as far as Scillonians were concerned. In the past when a line of livelihood failed they were accustomed to fall back on the traditional hard times. Kelping and then the illicit but widely-practised smuggling had all proved transitory and ephemeral; now piloting and ship-building, both of which had promised so much, had turned out disappointingly the same. But instead of the customary hardship which they might have so reasonably anticipated they now embarked on years which were to bring them an annual return the like of which even the most wildly optimistic of Scillonians would never have predicted.

By cruel experience islanders had been used to exploring every channel of making an income, and their adaptability proved invaluable at the time the new infant was struggling to find its feet. A small band of farsighted islanders recognized straight away that a new economic era was at hand and if the remainder did not immediately appreciate the transformation taking place and the extent to which the new industry was to change both their lives and the physical face of Scilly, they nevertheless cast in their lot happily with the winter trade. Anything was better than scratching for a living as they had done before: the breadline days of 1818 were still a painful memory in Scilly.

At this formative juncture Lieutenant T. A. Dorrien-Smith did as much as anyone to ensure that the new industry was established on a firm footing. Unostentatiously he gave his active backing; he brought his influence to bear both in the islands and in important spheres far removed from Scilly; he journeyed to Holland, Belgium and the Channel Islands to invest in large stocks of bulbs; he was largely responsible for recognizing the dangers of island winds and devised the characteristic Scillonian shelter belts, which in fact Augustus had already planted at the Abbey gardens; he enthusiastically probed into matters of freightage, shipping and land transport.

Export tonnages leapt up spectacularly, for the big mainland cities had just been hit by the demand for cut flowers. Sixty-five tons were shipped out of Scilly in 1885; two years later the 100-ton mark had been topped. In 1889 just under 200 tons were exported, and it was obvious the industry was racing towards full bloom. In 1925 650 tons left Scilly, while today well over a thousand tons are shipped off annually.

With the first tastes of success islanders began to devote all available land to flower-growing. Soil which had formerly provided for potatoes and purely domestic produce was given over to flower farming with a commercial end in view—and the manner in which the most unlikely parts of the islands, on cliff edge and sea-washed slope, were taken in, was ingenious. All the time wider and better bulb varieties were being embraced, successive Dorrien-Smith Lord Proprietors lent their energetic support and in quick time a group of islands whose main claim to fame was in its shipwrecks had made such an effective impact on the mainland and even further afield that Scilly was known as the "Islands of Flowers" and "The Fortunate Isles".

Today Mr. William Trevellick's brainchild, born of chance rather than design, is about a hundred years old: and flowers mean as much to the islands as they ever did. Although the business of "doing visitors", as one child put it, has reached such dimensions as to unseat flowers as the islands' number one money spinner, flower-growing is still almost universally practised. Scilly should judge itself fortunate. In flowers and tourists it has two fine industries which could prove to be complementary rather than competitive if approached with wisdom. One is a summer pursuit, the other a winter one: an all the year round income, but many dangers which will be discussed later are unfortunately lurking at hand.

The topographical appearance of modern day Scilly belies the sad, ever-increasing prophecies that the industry is on the way out. Walk along any of the roads that criss-cross St. Mary's and they will all be bordered, almost without exception, by box-like flower patches with their protective hedging. Walk along the very flanks of the island and one will see how every cultivable square yard has been incorporated right down to the rock-strewn shore and the sea itself. Weave through the pine belts that give the northern tip of St. Mary's such a Mediterranean flavour, and you will be suddenly surprised by tiny, secluded patches full of dancing daffodils with the blue sea shimmering through the foliage.

The rooted grip that flower culture has on Scilly is perhaps best illustrated by the off islands of Agnes, Bryher, Tresco and St. Martin's. There fields, sometimes only a few yards square, huddle side by side disputing every inch of the limited way along the sheltered southerly slopes away from the damaging winds.

The visitor in Scilly between November and April, the "season", cannot expect the islands to be a carpet of brilliant colour. The flowers are not allowed to bloom in the open and are picked in bud for export. However, he will certainly see enough colour to make his visit to the islands an unforgettable one: the deep gold of the "daffs" contrast strongly with the white varieties and the hundreds of in-between pastel shades, and always the marine backcloth heightens the impression. If the visitor does, by any chance, happen on a season when the fields are a riot of bloom, he can assume he has arrived at a poor season. He can assume that the erratic weather has caused all the varieties to come at once, with maybe two months' crop coming in one. Then the over-stretched pickers have inevitably fought a losing battle with the maturing properties of the sun, and when this calamity happens whole fields of gorgeous blooms go unpicked—a sad waste.

The "season" opens in November when the mainland just thirty miles across the water is habitually in the frosty grip of a British winter. The tourist season has tailed off, the lingering visitor has departed and a large part of each and every island, from Agnes in the west to St. Martin's in the east, turns *en bloc* to flowers. Everything is subordinated to the swift dispatch of the several processes which take the budding flowers from the fields to the mainland markets and the buying public itself, and all is sacrificed to speed. If the benefit of the advantages of climate are to be fully enjoyed the flowers must be put on the markets in advance of their mainland counterparts, and so scoop the price pool. Therefore, all available hands are welcome whether they belong to men, women or children; to navvy, guesthouse-keeper, or out-of-season boatmen. The men do all the outside work, and when island winds blow in winter, farming can be tough. To the uninitiated flower farming might seem a sinecure. It is not. Dressed often in oilskins and sea boots, which somehow poignantly reminds one of the islanders' traditional connection with the sea, they pick and place in baskets in all weathers. Later the men pack the flowers into boxes, but only after the blooms have gone through the intermediate handling stages of potting, bunching and tying, which are usually carried out by women. The female sex have definitely won their emancipation as far as the Scillonian context is concerned. If they were to withdraw from the packing sheds the industry would fold overnight.

The dominant varieties in the early stages of the season are the Scilly White, and our old friend the Soleil D'Or. The latter can accurately be described as the mainstay of the industry in Scilly, as barring the Channel Islands it will grow nowhere else in the British Isles. It hates frost. Every effort is made to place as many "Sols" as possible on the market before Christmas and it is said in the islands that to have good returns from the early Sol crop is being half way to having a profitable season over-all.

The flower season proper starts early in January and the main harvest of Soleil D'Or narcissus is followed towards the end of the month by the advance guard of the daffodils, the appropriately named Forerunner and the Magnificence ("Mag"). From this stage on there is little let up, with the hectic peak (weather always permitting) being reached between the last week in February and the third week in March. Altogether there are hundreds of bulb varieties grown in Scilly, but the species favoured most widely commercially are Pentewan, California, the trumpet daffodils King Alfred and Fortune, Golden Harvest, Brunswick, Aranjuez and Actaea. The Cheerfulness and the late Double White normally wind up the season which tapers to a close in mid-April with iris and tulips.

Scilly in March month is as hectic in its own way as is August when the islands are flooded with holidaymakers. But most of the

9

feverish activity goes unseen, taking place behind the closed doors of a hundred packing sheds, a hundred homes. A well-drilled team moves into annual action in the larger farms like Commander T. Dorrien-Smith's on Tresco and Normandy and Longstone on St. Mary's. Adjacent to the sheds which hold row upon row of potted flowers in bud are the bunching and tying rooms. Here a line of women sit at the benches, relentlessly selecting, discarding and banding the bunches of ten or twelve blooms ready to be packed into cardboard boxes of twenty-four bunches. A clublike atmosphere is provided by a radio. Some of the women may be relatives of the farmer, others may be "hardy annuals" who come back every year for employment in the season, while a few might have been engaged as extra hands to help out when the March rush is on.

The expert tyer reckons to account for a hundred bunches in the hour and all of them expect at one time or other to suffer from "lily rash", a skin irritation peculiar to the flower industry and which is caused by the sap of the blooms. At all times in the season the scent from the flowers is overpowering and after a while cloying. The bunched blooms are whisked away by the men for packing and, tied together in pairs, the boxes are loaded aboard the waiting lorries. In the old days wooden boxes were used. Gradually they became uneconomic while the growers had to wait for their return from the markets. Nowadays boxes of cardboard are used.

So far we have looked at the large grower, the man who farms forty to fifty acres. By mainland standards, of course, he is small. But the vast majority of the 200-odd island growers have only a few acres at their disposal. In the height of the season these rely almost wholly on members of their families to get the blooms off to market as quickly as possible, or a few might employ one extra hand. The tying and bunching is as often done in the home itself as in a specially made shed, and it can truly be called a family concern. Picking, bunching, tying and packing is done by father, mother and children, and if matters are getting out of hand it is no rare occurrence for the grower to take a basket to a friend's home for tying.

As with the larger farmer who employs, work goes on late into the night, for in the season special loading times are fixed with the Isles of Scilly Steamship Company. Up to midnight on St. Mary's traffic appears to be all one way—to the quay. Lorries, tractors and vans roll from all quarters of the "country" to load the "precious gold" as *Punch* called it, into the hold of the *Scillonian* or the *Queen of the Isles*. On the off islands a motley collection of vehicles stack the consignments on the little jetties well in advance of St. Mary's so that the Steamship Company launches can pick them up and ship them across to St. Mary's. The steamer sailings become erratic and confused at peak season as far as the passengers are concerned. The vessel might sail at 7 a.m.; it might sail at 8 or 9—all depending on the tides and the handling of the golden freight. This is winter, the flower season, and the few passengers around fully realize that they are subservient to the flowers.

March over, apart from the late varieties there is a general decline, a lessening of the hitherto hectic pace. May month arrives, the focus of attention swings from the "country" back to the "town" and the tourist, and the flower-grower is left with the bulb season from early May until August, when he lifts the bulbs in preparation for planting the following season. The Sol, the Mag and their beautiful fellows are a glamorous product of a singularly unglamorous and backbreaking business, and the bulb part of the year is perhaps the most taxing of all. A student friend of mine was quite recently employed in lifting and when after two weeks he was reduced to crawling along the "vaur" (furrow) on hands and knees in taking up the bulbs, his employer, not surprisingly, decided it was time to sever the short, and what promised to be uneconomic association!

In the bulb season the "Sols" are cut over, preheated in glass houses and replanted in June. These then form the basis of next year's early Sol crop. In addition to lifting, the bulbs are graded and a small but thriving dry bulb trade is done in the islands.

When planting takes place from August to October the bulbs are either "set up" in rows with a path between each or the small bulbs are put in the bottom in four-row beds. There is a tendency in this age of mechanization for machines to do the lifting and planting, but in Scilly conventional methods are still almost universally used. The traditional island manure of seaweed transported from the shores, is, however, giving way in some cases to rye grass. Many of the more substantial farms have sterilizing plants for the treatment of bulbs and the prevention of eel worm, also cold water dips.

Ideally bulbs should be lifted every two years, "Mags" for instance, are all the better for this practice, although "Sols" can be left in the ground for three, four or even five years without coming to harm. Many island farmers are now adopting a sort of "three-year-plan" lifting a third of their bulbs annually. Signs of bulb deterioration are evident either in the bulb itself or in the growing stalk.

A word here should be said of the Flower Show which used to take place every March on the first Friday and Saturday in the month in St. Mary's Town Hall. Unhappily it is no longer a feature of island life. It was referred to as "the oldest flower show in the country" and one can certainly believe this claim when one considers that the Scillonian grower was one of the advance guard of the industry in Britain. The show was generally attended by throngs of disbelieving visitors and the Press, and the brilliant array of blooms on display was proof of the well being of the industry and of the healthy competition taking place between the growers of the different islands.

The feverish activity in the "season", the large percentage of the population engaged in the industry, the annual success of the Flower Show and the number of flower fields that jigsaw the face of Scilly all go towards suggesting that the industry is as flourishing as it has ever been. Yet this healthy exterior masks an undercurrent of uncertainty which is becoming quite strong in some quarters. Everything in the flower garden is far from rosy, they say, and point to a succession of below average seasons, glutted markets in which prices were poor, and especially to the ominous, ever-increasing competition from the mainland and the chrysanthemum grower. The "golden-age" of the Scillonian farmer is over, they vow. As many are engaged in the flower business as ever, but the big paydays are a thing of the past. The grower's days are numbered. Forget flower farming, move with the times for the destiny of Scilly must surely be bound up from now on with the tourist.

It must be admitted that there have been some disturbing signs of late, but not enough to make these panicky predictions anything more than exaggerated. Pessimism and farming are old friends, not only in Scilly but the world over and perpetrators of gloom have been with the islands' flower industry from its very inception to the present day. Yet although untold calamities were supposed to fall on the heads of the growers the industry is still very much with Scilly. It should be noted that the current pessimism emanates from the fainthearted, for want of a better word "fringe man"—the man who shunts from farming in the winter to tourism in the summer, and who is more and more leaning towards the latter as a basic source of income. Whatever happens he will eventually throw in his lot with tourism anyway, so he should perhaps be considered apart from the dedicated flower farmer who has been reared to the land and who continues to regard flower farming as his one and only means of livelihood.

Nevertheless, whatever way one looks at the state of flowers in Scilly, it cannot be denied that island growers face an exacting future. The unpredictability of the weather and, more important, the modern scientific methods of forcing pre-cooled bulbs, now in a big way on the mainland, see to that. If Britain has a severe, frosty winter, followed by a hard spring with incessant winds then island growers usually have a good season. Scilly finds itself ahead of the mainland, is first on the market, and gains the top prices. But if a cold "snap" hits the islands at a crucial stage in the development of the season, and everything is held up, then disaster can all too easily ensue. The mainlander makes good his climatic disadvantage, while the Scillonian grower has his flowers coming all at once; he cannot handle them; finds the market glutted anyway, and prices nose-dive. When this sequence unravels the man who invariably receives the most hurt is not the bigger farmer, nor indeed the small three-acre grower, who has family labour at his disposal, but the unfortunate who farms, say, ten acres and is just large enough to employ. Unsupported by a cattle herd or anything as grand as that, he is finding an unremunerative season with the overheads which accompany employment, increasingly crippling, and with many of his colleagues in the same acreage bracket is looking to the visitor for a more stable and reliable form of income.

One would, perhaps, think the combination of farming and tourism, of winter and summer industry, a perfect answer to island economic problems: a dual-pronged assault as it were on income. Indeed these so totally different occupations can be complementary, but this second-string-to-the-bow technique could prove to be the "grower's" downfall in the long run.

If ever a calling demanded dedication and full attention, then it is flower-growing. From the time the first bulb is planted to the moment when the last blooms are picked there are countless problems and to split the attention between two things could prove disastrous. The tourist season falls right in the middle of the bulb season, the "engine room" of the industry when lifting, rotation and treatment of the bulbs is vital to the future welfare of the crop. It is logical to suppose that if the grower has turned guesthouse keeper for these all-important months, the basic processes which go into ensuring a successful harvest will inevitably suffer. Good land will be improperly treated, quality above all will deteriorate and the man with a dual income will find himself forced into becoming a full time guesthouse keeper. Nowadays flower farming is a specialist occupation and the overlapping approach of the guesthouse-keeper-cum-grower which seems to be becoming increasingly popular could be the downfall of an industry which above all else at this time needs united effort and a single-minded approach—and is getting the exact opposite.

What course of action should the Scillonian growers take to prevent the forecasts of the hotelliers, guesthouse people and their own disenchanted brethren wavering uncertainly between two forms of living, from having made a disastrously correct prediction? Firstly they must accept the fact that Scilly produces a mere fleabite of the percentage of Great Britain's flowers—under 1 per cent. Island flowers will hardly be missed. Obviously the Scillonian cannot operate on the same large turnover, small profit basis which is the trademark of the "forcers" and the Lincolnshire growers. The absolute reverse must necessarily be the case for him. He must realize that if the mainland has modern methods of bringing their flowers on earlier then his future lies in quality. The name of Scilly has always been synonymous with quality in the flower world and never before has it been so necessary to prove the veracity of this reputation (a not very encouraging prospect for the man of divided loyalties).

Many island farmers realize this all too well and are combining to operate under brand names, for they believe that co-operative growing could be the answer to their problems. They say it will favour capital re-investment and will aid them to "plough back" their money. In 1958 they got together to form the Isles of Scilly Growers in an attempt to reduce marketing costs. They rightly claim that Scilly as a whole will benefit from this as the money from flowers circulates within the islands, something which cannot be said for tourism.

The bad farmer can no longer get away with it. Standards are too high, competition too fierce. And nor will the man who fails to move with the times, who does not study constantly fluctuating public taste. Market trends must be noted and acted upon (white blooms are currently more in vogue than yellow, for example), sheltered land, long exhausted by continuous flower culture, must be given a rest, or better, fresh land, if that rarity can be found anywhere in Scilly, taken in. To succeed, the grower must come up with the requisite varieties, the new species, and it is also increasingly imperative that flowers should be sent in a younger state. The latter will ensure that Scilly's proud boast of being regularly first on the market in every variety which it had up until twenty years ago will be regained—and the buyer will get a longer vase life. The general public are more educated to flowers than they were formerly. They know what they want, they know that a natural bloom lasts longer than a forced bloom, and the successful Scillonian farmer will comply.

But all these things boil down to one—that the good, the efficient, the progressive grower will prosper, just as the bad, the haphazard, the old fashioned will surely be engulfed in the wave of competition.

Notwithstanding the uncertainty pregnant in the island air, and the somewhat depressing picture just painted, farming will die a hard and stubborn death in Scilly if economic circumstances ever push it that far. I, for one, could not conceive a Scilly without a flower industry. It would be akin to Dartmoor being shorn of its ponies!

Perhaps the men of Bryher, Agnes and St. Martin's face the most worrying time of all and can expect to feel the pinch more than their St. Mary's colleagues. For them everything is just that little bit more costly. The freightage and handling charges of his flower consignments are all over and above the economic handicap of living on such remote isles. A succession of bad seasons could well unite to put him out of business, and permanently. He cannot recoup his losses by potato growing as it clashes with the early bulb season; he has no second string to his bow as have the Cornish farmers who grow broccoli; and as yet the provision for off island tourism is nowhere near the scale that St. Mary's enjoys. His position and future can be described as uncertain.

The old saying goes "You can't have something for nothing", and this harsh but fundamental maxim could have been first coined in Scilly and expressly to meet the circumstances of today's grower. The island farmer will get in proportion to what he puts in, and no more. Much responsibility also lies with Duchy of Cornwall administration. If their tenants are allowed to farm badly then the industry will soon encounter troubled waters. The future format of the Scilly industry may lie in fewer farms and larger, more economic and more co-operative combines, which will be able to cope with increasing overheads.

I have never been to the annual Audit Dinner of the Duchy tenants held at St. Mary's, but if I did, I would reasonably expect one of the toasts to be *"Floreat Scillonia"*. One can equally reasonably expect that it will do just that if it faces squarely up to the present challenge in the manner it has tackled and dispatched past threats.

VI

ST. MARY'S, THE HUB

Of all the islands in the Scilly archipelago, St. Mary's, the group's hub, is certainly the least Scillonian. Slow infiltration of outside blood over the years has grown into a steady stream and a big percentage of those now living on St. Mary's are mainlanders. Tourism, more than anything else has robbed the island of its Scillonian characteristics, for it has altered the physical face until St. Mary's now smacks of the mainland. There are metalled roads, helicopters, camping sites, a volume of cars completely out of proportion to the size of the island, boundary marks and many other trappings of sophistication. When in Cardiff recently a Welshman said to me, "Don't go away with the idea you have seen Wales, Cardiff is the capital, but it is not Wales. The true country is inland, the valleys. There you can feel the pulse-beat of Wales." The same can be said of Scilly and St. Mary's. The off islands largely retain their Scillonian character, while "civilization" is doing its level best to destroy the soul of St. Mary's. The natural state is, after all, the prime attraction and at the moment it is in danger of being submerged under a welter of commercialization. St. Mary's folk are aware of the dangers in the air. They fear spoliation and the less savoury results of speculation, but tourism is now their bread and butter. . . .

Lest I drive prospective holidaymakers away from St. Mary's let me hasten to point out that even though the islands' capital is faced with problems which a hundred and one other resorts have had to contend with, and solved, the island is undoubtedly one of the most beautiful and underrated in the group. Visitors, eager to savour the attractions of the off islands, tend to use St. Mary's as a mere springboard without getting acquainted with it. A great pity, as the main island boasts a great physical variety and some of the most remarkable coastal scenery in Scilly. The granite headlands are magnificent. Forget the ever-present threat of over-commercialization and join me in the nine-mile ramble around this tiny island. It will not take long, much less than a day, and there is much to see.

After stepping ashore from the *Scillonian* or the *Queen*, a short walk along the quay puts one in Hugh Town. The plain granite quay which was started soon after the Duke of Leeds surrendered his lease and completed by Augustus Smith, stretches right out to, and incorporates the rocky half-acre of Rat Island at the back of which are the stores of the island coal merchant. The original jetty, the Godolphin-built "Old Quay" juts out from the main landing stage and is used by boatmen when the tide dictates.

Hugh Town is an uncomplicated settlement, consisting of just a main street which eventually splits up into two roads and which in turn lead out to the eastern sector of the island. Off this thoroughfare wind quaint, charmingly-named side streets such as Well Lane, Jerusalem Terrace, Back Lane and Silver Street. The town's buildings are a curious mixture of the old and the contemporary, seeming to epitomize the changing times of St. Mary's, the metamorphosis from Old Scilly to the new. Most are of grey, austere granite, with walls feet thick, while here and there are modern, brightly painted cottages, contrastingly gay.

In the early years of Hugh Town, the houses used only to be situated on the western end of the isthmus under the Star Castle guns. Gradually they straggled out on to the neck, until at one stage there were complaints that the Garrison artillery was being obstructed. The expansion has carried on apace and the former compactness of this self-supporting little settlement has, in recent years, taken on a sprawling character. A Council estate creeps up the Garrison Hill on land which was once known prettily as Parson's Field, Little Field, Prince's Field and Milkmaid's Walk; Ram's Valley, overlooking Porth Cressa, has been taken in by the developers and houses wind up the hill out of Hugh Town and threaten to join it with the islands' former capital of Old Town.

Hugh Town has most amenities. It has a post office (a remarkable granite arched edifice), two banks, hotels, an increasing number of guesthouses, some grocers, a butcher, drapers, a newsagent, bulb stores, a greengrocer, tobacconists, a milk bar, an electrical shop, a shoe shop, a chemist, a general stores, a Steamship Company office on the site of the old prison, and photographic studios, among other establishments. There are two resident doctors and a dentist.

In the summer the village, for my mainland standards it is really no more, is a seething mass of humanity. Most of those who are heading for the quay and the boats must pass through, and with the increase in island traffic it is a bottleneck of chaos. The congestion is no wit relieved by the momentous arrival of the airport bus with the daily papers which are ferried by an eager chain of helpers to the newsagent's shop.

In the main square of the village lies the back-garden-size Park where the rites of May Day are enacted faithfully every year. In the old days the square, or "Parade" was the drill ground for the Garrison military. The main street splits in two at the Park, one road (Church Street) leading out into the country via the parish church, the other, The Strand (aptly-named as it borders the town beach) passing also out into the centre of the island via the school. Among buildings situated in the park square are the police headquarters and the seat of local government,[1] the eighty-year-old Town Hall. Something must be said here about the Council of the Isles of Scilly.

As we saw in an earlier chapter an Act of Parliament in 1890 robbed the St. Mary's Select Vestry and its sister Vestries on the off islands of much of their powers and gave Scilly its properly-constituted local authority. The administrative change of 1890 was further corroborated in 1943, and today the Isles of Scilly Council is unique. As well as wielding the powers of an ordinary parish and rural authority, it also has County Council status. Among other things it conducts its own health, welfare and road matters, its planning and education affairs, its agriculture and, until fairly recently, was wholly responsible for policing St. Mary's. Today the peace is kept by the Devon and Cornwall Constabulary.

The Council can deal direct with the various ministries at Whitehall and on these occasions tiny Scilly is treated with the deference normally accorded to places the County Council size of Devon or Yorkshire! Each island, depending on its size, sends representatives to the Islands' Council, that is when tides and

---

[1] Nationally Scilly falls within the St. Ives constituency, and has for a number of years been represented in Parliament by a National-Liberal-Conservative member.

weather allow the crossing to St. Mary's. In poor conditions the trip cannot be made and the meeting is usually postponed. Always the sea rules.

The Isles of Scilly Council has peculiar, and I use the word advisedly in both senses, problems, not the least being its strange and at times, complex relationship with the Duchy of Cornwall. The Council administers the affairs of a people who are, in turn, mainly tenants of the Crown estates of Scilly. On the one hand a democratically elected local authority, on the other the Duchy, privileged, longtime landlords who own 99 per cent of Scilly. The remaining 1 per cent, the freehold area of Hugh Town, was sold to the sitting tenants four years after a celebrated letter (later withdrawn) had been written to the King following some friction between the Council and the Duchy. Many Hugh Town freeholders today do not know the history of what some wags term "their liberation".

For the most part a harmonious relationship exists between the Council and the Duchy, but occasionally friction and a "cold war" atmosphere mar their mutual dealings, as they are bound to do between two such bodies, a dual-type authority. I say authority purposely, for although the Duchy have no actual administrative sway in Scilly, they have the power to influence indirectly. For they own the land, the all-important key, and in an expanding Scilly with, among other things, its pressing housing problems, the Council understandably feels its power shackled—that is unless it gets really democratic and forces an issue, which, of course, it can always do in the end. Actually the Duchy still have the nominal right to put their representative on the Islands' Council. Needless to say, they do not exercise it. Islanders, only relatively recently refreshed by the winds of democracy which established an elected chairman in what had always been a Dorrien-Smith inherited post, would hardly stand for it.

Farce, unfortunately, seems to be a close associate of many happenings in Scilly, and it even touches upon the grave sphere of local politics. The strangest of situations can crop up. The case of the water supply is a random example. In its attempts to give piped water to everyone on St. Mary's, the Council found that its wells were—leasehold! Obviously no authority could put up with having to pay "X" royalties per number of gallons consumed and the Duchy duly sold the freehold of the wells. In these aggravating situations the landlords are usually understanding and accommodating, but nevertheless the basis for disagreement is ever present, as it must be—the direct result of the singular constitution of the islands.

It is, perhaps, in the matter of compulsory purchase that the Council feels itself most baulked and embarrassed. As the Duchy, that is the Crown, is exempt in practically every Act, the Council finds its County Council powers ineffective, and cannot employ compulsion as mainland councils can. If it wishes to buy out a Hugh Town freeholder in the interests of the public good, it may, of course, do so; if it wished to do the same to land belonging to a private landowner, it could also do so. But the Duchy of Cornwall are no ordinary landlords. They are immune, generally beyond the legal pale. On this score it truly seems as though a Scillonian "iron curtain" has dropped between the freehold and leasehold tracts! This type of inequality has in many cases caused mounting resentment against the Duchy in Scilly, although the worth of the Prince's Council as landlords is for the most part unquestioned. The Duchy are, in fact, benevolent landlords, and as will be outlined in a later chapter, are vital to Scilly's future welfare.

Before leaving the Council to its headaches in order to take a look at the Hugh Peninsula above Hugh Town, mention must be made of the local bench of six magistrates who hold their infrequent sessions at St. Mary's Town Hall. The incidence and severity of crime in Scilly can, I think, be gauged from a session when two islanders were fined £1 each for shooting shags. . . .

The Hugh, topped by the Elizabethan fort-turned-hotel, Star Castle and surrounded by the thick eighteenth-century granite walls which gave the area its common name of The Garrison, is prominent anywhere in the islands. Entry from Hugh Town is gained through the rebuilt impressive archway which bears the initials A.T. after Abraham Tovey, a Master Gunner who was responsible for much of the fortifications in the 1700s. Until fairly recently the area of the Garrison was shut for one day in the year to islanders, except those living within the "lines", a tradition dating back hundreds of years. The obvious antiquity of the Garrison archway contrasts strongly with a notice reading "Speed Limit 5 m.p.h.". The top of the Garrison hill is a favourite vantage point for visitors who watch Scilly's famed sunsets. A sweeping panoramic view of the archipelago can be gained from this spot, close to Star Castle and the blood-red sun sinking behind Samson is an unforgettable sight.

From Star Castle the road leads past a pine wood to the island sports field and lone tennis court. Near the field is the old Lloyd's signal building, from which home-bound shipping used to receive their orders. Branch right before this, however, and take the cliff path which winds around the peninsula. The hour-long stroll around the Garrison is one of the most lovely in Scilly and was called "The Mall" by Troutbeck. A truly superb view of Samson and the Minalto Rocks is followed by one of Agnes, Gugh, Annet and the Western Rocks, with the lonely Bishop standing sentinel far out to sea. Like most of the coastline of Scilly, granite, bracken and bramble argue right down to the eroded shore and the sea edge, fringed by the offshore rocks of Steval, Barrel of Butter and the Newman.

At the furthest extremity of the headland is the lone surviving Garrison battery, the Woolpack Battery,[1] where there are two of the original cannons, now rusty with age and with the savaging of a thousand gales. The guns point dumbly out over St. Mary's Sound through which the *Scillonian* and most shipping pass to reach St. Mary's harbour. In this Sound thrust up from the seabed are the dangerous Bartholomew Ledge, Woodcock's Ledge, Woolpack Rock, and the Spanish Ledges. The latter are a great hazard to shipping entering this channel but their fangs have been largely drawn by a bellbuoy. A typical sound when the wind is blowing (which is most of the time) is the dirge-like tolling of this Trinity House warning device, poignant and somehow inescapably Scillonian. In calm weather St. Mary's Sound is beautiful, the blue waters caressing the Garrison shore and the sands across the way at Porth Conger Bay, Agnes. But when a norwester tears over this quarter the sea is whipped into a frenzy and the rocks on the point are covered white with soap-sud-like spray.

Further around the headland at Morning Point the bareness gives way to surprising lushness and verdure as can so easily happen in the changing world of Scilly. Protected from the cruel norwester, here mesembrianthemum trails down the cliffs and over rock and ledge, pretty plants flourish, while palm and

[1] There are few remnants of the other batteries—Steval, Morning Point, etc.

pine grow side by side. Off the Point lies the Wrasse Rock. On the way back to the archway entrance to the Garrison past the Trinity House cottages, the Duchy of Cornwall's Land Steward's offices are reached. Massive granite, their dominant position seeming to symbolize the Duchy's sway over greater Scilly, they overlook Hugh Town, and the waters of Porth Cressa Bay, which is the most popular St. Mary's beach as it is so central. Through the archway, down the hill past houses nestling into the slope and the side of the Garrison hill, and we are in Hugh Town again. Scilly's muralled Mall has been circled within the hour.

Before leaving the Garrison it is as well to note that from its commanding position a real understanding of the narrowness of the Hugh Town isthmus can be gained. Looking left from the Duchy Offices at the time of high tides the waters of the Pool wash the back gates of the houses, while the sea at the Porth Cressa side is well up towards the bank. The distance between Porth Cressa and contiguous Little Porth and the Pool can be no more than 150 yards. Also one can see from this point just how much everything centres around the quay and the steamer. When she is tied up alongside the quay, looking almost toylike from a distance, there is a great bustle in Hugh Town. St. Mary's wakes up, the boat is in.

Now for the eastern part of the island. The right-hand fork from the Park in Hugh Town takes one up Church Street past the Methodist Chapel (there is a strong Wesleyan following in the islands) to the Parish Church. The latter, started by William IV and finished by Augustus Smith in 1837, is a plain granite building and fits in tastefully with its environment. On either side of the main door are lead tanks, which stood for 200 years at Star Castle and which bear the coat of arms of George II. Near the church is an imposing house built by an Italian count who settled in Scilly before the Great War.

Continuing right, past the vicarage, the road leads up to Pilot's Retreat, an area of high ground where the sea pilots of old used to gather to discuss business in hand. Tucked into an old quarry underneath the hill is the island power station, now connected with the South Western Electricity Board. Many years ago, when it was run privately, lights would be dipped at 11.55 p.m. to warn islanders of the impending black-out at midnight! On the top of the hill is Buzza Tower, and nearby the hospital. Originally an old Spanish windmill built in 1821 and used for grinding island corn, Buzza was converted into a tower to commemorate the visit of King Edward VII to Scilly in 1902. Its prominent position has made it a landmark for sailors out in the Roadstead when navigating for St. Mary's. As good a view down on Hugh Town can be gained from Buzza Hill as from the Garrison on the western side of the isthmus.

St. Mary's hospital is one of the prides of the island and of Scilly as a whole. With the island dentist and doctors working side by side under one roof, the hospital is regarded as a near-perfect example of how a National Health establishment should operate. Before it was built in 1938 as St. Mary's Emergency Hospital, cases such as appendicitis which could not be treated locally had to be sent across to Penzance; and sometimes in the dead of night the lifeboat would have to take a suffering patient over in gale force conditions, that following a gig trip down from the off islands. Recently extended, the hospital can meet most emergencies, and the little building overlooking Porth Cressa Bay is, indeed, a credit to such a small community.

From the hospital a track bumps through a granite-walled lane, over stone and pothole and a Cornish stile to heathland of springy turf which culminates in Peninnis Head, the southernmost extremity of St. Mary's.

Of all the magnificent sights in the islands Peninnis Head reigns supreme. Scilly granite takes on many weird and strange forms under the torturing influence of weathering, but this headland has been affected more fantastically than any other spot, save possibly Agnes, for it is utterly exposed, a prey to the prevailing winds and the Atlantic waves. I never tire of looking at the rocks of Peninnis, and wondering at their originality. Ton upon ton of rock tower up into the sky like a rude gigantic fortress or castle, here turreted and buttressed, there pinnacled and domed. Sometimes a great mountainside of rock presents its bold face, elsewhere a mass is built up of individual rocks of every conceivable shape and size, but all seemingly welded together. The action of the wind and weather over thousands of years has deeply scarred and furrowed the lichen-barnacled granite into most remarkable forms many of which have been given names by islanders. The Tooth Rock is one such rock. Fined down into an amazing likeness of a tooth, it thrusts itself forty feet conically into the air, a perfect

Bishop Rock lighthouse

example of the vertical decomposition of granite. The most celebrated of the Peninnis rocks is the Pulpit, pictures of which have appeared in just about every geographical and geological magazine in the world. The Pulpit is the horizontal equivalent of the "Tooth", a great tabular granite slab which rests, seemingly precariously, on a smaller fulcrum before jutting out towards the sea.

Many other rocks have been chiselled by the elements into recognizable forms, such as the Nubians Head, the Tuskless Elephant, the Monks Cowl—so called because of its hooded appearance—the Toast-rack and the Kettle and Pans, a group of rocks hollowed out deeply by water. The latter furnish a fine example of the famed Peninnis rock basins where quartz and felspar have been worn away into cylindrical, rounded scoops, often many feet in depth and circumference. Sometimes the elements have cut through the rim of the basin to form a lip, and one may sit in the armchair-like depressions with one's feet trailing over the side.

So remarkably smooth are the rock basins that past writers attributed their origins to human hands. All this is nonsense. The rock basin phenomenon is purely and simply an indication of the mighty eroding powers of the elements.

Further down, nearer the southernmost tip of the Peninnis promontory and the sea itself, any individual characteristics the rocks may have become lost in a shambles of strewn granite, as if gargantuan trucks have summarily dumped loads of rocks without plan or order. Somewhere in this igneous waste, so they say, lies the Logan Rock, a twenty-one-foot-high, 313-ton monolith, which can be rocked because it is so finely balanced. For years I have been putting my shoulder to every rock in the vicinity, but the mighty Logan still eludes me!

A few words must be said about the processes which have gone into the forming of the granite shapes of Peninnis and Scilly as a whole. Most of the granite in the islands has fault-lines or joins sometimes barely visible, along which the elements have acted. When the fault is vertical, with few horizontal joins, then the result is a columnar, pillar-like rock. On the other hand when the joins are mainly horizontal the eroding power of the winds and water produce flat slabs, often balanced upon smaller rocks (like the Pulpit). When there are many vertical and horizontal faults in

10

Agnes lighthouse with "home-made" road in the foreground

one rock-mass decomposition goes on until sections are completely separated from the original, and in some cases drop to the foot of the mass or roll further away (as in the chaotic mess at the tip of the head). As far as the rock basins are concerned, decomposition is still in progress, as can be seen from the minute particles of quartz and felspar which often lie at the bottom of the basins.

There are a number of eroded indentations under the outer cliffs of Peninnis, all, of course, which bear names such as Pitts Parlour, Izzacumpucca and Piper's Hole. The latter is said to be joined by a subterranean tunnel to its more famous namesake at Tresco.

Out from the cliffs of Peninnis lie the rocky appendages of Carrickstarne and the little and big High Jolly Rocks which are strangely shaped as befitting this distorted world, the largest mass lying to the seaward gradually sloping downwards towards the land.

Peninnis is not a beauty spot in the conventional meaning of the word. The granite is too severe, its outline too harsh and jarring; "magnificent" or "impressive" are apt words to describe the promontory, even awe-inspiring, especially when storm whips the sea into a frenzy to crash landwards over the Jolly Rocks, into the gurgling funnels of Izzacumpucca and Piper's Hole, to send spray cascading far up into the interior heathland. The only man-made intrusion into this chilling ruin of rock is the white tower of the automatic Peninnis Lighthouse which stands on the cliffs and projects its comforting beam far out into the southern seas. The mechanism is set each day by a keeper living on St. Mary's and whose daily excursion with his dog is a familiar sight to Scillonians.

A cliff path leads from Peninnis Head via Dutchman's Carn and Carn Mahale back to Porth Cressa and Hugh Town, but continuing anti-clockwise around St. Mary's there are a succession of bays, the first of which is Old Town. Originally the buildings fringing this attractive little bay formed the main settlement of St. Mary's, but the rise of Star Castle and Hugh Town, and the deterioration of Ennor Castle above Old Town relegated it to secondary status. Today the erection of flats and houses promises to regain it some of its pristine importance, but, to me, this settlement is little more than a hamlet.

Like so many spots in Scilly, Old Town is a place of contrast.

At high tide it is incredibly beautiful, at low incredibly ugly. In summer calm the blue waters of the bay flanked by Carn Leh and the Pulpit Rock silhouette of Peninnis Head on the right and Tolman[1] Point on the left, are lagoon-like. Boats lilt gently at anchor, Old Townites sit in a row on a bench overlooking the beach as they have done for centuries, the water caresses the sand and laps against the Old Quay. Time stands still.

That is the peaceful side of Old Town, but when the bay turns nasty it is very nasty indeed. I remember one day walking down the hill from Pilot's Retreat and being awed by the mass of water which had been piling up in front of a southerly gale and which was thundering into the bay to explode in a cloud of spume on the Gull Rock which guards the entrance. It seemed to me then that there was nothing to stop the rollers from crashing in over the beach, the bordering flower fields and engulfing me.

Old Town is one of the lowest-lying places on St. Mary's, a situation which has surrounded the hamlet with a strange atmosphere. One can get a sad, lonely feeling when down in Old Town and it seems to disappear immediately on reaching the high ground on either side.

Just about the major attraction, if a cemetery can be so exalted, is the church and churchyard situated under the hill on the westerly fringe of the bay. The quaint little church, dating from the twelfth century and re-designed on the Restoration, was the original place of worship in St. Mary's (a bell at the Guard Gate on the Garrison summoned worshippers) before a move was made over the hill to settle in Hugh Town. Occasionally services are still held there. In the churchyard, amid strange-looking sub-tropical plants and trees—aloe, draecanas, Australian ironwood and palm—lie the bones of generations of St. Mary's folk often in clans.

As one wanders around the belichened gravestones, the plundering role the sea has played in the lives of Scillonians makes itself only too evident; grave after grave bears the epitaph of sailor and seaman, tells the horrors of shipwreck and drowning. Here

[1] It has been claimed that Tolman Rock, no longer there but giving its name to the promontory, was so-called as the early monks, whose St. Mary's "base" was Holy Vale, put a chain across the mouth of the bay to extract a toll from incoming shipping. As Old Town, although the one time capital, was never a place of disembarkation, this is unlikely. The name probably has Celtic origins.

lie the bodies of some of the men of Sir Cloudesley Shovel's fleet, among them notably Henry Trelawny, son of the famed Bishop Trelawny and who was captain of one of the ill-fated ships. This seaside spot is a fitting last resting place.

Here, also, lie the victims of the *Schiller* disaster in a mass grave. The most dominating monument in this tiny terraced churchyard is a granite obelisk which carries the inscription: "In memory of Louise Holzmaister, born at New York, 15th May, 1851, who lost her life in the wreck of the S.S. *Schiller*, off the Scilly Isles, 7th May, 1875." Two other epitaphs read *"Ruhe sanst die schöne seele"* (Rest gently, thou beautiful soul) and *"Unvergesslich den deinigen"* (The unforgettable family). Old Town cemetery also contains a memorial to those who fell in the two World Wars and a monument to Augustus Smith.

Perhaps the sadness which seems to pervade Old Town springs from the tragedies of this graveyard.

Round from Old Town is another little rocky inlet, Porth Minick, of little significance save for a one-time association with the island garbage dump! While inland from this coastal area, at what was originally known as High Cross, lies St. Mary's airport, An air service first came to Scilly in 1937 and the planes which linked the islands with Kelynack, Cornwall, were the two-winged, eight-seater de Havilland Rapides, until 1964 when helicopters were introduced. The airport at St. Mary's has remained the landing ground, but the St. Just airfield has given way to a heliport at Eastern Green. Penzance,

The Rapides rendered gallant service over the years. Although tiny, and causing an average-sized person to feel he had been prised from a sardine tin on alighting, only once was there an accident. That was at St. Just when the aircraft over-ran the strip, but nobody was hurt.

The present service, maintained by two twenty-six-seater twin turbine amphibious S.61.N Sikorsky helicopters, is a far more pleasant way of travel. A hovering descent on St. Mary's is much less trying on the nerves than as formerly when the ancient-looking planes used to swoop straight for the cliff face, miss as if by miracle, only to give the impression of taxi-ing crazily on straight into St. Mary's Pool!

Below St. Mary's airport lie the granite boss of Blue Carn and the tumuli-sprinkled cliffs of Giant's Castle and Church Point where the Peninnis Light was nearly sited. Giant's Castle is believed to be an example of the cliff castles of old, and was said by Troutbeck to have been probably designed by the Danes as a retreat from the Saxons. There are still traces, admittedly faint, of the cliff-work construction, and the view of the surrounding area is a fine one. The tumuli referred to earlier are much in evidence on this strip of shore. Some of the barrows are in a good state of preservation, others not.

Round Port Loggos and Newfoundland Point the coastline turns in to enclose Porth Hellick Bay, where, as has been noted, two of Scilly's most famous wrecking dramas were enacted. Porth Hellick or in Cornish "Willow Cove" is, like Old Town, contrastingly the least and the most attractive of St. Mary's inlets. It is very low-lying and the retreating tide leaves an ugly waste of ochre sand and weed-covered rocks, but at high water there is a beautiful volte-face—a perfect example of Scilly's changefulness. Beyond the beach there is a brackish lake where island marksmen discharge at duck and woodcock, while in the winter months the bank of the bay is lined with boats drawn up for their annual overhaul. Here is the monument to Sir Cloudesley Shovel made of quartz from nearby Normandy Downs. On the gorse-clad downs adjoining is located the celebrated Porth Hellick Bronze Age burial chamber.

Porth Hellick Bay, like most bays in Scilly, is encased by crags of granite, many of them, as at Peninnis, bearing names. The celebrated Loaded Camel is, alas, no more, tons of granite summarily destroyed by vandals—but Dick's Carn, which has a striking similarity to the original Loaded Camel, has conveniently taken over the mantle, and everyone is happy. Other Porth Hellick showpieces are the Clapper Rocks which serve with the already mentioned Pulpit as examples of the horizontal action of weather; steps chiselled from the granite point to enable a safe ramble for a former Prince of Wales visiting St. Mary's; and the Arch Druid's Chair, a rock basin which is supposed to have been the seat of an arch druid of old.

Inland from Porth Hellick lie the leasehold farm areas of Salakee,[1] Carn Friars, Tremelethen, Longstone, Mount Todden, Lunnon and Normandy, and the downs of the latter takes us past Perwreck

[1] This strange name probably originated in the days when the rovers of Salee scoured the English Channel.

(Porth Wreck) where there is a ram quarry, to Jacky's Rock, Great Britain Rock and to the most easterly point of St. Mary's, Deep Point. From this vantage point the various eastern islands can be seen. Great Arthur, Great Innisvouls and Menawethan. This part of the St. Mary's coastline, where the first telegraph cable came ashore in 1869, is one of the most rugged of the island. The granite overhangs the water and drops in places sheer to the sea.

The first telegraph cable linked St. Mary's with Millbay, Lands End and later with Porthcurno. It broke on a number of occasions and the last time it happened, in 1877, the Isles of Scilly Telegraph Company closed down, and communications were taken over by the G.P.O. Morse telegraph was an expensive and never very efficient means of communication, wholesale chaos ensuing in the tiny office the night the *Schiller* went down, and it was not until 1935 that the service improved. In that year there was a decrease in costs. So elated were islanders, that in honour of the occasion the Council vice-chairman's wife was delegated to send to the Prince of Wales what must have been one of the strangest telegrams that worthy gentleman ever received: "I have the honour to address to your Royal Highness the first telegram from St. Mary's, Isles of Scilly, at the new rate of nine words for sixpence!" The undoubtedly taken-aback recipient countered in more conventional and sober terms: "Much appreciate St. Mary's inaugural telegram." Morse telegraph communication gave way eventually in 1938 to telephone.

Further around from Deep Point, Tolls island juts out from the corner of Pelistry Bay, an island at high water, but at low joined by a sandbar. Tolls island was the site of Pellew's Redoubt in the Civil War and is just about an acre in area, but is a favourite spot for picnicking visitors who have to be reminded of the caprices of the tide or they will be cut off. Pelistry sand is beautiful, a mixture of disintegrated felspar and quartz and the sea and view eastwards hard to beat. A succession of coastal indentations takes one through picturesque Watermill (a bay where the *Scillonian* and *Queen of the Isles* occasionally shelter in adverse conditions) past Block House point, the Inisdigen burial area Bar Point to the attractively pine-fringed northern tip of St. Mary's. Some of the best bathing can be had at Bar.

The rough cliff slopes which continue unchanged past Halangy Point, with the Creeb Rock lying off shore, takes us to Bants

Carn, celebrated in Scilly not only for its Bronze Age burial chamber, but also for its Roman Village dating from the early centuries A.D. This part of St. Mary's has attracted a number of eminent archaeologists in recent years (notably Mr. Paul Ashbee), who have conducted digs in an effort to bare more of Scillys' mysterious past. Inland from Bants Carn are the farm areas of Trenoweth and Newford and also Telegraph where the prominent coastguard station with its navigation and meteorological units stands on the most elevated ground in Scilly. The Telegraph building was, like the Lloyd's Signal structure on the Garrison, a gun tower built soon after the turn of the nineteenth century and resembles the Martello Towers of the Napoleonic Wars era. It is here that Marconi was said to have proved his theory of the wireless transmission of morse signals by receiving same from a mast with aerial erected on the hill above Porthcurno. Down by the coast is Pendrathen Quarry, the only workings currently operating in Scilly.

Moving down towards Hugh Town the coastal heathland, which we have encountered continually in our island travel, gives way to a more ordered appearance: the Isles of Scilly Golf Club has been reached.

The links were laid out in 1904 through the efforts of a sports-minded local doctor and an army of industrious flower farmers who cleared away gorse and heath to form the present nine holes. It must command one of the finest views in Britain. The course stretches along the north-western part of the island and a panorama from St. Martin's in the east to Agnes in the west can be seen. Many a frayed temper has been appeased by such beautiful surroundings.

The club boasts a 100-plus membership, an incredible achievement when the total population of the island is only 1,500. Most of the maintenance work is done by voluntary labour and poor greens do not detract one jot from a pleasant state of affairs where boatman plays with bank manager, farmer with shopkeeper. Class distinction, in the mainland meaning of the word, does not exist on St. Mary's and the general classlessness of the Isles of Scilly Golf Club is a welcome relief from the barriers so often encountered on mainland courses.

In the pioneering days of Sir Alan Cobham the golf course was used as a landing ground for the first aircraft to serve Scilly regularly. In 1934 a notice was given islanders that their support was required to back a first-class service to be provided by "a multi-engined aeroplane". Major Dorrien-Smith, at the time performing the opening of the new clubhouse, said: "I hear that there is an idea of the course being used as a landing ground for flying machines, and if this materializes I would strongly urge our committee to draw up rules for taking cover when a machine is sighted. I think Belisha Beacons, grids and chalk marks are what you want, and that you should have really asked the inventor of these atrocities to come and perform this opening for you."

In 1937 despite disapproval from certain quarters, the "flying machines" of the Channel Air Ferries descended on the fairways of the golf course. The links were cleared three times a day, a warning bell was tolled on the approach of an aircraft, brassie and niblick were hastily discarded and the golfers retired to the side lines. The maiden flight was marked by shocking gale force conditions, and occasioned a most "unroyal and ancient" procedure, one which, in fact, was to happen regularly until planes stopped using the course. When the aircraft taxied to a halt the golfers surged forward to hold down the wings as the wind buffeted the flimsy machine and the passengers alighted! When the plane had safely departed the golfers were free to return to their game, line up their club on the fifth green by taking the Bishop Rock lighthouse or the Haycocks off Annet island as a mark, and fire away!

The Great Western and Southern Airlines Limited took over the service and after using the golf course as an airport for twenty-two months, aviation moved on in 1939 to the present airport. Bunkers and hazards were restored, the booking hut by the second green disappeared, and apart from the course being used by the airforce and deteriorating somewhat during the Second World War, through the encroachment of gorse, the game has been played without further break or mishap up to the present day.

While discussing the golf club mention should be made of the Mal de Mers, a small group of sportsminded businessmen who have been visiting the islands annually for a long time now. As their name suggests the inaugural party experienced considerable discomfort on the old *Scillonian*, but they have survived to do yearly battle with islanders not only on the golf course, but on the cricket field, soccer pitch and in other spheres.

From the golf course and the cliffs of Carn Morval, the coast dives in and out of three more bays before the Pool and Hugh Town are reached and the circuit of St. Mary's has been done. In Porthloo bay lies tiny Taylors island, its granite taking on a forted shape, as so often happens in Scilly, while the equally minute Newford island separates Porthloo from the neighbouring bay, Shark's Pit. Newford island, like Tolls island, is only cut off from the mainland of St. Mary's at the flood, but at low water one can easily reach it over the rocks.

Above Shark's Pit, or Grenofen as it is often called, on the raised ground of Mount Flagon is situated the sixteenth-century fort of Harry's Walls, or rather what is left of it. The name is misleading as it was not built in the reign of Henry VIII as it implies, but was part of the general plan of fortification undertaken later in the reign of King Edward VI. Harry's Walls was abandoned well before completion because of faulty siting, but the two bastions, which can be discerned from the mass of stone, are regarded as an example of a rare building of those days.

The next "par" Porth Mellin Bay, is separated from the Pool by an outcrop of rock known as Carn Thomas, from which is situated on the landward side, Carn Thomas School, and the seaward side the lifeboat house and slipway. Not so very long ago the mahogany cargo of the wrecked *Fantee* was allowed to rot away on this beach.

Porth Mellin beach provides a fine natural playground for the pupils of Carn Thomas School, which for many years has provided good, if in the old days effectively crude, education for St. Mary's children up to Primary level. But for many years there has been an obvious need for further education in the shape of a Secondary School. Such a school has at long last been achieved, built opposite Carn Thomas, at the foot of Jackson's Hill, and following heated local controversy which found expression in both Press and television the Education Committee voted it should provide for comprehensive education. Off island children board at a St. Mary's hostel. Previously children who passed the Eleven-Plus went away at the Council's expense to mainland grammar, even public schools, while those who failed either went to mainland technical colleges, or stayed in the islands until leaving age without having any further education to speak of.

Despite the hotly divided opinion on Scillonian education, one cannot help but recall the opposition which Augustus's compulsory scheme aroused over a century ago, and feel that the great man himself would have given his whole-hearted approval. Islanders seem as wary of innovation as their brethren across the water.

St. Mary's lifeboat house behind Carn Thomas is a favourite spot for visitors. The *Guy and Clare Hunter* may be seen at various times as well as the wall plaques telling of the rescues and heroism of the past.

Our tour of St. Mary's ends with a walk along the Strand past the old Rechabite[1] slip, the tiny Roman Catholic Church (the Star of the Sea) built by Augustus Smith in 1860, and the Scillonian Club. We have now reached the Park and Hugh Town once again.

The ramble just completed around the extremities of St. Mary's provides few signs of cultivation, puzzling when one stops to consider the impression gained from the air. Then the island seemed a mass of little flower patches, sandwiched side by side and sheltered from the winds by man-made belts of trees; greenhouses and packing sheds gave further indication that every available acre had been harnessed by the farmer. However, the coastal areas, apart from those sheltered parts where patches jostle with each other down the slopes, are still very much as nature intended.

Perhaps the roads help to give a somewhat misleading effect of sophistication. An aerial view sees them criss-crossing each other all over the island, signs that every square yard has been developed. However, the majority of these roads are no more than tracks, barring the main metalled ones that are rather more indifferent than the maps claim. The main St. Mary's "arterial highway" leads from Hugh Town and encompasses the inland areas of Parting Carn, Lunnon, Porthloo, Maypole, Telegraph and Old Town among other places, while the roads branching off and leading to the outer parts of St. Mary's are little more than potholed tracks. So do not be misled. Much of St. Mary's is still wild

[1] The Rechabites (motto: "Peace and Plenty the reward of Temperance") once played a big part in the Scillonian community.

heathland, although much unfarm-like land has been ingeniously gobbled up by the cultivator.

One of the most surprising features of St. Mary's is the interior of the eastern bulge of the island or the country as it is called. In certain spots in this area one can easily forget one is on an island because they have a distinctly rural touch about them. Holy Vale is such a place. It is situated in a hollow in the "well" of the island and is surrounded by lush, sub-tropical vegetation. It is further from the sea than any spot on the island. Here the influence of the water is remote; it cannot be seen, nor can it be heard. One could be in a little country hamlet instead of being on an island with the cliffs and heathland only minutes away.

The countrified atmosphere of this part of St. Mary's can also be seen in other inland nooks and crannies, like Lunnon, and Maypole. Here there are fir belts and other trees, an uncharacteristic sight in Scilly, barring Tresco. It should be noted that these places are tiny, consisting often of just a few cottages. Most of them take their names from farms, rather than from the settlements.

I have always sensed, rather than noticed, a peculiar division and separateness between the country of St. Mary's and Hugh Town and its immediate environment. In the old days of Scilly, as we saw earlier, islanders gained their livelihood from the land or the sea. The country represented the farming element, the town, those concerned with water. It is the same today. The two dominant industries are flower farming and the tourist trade. The country is still associated with the former, the town and its connection with boats, with the latter. To say "never the twain shall meet" would be inaccurate. In the past the farmer was equally at home in a boat as on the land, and vice versa, while today many country people work in connection with the boats and many Hugh Townites labour on the land in the flower season. Nevertheless, although the two do meet, the distinction is there, felt rather than seen, a state of affairs underlined by the influx of mainlanders into Hugh Town to set up guesthouses, while the leasehold areas of the country stay almost predominantly "native". The only time the difference between the two areas developed into any sort of reality was when Hugh Town and the country were split up for rating purposes, and when the areas had their respective teams which did battle on the Garrison field. These sporting divisions no longer exist, and the strange apartness of these two areas and their peoples is really difficult to comprehend when the size of the island is taken into account. But everything in this Lilliputian world is scaled down accordingly, and one becomes exaggeratedly aware of difference.

Notwithstanding "town" and "country" whose dividing line is when the forty freehold acres of Hugh Town merge with the greater leasehold area, there are few social barriers; everyone on St. Mary's knows everyone else. Even the new settler (and today he is threatening to outnumber the born islander) is soon known and to walk through Hugh Town is to be forever saying "hello" and answering that peculiar Scillonian greeting of simply, "All right?" (Islanders do not reply " 'Andsome, my cock" or "Proper job" as do the stage Cornish). To the visitor accustomed to the impersonal anonymity of big mainland cities, the friendliness of islanders is a revelation. The status of a person's job is unimportant. It is the person who counts.

The standard of living on St. Mary's today is good, far removed, I am sure, from the mainland's conception of the way of life on a British offshore island. The flower trade, and to a greater extent, the tourist trade, have lifted islanders from what was once a subsistence-type living to a moneyed and commercial one. Despite the fears that arose when Mr. R. A. Butler introduced income tax to Scilly for the first time in 1954, islanders have never had better times.

When the Chancellor imposed the tax there was immediately a justifiable outcry. In his Budget speech Mr. Butler said: "Owing to defective machinery of assessment residents in the Scilly Isles have enjoyed exemption from tax on incomes and profits arising there. A clause in the Finance Bill will bring this happy state of affairs to an end." Scillonians, up in arms, forecast the tax would be crippling and would drive people away from the islands. Higher freightage and transport charges were put forward as the higher cost of living, with the even more remote off islanders well to the fore. A moderated tax, if one was needed at all, was only fair, they said, and councillors frequently went to London to seek redress, albeit fruitlessly.

Despite the money now coming to the islands through the tourist trade, the situation has changed little. The cost of living on St. Mary's has been estimated as over 20 per cent higher than the

mainland and even higher on the off islands, and of course
Scillonians are denied many of the everyday amenities that their
tax-paying colleagues on the mainland take for granted.

Notwithstanding tax inequality, St. Mary's people are not
badly catered for. Although theatres, nightclubs and other trappings of the mainland social scene are absent they have a beautiful
unspoilt landscape—the very breath of life for islanders. And St.
Mary's has a Women's Institute, Choral Society, a cinema (somewhat unoriginally called The Plaza), dances held in the Town Hall
throughout the summer, a Round Table, a Freemasons Lodge, a
Playreading Society, a badminton club, camera and sailing clubs, a
museum, the Scillonian Club where billiards, bingo and bridge
can be played. Soccer and cricket are also played, even though the
irregularities of the former, demonstrated in the following Press
report, have to be taken into account: "The delay caused in the
playing of the cup final is owing to the Tresco team being unable
to get time off from picking flowers!"

On the debit side there are always the delays and inconsistencies inevitably consequent on living on an island. Goods
ordered from the mainland are held up by train delays; the boats'
sailing times may be put back; fog grounds the helicopters. When
the latter happens there are no papers unless they have been rushed
from the heliport in Penzance to catch the *Scillonian*—and often
three days' papers arrive on the same day. But this is island life.
As someone said, "To live in Scilly is to live for the unusual"—
and indeed there are problems which the mainlander could not
even conceive.

VII

DOWN TO WEST'ARD

Animate Agnes

The inhabited islands in the Scilly archipelago all have their distinctive characteristics despite being set in such a confined area. Tresco is only a few hundred yards across the channel from Bryher, yet it is different and has an indefinable quality that is peculiarly its own. The same is true of St. Martin's. Again it is situated on the back doorstep of Tresco, but it, too, has its own special stamp. However, no one island in the group can boast the extraordinary individuality of Agnes, tucked away on its own in the western corner. Tresco, Bryher and St. Martin's being so close to each other, have inevitably lost bits of their personality to their fellows, and individual atmosphere has, in some cases, become merged and blurred. St. Mary's, of course, has been absorbed, or is in the process of being, by the mainland. Agnes is different. It stands off on its own, disdainful and aloof with no neighbours to influence it and rob it of its individuality. It shares with no one but the boundless Atlantic and the labyrinth of rocks and reefs on its western shores.

Straightaway I must admit to a partiality towards Agnes, possibly because my forebears were Hicks' from that island. I find it infinitely the most Scillonian of spots. Moreover, it can claim to be unique. The island has more than just springy turf, rocks and beaches, it has a soul, a near-human personality of which I am aware the minute I step ashore at rocky Porth Conger. To me, visiting the island is like visiting a long-known friend, so curiously animate is the island of Agnes. Being untouched and uninfluenced the island has thrown itself open to nature and has allowed itself to assimilate the absolute essence of its environment. In this way it has built up its own personality composed of the savagery of the seas that surround it; of the wildness of the heathland; of the bleakness of granite; of the sadness and melancholy which shrouds its solitude and loneliness.

To get to Agnes from St. Mary's one must cross St. Mary's Sound, and the swift tides of this narrow stretch of water, treacherous in bad weather, are formidable enough even in fine when there is a swell on the great cross-seas rolling into the Roadstead from the south-west. When conditions are really bad trips to and from Agnes are inadvisable; islanders are therefore cut off and in yet another way that peculiar singularity of Agnes is maintained. Imagine, however, that it is a fine day with only a mild sea running in St. Mary's Sound as the boat chugs out of St. Mary's Pool and turns her bows westward. The dangerous Bacon Ledge at the back of the quay is passed, and the boat skirts the Newman, the Garrison shore and the Steval. Agnes has, by now, come into full view and from a distance its landscape is uninteresting. The only distinctive landmark is the whitewashed lighthouse which stands on the high ground and dwarfs everything around it.

The fifteen-to-twenty-minute trip ends in the bay of Porth Conger, situated in the north-eastern tip of the island. Porth Conger is the main landing ground of Agnes although there is a little-used place at Priglis on the other side of the island. Porth Conger is a delightful spot. At low water it is almost completely landlocked as on the left is Gugh island, on the right Agnes itself, while the sand bar joining these two islands forms the third "boundary". At the flood the sea covers the bar, and then, of course, the two places are individual islands. Before arriving at the jetty two rocks which guard the entrance to the bay have to be passed. Rigorously observing their practice of recognizing the merest of details, islanders have faithfully given names to these two stumps of granite. The larger of the two is the Cow, the smaller, naturally, the Calf!

The jetty at Agnes, like the quay at St. Mary's and the landing stages on the other inhabited islands, is a focal point. Here visitor and islander land, and here the mail, foodstuffs and other vital day-to-day necessities are brought ashore from Steamship Company launches following the arrival of the *Scillonian* or the *Queen* at St. Mary's. Until fairly recently only a straggling protuberance of rough granite rocks served as a quay, and the tidal currents of that area made landing and mooring an often tricky task. At high water, with a northerly ground sea running, the little quay was often awash, even submerged at its extremities, but now Agnes has another and better jetty, plus a surge wall, thanks to their Duchy of Cornwall landlords.

A concrete road a few yards wide winds pleasantly up from the quay, through fields and flower patches to Higher Town and Middle Town, admirably situated little villages for they nestle into the contours of the Hill with absolute harmony. Here, in the vicinity of the disused lighthouse, most of the fifty Agnes people live and farm their few plots of land. There is a post office-cum-general stores, a school for a handful of children, a village green; little flapping windmills generate electricity and a number of television aerials contrast grotesquely with the unsophisticated surroundings.

Materially that is all. Although there is an off licence, there is no pub (the famed "Turk's Head" has long been closed), no cinema, in fact little of what one has become accustomed to accept as the normal things of life. Time after time one hears the cry from visitors "What a heavenly little place; how I would love to live here". But would they? The city dweller, forever surrounded by the stresses of modern life, finds Agnes in all its beauty and naturalness a veritable heaven—in relief. If he had to live there all the year round with none of the push-button conveniences he is so used to, even dependent upon, his enthusiasm, I suspect, would rapidly wane.

What then, is the secret of the obvious contentment which Agnes folk find on their rocky island home? I believe their indigenousness is the master key. Most of the families have been rooted to the soil of this western isle for centuries. It is their home, their heritage and the way of island life is in their blood. The appreciation of their environment goes deeper than that of the stranger which tends to be superficial. They love, and more important, understand their island home in all its varying moods, in tranquillity and ugly storm. They have the inborn gift of being able to enjoy the bare bones of life, an ability which most of us have lost. The lure of modern luxury would never, I feel, induce a true Agnesite to leave his native rock. That would be betraying his antecedents. Probably he could never live happily anywhere else. And yet do not think for a minute that his experience is limited to the narrow confines of his island. Many have travelled

Gugh, and sand-bar connecting it with Agnes

the world and possess the resulting wisdom and farsightedness. Yet they always come back. . . .

One of the things which puzzles mainlanders, even St. Mary's people, is how Agnes folk pass their time. To the gregarious among us, living on Agnes would be like staring boredom in the face. But not so with Agnes people. The lack of numbers and variety is offset by a quite remarkable gift for occupying themselves and a family atmosphere. Everyone is known on the island and everyone pulls together to improve the common lot.

A perfect example of the Agnes community spirit is the case of the main road which winds round the little Hill from the quay at Porth Conger to the lighthouse. Until fairly recently it was no more than a cart-track of bumps, originally laid by islanders at the order of Augustus Smith. No one cared much about its condition as there were no cars on the island and little damage was done. But Agnes people are inordinately proud of their tiny island and they wanted a better surface to traverse with their varied assortment of carts and receptacles when they went to the quay to fetch their goods. And so, magnificently independent, they set aside a couple of weeks a year to build a road themselves, lacking in many of the implements needed for such a job. Progress was slow, only yards of concreted pathway being laid at a time, but eventually the job was done. The "rolling Agnes road" stands as a tribute to the selflessness and spirit of pulling together. Could this happen on the mainland? I doubt it.

Agnes is about a mile long at its furthest point, a half a mile across, and can be walked around comfortably in a few hours. Apart from the limited area of habitation and the few plots fit for cultivation, the island is in possession of moorland and granite, for it is probably the most barren of the Scilly group and certainly the most rocky.

Before circumscribing Agnes, let us take a look at the old lighthouse and if Mr. Lewis Hicks, formerly the island's senior councillor, who lives in the house attached, permits, the interior of the building itself. Entry to the tower proper is effected by Mr. Hicks stepping up to one of his walls and opening what seems like a large cupboard. "Not many people can boast a lighthouse in their cupboard," he so rightly jokes, as the spiral stairway is ascended.

The lighthouse is no longer used for anything other than the

11

Bryher and the Norrad Rocks
Bryher

storing of lifesaving gear, as the Peninnis light took over in 1911. The original cresset burner now languishes in the Valhalla at Tresco Abbey Gardens.

Although its use has been superannuated, Agnes lighthouse, its whitewashed casing still serving as a useful daymark, is one of the few remaining links Scilly has with its wreck-strewn past, and what is more, from the platform at the top of the stairway one can gain an unparalleled view of the archipelago. To the east over Porth Conger the brilliant gorse-clad slopes of the Garrison give way to the distant beaches of St. Martin's, Tresco with its belts of firs and Bryher and Samson. But the western scene tops everything. The tortuous maze of rocks and reefs culminating with the pyramid of Bishop, can be appreciated from no better spot in Scilly, and from the tower of the Agnes light one cannot but understand why the granite tangle was feared the world over by mariners.

One path leads from the lighthouse to the western downs, while another winds down through hedges of tamarisk and other exotic plants, past the Bird Observatory, out to Priglis and the flattened, almost sea-level northern extremity of the island. Agnes' church stands near this bay and it is claimed that Priglis derives its name from Portus Ecclesiae or Church Bay.

The origin of the church is interesting. A French ship was supposed to have been wrecked off Priglis in 1685 and islanders assisted salvage operations. With the proceeds of their work a church was built and topped by the bell of the foundered vessel. The same building stands to this day, although much improved and strengthened in 1860 by voluntary labour and monetary help from the S.P.C.K., and its font is made of a solid piece of granite from Wingletang Downs. No better indication of the deep "roots" of Agnes people can be gained than by studying the inscriptions of the gravestones in the churchyard. The same family names crop up time after time with the Hicks clan dominating, and like the stones of Old Town Churchyard, St. Mary's, they tell the story of many a sea tragedy. Another point of interest lies in the Christian names on the stones. Seafaring folk have always been regarded as God-fearing people and Agnes islanders are no exception for there is a preponderance of strangely biblical-sounding names such as Uriah, Abraham, Obediah, Israel, Bathsheba and Amos.

Alongside picturesque Priglis with its long lifeboat slip and punts gently rocking on the pool, is Agnes Meadow, where island social and sporting functions take place. Bordered by the bank of the bay on the west, granite-walled fields, a grass tennis court and the pool, the Meadow is an acre or so of very uneven sandy-soiled heathland, and was the setting for the visit of the Duke of Edinburgh to Agnes in 1956. The Duke's helicopter alighted there where the entire population of the island was assembled to meet the royal visitor.

Agnes once ran a thriving cricket side which, bolstered by any visitor who happened to be staying on the island at the time, used to play teams from St. Mary's, Tresco, St. Martin's and Bryher on the Meadow "pitch" in an inter-island shield competition. The dangers of the pot-holed pitch were to some extent eliminated by the use of coconut matting, but nevertheless it was often a traumatic experience to face the Agnes Larwood on the Meadow wicket! In addition, many have lamented the failure of the M.C.C. to have a ruling to cover the disappearance of a cricket ball down a rabbit hole!

From the Priglis end, deep long-on was smack in the middle of Agnes Pool which books claim to be a fresh water lake, but which, in fact, is extremely brackish. Not surprisingly, when the proximity of the sea on all sides is taken into account and when the Meadow itself is often flooded. North of the Pool is the perimeter of the island with the two bays of Porth Killier, and Porth Coose and the furthest extremity, Browarth Point. West of this point, separated by Smith Sound, lies Annet.

A notable feature of the Agnes coastline is the sequence of bays. In this little north end of the island there are no less than four, Porth Conger, Porth Killier, Porth Coose and Priglis. "Porth" (bay) is a common name in Scilly, and is usually shortened to "per". So we get Perconger, Perkillier (or Perkillya), Percoose, even Periglis, as on St. Mary's we get Percressa for Porth Cressa and Permellin for Porth Mellin.

The western coast of Agnes from Priglis to the southern tip of Horse Point is primitive and stark. Some measure of protection can be found in Priglis and the habited area of the island, but the west shore of the island is an open wasteland of granite and gorse, a prey to the Atlantic winds and seas. Here the rocks take on agonized forms found nowhere else in Scilly, save at Peninnis

Head, St. Mary's, and their wildness is tinged with the loneliness I was earlier trying to explain when one looks out to the western reefs and realizes that there is nothing but sea between you and America, 3,000 miles away.

I well remember a sleepy afternoon a number of years ago when I really came to terms with the elusive personality of Agnes. It was a hot cloudless day and I was stretched out on a little carpet of pink seathrift, imprisoned on all sides by gorse and carns of twisted, belichened granite. The day before there had been a south-westerly gale, but now the sea was asleep, its energy dissipated, gently caressing a jagged shore still littered with flotsam of wood and boxes and one large battered oil drum. As I took in the panorama of rocky fragments which made up the Western Isles, I had never experienced such peace. There was not a sound save the faint whirring of wings as a lesser blackbacked gull homed in to land on the carn behind me, and the moan of the sea. The bustle and rush of city and town was so remote as to be non-existent. I was overwhelmed by a great sense of timelessness. The huge carns had survived a thousand storms, and would continue to do so long after I was gone and forgotten. The puny stature of man was brought home to me by that ageless scene; his short span of life with all its contrasting elations, depressions and worries, was ephemeral, insignificant. How many had looked on the same scene before me, and how many would do so after? All was infinity.

Ebb tide and the gradual baring of weed-covered rocks somehow heightened the feeling of desolation and loneliness. An end-of-the-world pall hung over everything. An isle of "savage melancholy". Far out to sea a liner appeared up over the curve of the horizon, while the hoot of the *Scillonian* drifted faintly over from the east, warning trippers of the vessel's imminent departure for Penzance and of yet another of those pressing deadlines which seem to constitute so much of our lives. If ever a spot belonged body and soul to Nature, then this was it.

Only a few hundred yards from where I lay was the strangest of incongruities, a miniature circle of tiny stones worked out in the turf of the shore so as to form a maze. It serves, I suppose, as light relief from the starkness of the general environment, but it seems somehow pathetic.

A word must be said here of this strange little rock pattern which bears the name of the Troy Town Maze from which the adjacent Troy Town farm is supposed to have taken its name. The maze is claimed by some to be similar to the classical Cretan Labyrinth pattern which was known in the Eastern Mediterranean in the Bronze Age, and which was called "The Walls of Troy". There are many similar maze designs around western Europe. Apparently all such mazes were given the name Troy, although the ancient city of Troy was not constructed in any way resembling a maze.

The school of thought who attribute this illustrious antiquity to Agnes' pattern of stones, are, however, confounded by the simple island claim that one Amor Clarke, a local lighthouse keeper who married into the Hicks clan, constructed it in 1729. The others retaliate by saying Clarke and probably those who followed him renovated the pattern and kept it in order, and are adamant that the maze had much earlier origins. However, the scales are tilted Amor's way by the writings of Heath, Borlase, Troutbeck and Woodley, all of whom did not even mention the maze. Probably it was regarded as too recent to merit recording.

The work of classical antiquity or of one Amor Clarke? The wrangle will probably never be settled, but the maze is still there today on the westerly reaches of Agnes and, as I have said, an incongruous and rather forlorn touch in such elemental surroundings. It seems to epitomize the often unequal struggle Agnes and its people wage against the wildness of their environment.

The rocks in the vicinity of this, the most southerly-inhabited point of Great Britain, are magnificent; Gamperdizl Point, another granite pile called Gampergurling and a grimmacing carn named Kestillier (or Castella). Offshore lurk the advance battery of the western reefs, Menglow, Buccabu, Ragged Rock, the Thickeses and countless more in an ironbound ring around the shore. The Troy Town area, which dips into the sea at Gamperdizl Point, is separated from the southern peninsula of Wingletang Downs by Santa Warna Cove, better-known as St. Warna's Cove, the largest bay around the much-indented coast of Agnes.

St. Warna was the patron saint of wrecks, who, legend tells us, sailed to Agnes from Ireland in a little coracle made of hides and her place of disembarkation was given her name. On the shores of the bay there is an old well, St. Warna's wishing well, into which islanders, in past days, were said to have cast their coins to solicit the saint's benevolence in sending them a wreck. St. Warna more often than not readily obliged. Some writers claim St. Warna's Island as the original name of Agnes. This is untrue. It has always been Agnes, or earlier Celtic Ag-Innis.

The landscape becomes even more primitive as the bay is skirted and the downs of Wingletang are reached. How superbly suggestive of wildness are the names of Scilly's western rocks; Camperdizl, Campergurling, Kestillier, Perkylla—and as savage by nature as by name, Wingletang. One can almost taste the salt air and smell the dankness of the weed covered ledges! Here Agnes granite surpasses itself in ingenious formation with the Giant's Punch Bowl outstanding.

Agnes, the supreme individual, even has its own special brand of weathered formations. Many rocks are vertical pillars, eroded and fined in their lower extremities to resemble, as one writer graphically noted, "petrified mushrooms". Nowhere else in Scilly are these singular contortions found.

The most southerly tip of the island is Horse Point, while just off shore lie the dangerous Wingletang ledges. As recently as 1951 Wingletang was nearly the scene of a major Scillonian disaster, for the steamer went aground on her ledges. She was refloated, but had she been extensively damaged islanders would have been in serious trouble. It was thick fog that day, comparable with conditions when the *Plympton* went down, and islanders knew all was not well when they heard the *Scillonian*'s siren bleating as she tried to grope her way along the southerly shore of St. Mary's. In such blanketing conditions and with no radar aid, the time-honoured procedure was for the chairman of the Steamship Company to discharge a shotgun off Normandy Downs, St. Mary's, and the island's garage owner "Vic" (well-known to countless tourists) to sound a bugle at Peninnis Head. The *Scillonian*'s master, heard the former, but in the sound-proofing mist, missed the latter, and also the Spanish bellbuoy, and found himself steaming up the westerly shore of Agnes towards the rock of Melledgan, radically off course. Realizing his error, he turned around and went hard and fast on the Wingletang Point.

Some Agnes men had hurried from the village to warn her off, but too late. However, all ended well as passengers were all safely taken off. The *Scillonian* was found to have suffered no more than some buckled plates, and islanders breathed again.

Looking south from Horse Point as far as the eye can see is water. Water everywhere, nothing breaks its monotony and one gets tired of the changelessness of aspect. Even in fine weather there is a southerly heave off this point, with the mass of water building up into a rhythmic, sucking swell. At Horse Point one can begin to appreciate the meaning of the words of Oliver Wendall Holmes:

> The sea is like a great liquid metronome,
> Beats out her solemn measure.

Around on the east shore of Wingletang is Beady Pool named after a Venetian ship carrying a cargo of beads and trinkets which went aground there. Occasionally people still find beads in the adjacent fields or in seaweed brought up from the shore.

Near Beady Pool can be found Boy's Rock which serves as yet another link with Agnes and her days of shipwreck. Islanders beachcombing along the shores following a bad storm found the body of a little sailor boy lodged between a rock, whose name now commemorates the tragedy. Further along the coast they came across pieces of wreckage, proof of an unknown wreck during the night.

The shore stutters from Beady Pool in and around the bay of Wingletang itself and soon the lee of Gugh island is reached. The southerly bay formed by the sand bar and the two islands is the Cove of Agnes, and here for many years islanders hauled their seines for scads and mullet. The northern bay caused by the bar is, of course, the landing ground of Porth Conger. The bar itself is one of the finest strands in Scilly, but visitors should beware of the tides before bathing. One minute the bar is dry, the next covered by feet of swirling water. When the tide is safe the bathing is exceptional, even if a recent guidebook's claim of "the finest bathing beach in Europe" is a little extravagant.

Gugh itself is about the size of St. Mary's Garrison peninsula, or Hugh. Gugh, Hugh, Heugh or Hoe (as found at Plymouth) and other sundry corruptions all stem from the Cornish word meaning headland. Although parts of Gugh island have been brought under cultivation, it is largely barren and perhaps the most remarkable feature is the number of megaliths dotted all over the tiny island. The most notable is "The Old Man of Gugh", a nine-feet-high standing stone.

The strange-sounding names of this western quarter of Scilly are again in evidence. The most southerly extremity is Hoe Point, with the Hakestone rock nearby, while round on the eastern shore is Dropnose Point (pronounced Droppynose) with a rock bearing the same curious name lying off-shore. Another strange-sounding point is Carnkimbra, while lying off the coast are Wetnose and Cuckolds Ledge. The northern part of Gugh towers up into a big granite pile of the Kittern.

For many years Gugh has been inhabited. There is a farmhouse close to the spot where the bar joins with Agnes. Currently living on Gugh are a family, who bear an appropriate name for this part of Scilly—Hick—albeit without the S!

It is time to leave this modern Swiss Family Robinson to their island home, as the tide is "making" over the bar.

The tempo of life on these lonely islands in the western corner of Scilly has not changed much over the years. There is still a characteristic aura of *mañana* in the salt air. True, increased dabbling in the tourist trade has brought a hitherto unaccustomed burst of seasonal activity, but this can be said to be offset by the falling away of Agnes as an active seafaring community. The island was once the traditional home of the pilots, but now she has none. Once upon a time all was fishing bustle with the seines being hauled in the Cove and Sennen fisher folk arriving every year for the lobster season. This, too, is just a memory.

Nevertheless, Agnes still retains her interest in the sea, even if she is relegated to the passive role of onlooker. The course taken by the St. Mary's pleasure boats to the Bishop is noted with lazy interest, and the island's inbred concern with boats and navigation extends to the distant horizon where today's modern diesel vessels plough the shipping lanes as did their forerunners in the days of sail and steam.

Many of the great transatlantic liners are familiar with Agnes people. The *Rotterdam*, a big Dutch liner, regularly used to slow down off the back of Agnes to allow the pleasure craft to get a closer look. The skipper's farewell voyage was a famous occasion. The St. Mary's peglegged town cryer informed islanders that "Commodore Bouman, captain of the Dutch liner *Rotterdam* will say farewell to the islands today", and when the liner arrived off

Scilly she completely stopped. The little boats swarmed all round, giving the popular captain a rousing send-off. The *Rotterdam* responded with blasts of her siren, and the chimney of the house belonging to the retired Agnes pilot was seen to be sporting a voluminous white sheet, one old sea dog's salute to another.

Of all the off islands, Agnes would perhaps seem the last to succumb to the tourist traffic and its attendant changes, but already there are signs that it is stepping in line with the rest of Scilly. The main means of livelihood for Agnes people has, for years, been the cultivating of early potatoes and flowers, but the latter these days tends to be a precarious business. Inconsistencies and market fluctuations are an ever present danger, and while they can be borne without undue hurt by the larger grower on St. Mary's, they can have serious effects on the small man—and most of the Agnes farmers operate by necessity on a small scale.

More and more in recent years the Agnes person has leant towards the tourist and when he hears St. Mary's councillors talking of keeping the island unspoilt and of resolving to prevent the spread of commercialization, he is at the same time in agreement, and in opposition. He would hate to see Scilly ruined in the quest for a "fast buck" but to him "keeping the island unspoilt" does not mean the refusal to grant the trappings of normal progress. It is all very well for a visitor to see an off island cottage and exclaim "what a beautiful little place", but if he had to live there he would soon change his tune when he found there was no main drainage, no piped water and that he had to generate his electricity by wind blown mill. One Agnes man said accusingly, "They want to keep us in picturesque poverty," while another hinted darkly that the local authority seemed to have no objection to Agnes being turned into a Whipsnade: see the islanders, a penny a peep!

Already the indications are there that Agnes is turning to the visitor, for the all-important extras of income: more visitors than ever are being taken in. But perhaps conclusive proof that Agnes is doing her best to throw away associations with her former way of life is found in the singular Case of the Public Convenience.

In the past there was no such luxury on Agnes. It was unnecessary, as part of the "back to nature" appeal for visitors was diving into the ferns or darting behind one of the many rocky carns that cover the island. *Tempora mutantur*, sadly perhaps. Now boatloads of humanity get off at Agnes on their way to and from trips to the western rocks and the lack of a latrine came to be an obvious embarrassment. The Duchy decided to meet the need, supported by the Council by erecting an elaborate building at Porth Conger, above the quay, but as so often happens in the unique world of Scilly, the unusual was not catered for. The original estimate proved wrong, the price soared and at one stage it was found that water could not be pumped up from the sea! The cost rocketed to the region of £6,000 and so indignant was one St. Mary's man (why, I do not know as the Duchy, not the rates were in the main footing the bill), that he suggested there should be a civic opening Clochmerle-style, with one of the Agnes councillors passing the first motion ... !

Annet and the Western Rocks

Agnes island and the western rocks have often been discussed in books under separate chapter headings, and by doing so the writers have unwittingly severed the strong links which have always and will always unite the two. Agnes and her rocks can never be dissociated, for not only have they a physical affinity, but also a definite influence on each other. The folk who live on the lighthouse island must always be aware of their rocky neighbours, for they live out their lives to the sound of the Atlantic surf pounding over them and boiling into her western shores. Moreover for centuries they earned their meagre livelihoods by potting and navigating the reef strewn waters where many of their kin lost their lives. It is no exaggeration to say that the proximity of the rocks wholly conditioned the *modus vivendi* of Agnes people in days gone by. They presented shipping with a dangerous hazard which called for the services of a channel pilot. And so Agnes became the pilot's isle; pilots expressly settled there to ply their trade and in its heyday piloting boomed solely because of the money-making maze of rocks to the west of the island. In addition these reefs claimed countless ships, which directly or indirectly went to stave off extreme hardship which so often threatened the Agnesite.

No, Agnes and the western rocks must be treated as an intrinsic whole, one having bearing on the other. To talk of Agnes and its rocks is indeed to talk of cause and effect.

For the sake of identification the western rocks start with Annet island and a line down the back of Agnes to the "Thickeses" and stretch away westwards to the Bishop Rock and the Crebbinicks, an area of about twenty square miles. In this sea area there are more rocks than anywhere in the archipelago. Here the full weight of the Atlantic is felt as it is nowhere else in Scilly, and even on a calm day, when the waters of the Roadstead are "a pan of milk", there is still ominous movement. The sea is sucking and boils around the reefs which, depending on the tide, are submerged or above the water; and when the weather turns foul, then to look out from Agnes is to see an awesome spectacle. Great breakers thunder in like a tidal wave, exploding in a cloud of foam; the entire area is a sea of white; the turmoil and noise is quite deafening, and even the regal Bishop, towering above the maelstrom, trembles, literally.

The names of some of the rocks in the western group reflect the savagery of the seas, Hellweathers, Crebbinicks, Crim, Gorregan, Malledgan, Crebawethan, Inisvrank, Minmanueth. And typical of paradoxical Scilly we get other hopelessly inappropriate names like the Daisy, Silver Carn, Rosevean, Jack's Rock, Trenemene.

Let us start with Annet and work westwards to the Bishop. Annet island lies west of Priglis Bay, Agnes across the waters of Smith Sound. Its name is not in any way connected with neighbouring Agnes as may be reasonably supposed, nor has it any French origin. Like Agnes, it derives its strange name from old Celtic.

Annet's main claim to fame lies in its birds. The island is the nesting ground for several species of sea bird, and at certain times in the year it is literally impossible to walk without stepping on a nest. For this reason the island is classed as a bird sanctuary and a licence has to be obtained from the lessee, Commander T. Dorrien-Smith, before a visit can be made. Annet's fifty acres are covered with sea pinks, fern and riddled with nesting holes. The coast line is pock-marked with indentations, and the shores strewn with granite boulders. The northern end of the island is, perhaps, best known as it meets the sea at Annet Head and the contiguous string of pointed rocks, the Haycocks. Looking from St. Mary's over to the west the points of this end of Annet are unmistakable.

In the nesting season, when, in fact, Annet cannot be visited, the all-pervading smell of bird and effluvia assails the nostrils. They are everywhere, along the shores in the tufts of grass, burrowing in the ground, their harsh cries contributing to a clamour that deafens. Just about every sea bird known in the British Isles can be found on Annet. Greater blackbacked gull, lesser blackbacked gull, cormorant, razorbill, tern, petrel, sheer-water, guillemot, oystercatcher and puffins are to be found. After the nesting season the island is a battlefield of dead gulls who failed to survive birth and the stench of decaying flesh is very unpleasant.

Off the north tip of the island lay the aptly-named Halftide ledges and the Smith rocks, Great and Little Smith. These rocks stand at the northern entrance to the channel which separates Agnes and Annet, and give their name to Smith Sound.

Fringing Annet's western shores are the Minmanueths which are known to all and sundry as the "dogs of Scilly"; and how they live up to their onomatopoeic nickname! Their jagged tops protrude just above the surface of the water, like fangs. Min-manueth and nearby Ranneys gave their names to two vessels which operated out of Scilly in the islands' ship-building days.

Off the southern tip of Annet one gets a foretaste of the rock tangle which, in fact, gets even more confusing as one moves further west. Annet is separated from Hellweathers by Annet Neck; Hellweathers is, in turn, broken from a neighbouring reef by Hellweathers Neck; a little bit further south there are the Brow, Hale Rock, Brothers and Inisvrank, and some more narrow channels Shoal Neck and Muncoy Neck. It can be readily under-stood that a novice who presumes to navigate in these waters would be courting disaster. The necks and channels are in some places as narrow as the proverbial eye of a needle, and conning through them is made more difficult by the confusing disap-pearance and reappearance of the rocks on the movement of the tiders. Only the most experienced boatmen thread their way though this maze.

With Agnes and her lighthouse dropping further astern the largest isle of the group is encountered, Malledgan. By largest I mean precisely two acres! North of Malledgan are the dangerous Muncoy ledges, and south a stretch of water separates the rock from Gorregan. Gorregan is an ugly, scarred pile of granite.

It is continually washed by the waves, and is as sinister as the sound of the name it bears. Many of the rocks in Scilly go in pairs, and when this happens the smaller one is given the name Biggal. So with Gorregan, which is the Biggal of Gorregan standing nearby.

Near Gorregan the reefs become even thicker, Trenemene, Pednathise Head, Daisy, The Rags, Rosevean, all with their accompanying necks—Shoal Neck, Broad Neck and Gorregan Neck. In this area lies Rosevear, which for an insignificant isle boasts a remarkable history and which is far and away the most interesting of the western rocks. Rosevear, which in Cornish means large headland(!), just as Rosevean means small headland, might well have been the site of the lighthouse which guard these rocks. Instead of the Bishop Rock lighthouse, we might have had Rosevear lighthouse. Of all the rocks considered for the building of a lighthouse by Douglas, the choice was narrowed down to Rosevear and the Bishop. The latter got the vote, but Rosevear had very real claims. It lies that all important bit more south than the Bishop, and as the majority of the shipping carnage was caused by vessels approaching from the south, a light would have been as effective there as on the Bishop.

Although Rosevear was not chosen as the site for the lighthouse, the rocky islet served as a base for the men engaged on the Bishop construction work. Looking at the meagre acreage of Rosevear today, it is difficult to credit that a gang of Cornish workmen lived there for a quite extensive period of time; that they managed to grow their own vegetables there; that a blacksmith's shop was erected as well as other sheds. There are few signs left of Rosevear's brief period of habitation, and it surpasses belief that men could live here and go about the exacting job of building a lighthouse in this exposed quarter. There was little protection from the winds, and no shelter from neighbouring islands. For this was the unsafe world beyond the ten-fathom line.

Rosevear was occupied during the years 1847–50 which culminated disastrously with the washing away of the Bishop Rock's first iron structure. There is reason, too, to believe that Rosevear was still inhabited during the remaining two stages which were required before the lighthouse was finished. One fact is certain, however. There was a ball on tiny Rosevear. The sheds and workmen's living quarters were decorated, music supplied, guests invited from St. Mary's and other islands and a moonlit night was danced away to the moan of the wind and the boom of the sea. Surely the strangest and most romantic ball of all time.

Alongside Rosevear are the Jolly Rocks, Jacky's Rock, a reef known as the Brow of the Ponds, and Crebawethan with, of course, Little Crebawethan and the inevitable neck. We are now on the edge of Scilly. Just four rocks lie westward bringing up the perimeter—four of the most fearsome. The Gilstone, whose surrounds mark the graveyard of Sir Cloudesley Shovel's ship, and whose waters are as deep as anywhere in Scilly; the Retarrier Ledges, of *Schiller* notoriety; the vicious sounding Crebinicks and the Bishop Rock itself.

North of the Bishop, curiously dissociated with the main group, lie the Crim Rocks, Zantman's and the Gunners. Westward as far as the eye can see is water. Looking in the opposite direction Agnes can be seen in the distance, but there is little hint of St. Mary's and of the oval of islands circling the Roadstead beyond. The shelter of the archipelago has been left behind; we are out in the open Atlantic.

One of the great attractions to visitors going to this corner of Scilly are the seals. Colonies frequent the area and when there is not too much drag in the water boats cut off their motors and coast in close to the rocks where the seals bask in the sun.

Mention of these creatures recalls the most celebrated of the species in Scillonian waters. A number of years ago a seal had the misfortune to surface straight into a car tyre floating on the surface of the water. Being unable to dive because of the buoyant ring she was faced with starvation, and soon the story was given national Press coverage. The seal was given the name Sally and boatmen did a thriving business as trippers went out daily hoping to catch a glimpse of her; inevitably a mate of the distressed Sally, Sammy, was cooked up! The affair attracted the attention of the R.S.P.C.A. and unavailing attempts to feed the seal were made. I never found out what actually happened to Sally. Presumably she got rid of the offending tyre and she and Sammy lived happily ever after, if that is what seals do. In retrospect, one thing is certain. The Sally episode did as much to bring Scilly to the notice of the public as any other event in those early days of the tourist industry.

Crebawethan, Rosevear, Gorregan and their colleagues **are** haunted by sea birds as well as seals. They perch on ledges in perfect rows "line astern" and fill every nook and cranny, the same bewildering mixture that throngs Annet. The shag is much in evidence, a sad-looking bird with the emaciated appearance of the very rocks it inhabits. When disturbed the shag flies off low, hugging the surface of the water and looking every bit the predator it is.

A landing can be brought off on some of the more sizeable of the western rocks, but only if the seas are not too rough. The layman is advised to leave this part of Scilly severely alone.

VIII

FAIRY-TALE BRYHER

Heathy Hill, Rushy Bay and Broomy Field, Stony Porth, Timmy's Hill and—Stinking Porth: these picturesque and impossible names spank absurdly of the children's story book, of Rupert and Nutwood Common, of Sailor Sam and other creations of fiction. And indeed when one happens upon the tiny Scillonian island of Bryher, shimmering in the blue sea three miles north-west of St. Mary's and a third of a mile across New Grimsby Channel from Tresco, one cannot but feel that one has intruded into a world of make-believe.

Bryher's place names are just one facet, for the general island framework seems altogether divorced from reality and all that is conventional. Bryher is thumb-nail size, a mere 317 acres into which are squeezed no less than five hills (Scillonian scale), a pool, a town, a chapel, a church, a reading room, a quite considerable number of flower patches, a post office and a school which currently houses nine children—and there is still room to move. Roads, in the accepted sense of the word, do not exist, nor do cars. Sandy lanes traverse the island over hillock and through outcrops of gorse and granite, while tractor affords the most sophisticated form of transport. The post office is Bryher's focal point, and the only mainland touch, yet even this has become assimilated by the off-island way of life since it fulfils a dual role, being the general stores as well. There is no public house on the island, Bryher people who want a pint having to punt across the channel to Tresco—a pleasant enough chore on a summer's evening.

The majority of a dwindling island population, now just under fifty, live in what is somewhat grandly called Bryher Town, a tiny hamlet of about fifteen houses which line the one lane. The remainder live in spots dotted around the island, in a northern

176

part, a southern, and near the pool. When referred to locally they live "up to Nor'rard", "Down to South'ard" or "over to Pool".

The final incongruity of this strange island of Bryher belongs, perhaps, more to the past than to the present—namely its long association with the family surname of Jenkins. Once upon a time nearly everyone on Bryher was a Jenkins—literally—and although this is no longer quite the case in a fast-changing Scilly, the Bryher-Jenkins love affair is every bit as remarkable as the indigenousness of the Agnes' Hicks.

Bryher, together with Agnes, is the smallest of the inhabited islands of Scilly, and like Agnes its main appeal lies in its pre-carious man-versus-environment position. It is an island roman-tically cliff-hanging between cultivation and civilization on the one hand and return to nature and depopulation on the other. If the inhabitants lose the fight it will be a tragedy for Scilly. They will not, I hope, for many years yet, but the warning cones have already been hoisted. The cultivable parts of the island are regularly threatened by the encroaching sea, and this together with the fact that general amenities and facilities are foreign to the island community could eventually unite to depopulate Bryher.

If the main attrac tion of Agnes can be said to lie in its solitude and wildness, then Bryher's appeal rests in its contrasts. For such a tiny island the discrepancies of topography are incredible. To the north and west Bryher is rugged and exposed, a fitting bul-wark to the winds and seas that sweep in over the Norrad rocks. To the east and south, in the sheltered lee of neighbouring Tresco, it is the most docile and entrancing place imaginable, at times the quietest spot in Scilly and a place where cream teas are the order of the day. *Multum in parvo* once again.

There are two landing grounds on Bryher, three if Rushy Bay beach is included. In the past when visiting Bryher for the day, we used to go ashore at Rushy in the south of the island and play cricket on Rushy Bay green above the beach, a flower box serving as a wicket. Sadly Bryher can no longer raise a side. Their great moment came in 1924 when they vanquished mighty St. Mary's and Tresco to win the Inter-island Shield. But these days the bay seems little used. The main spots are both on the more secluded eastern flank facing into New Grimsby channel with Tresco's New Grimsby Harbour just across the water. Tides dictate the

12

New Grimsby Harbour, Tresco
Old Grimsby Harbour, Tresco

landing ground. The whole area to the south of Bryher between that island and Tresco is riddled with sandbars and at dead low water people often have to alight on the beach north of the regular jetty. The latter juts out from a small promontory erroneously yet typically called the "island" by locals. Originally it was like the Agnes quay, a jumble of badly shaped stones, but since the war the Duchy of Cornwall have encased it in concrete and extended it. It is of great convenience to Bryher islanders, as the inter-island launches and visitor boats can come alongside instead of having to conduct laborious operations from the beach as was the case in former days. Despite the improvement, there is a humorous side to the Bryher jetty, although perhaps not quite as amusing as the Agnes Clochmerle. The constructors surprisingly overlooked the rise and fall of tides and at low water the quay is high and dry, a forlorn appendage to the island.

On alighting at the "island" quay the capital of Bryher Town can be easily seen. The few houses, flower sheds and beneath them the rows of flower patches nestle into Watch Hill, which dominates not only this part of the island, but also this area of the New Grimsby channel. "Dominates" might seem an inappropriate word in low-lying Scilly, but surprisingly, not in the Bryher context. Although only 138 feet above sea level, Watch Hill is remarkably steepsided, is the highest point on the island, and gives a misleading impression of greater height.

Just fifty yards from the jetty is Bryher's All Saints Church, a tiny granite building with its roof belichened and weathered yellow. Flanking its tiny cemetery on one side are flower fields, while on the other is the sandy bank of the beach. The church was first built in 1742, and later renovated and enlarged in 1821. On its bell is inscribed in Swedish "Frigate ship Aurora, 1746" and although it is conjectural, it might have come from the *Aurora* which was wrecked in St. Helen's Gap in 1784. Only recently has Bryher church received a licence to marry. Formerly island couples were rowed across the channel to St. Nicholas' Church Tresco in a bridal gig. A glance at the gravestones in the churchyard bears out Bryher's one-time subjugation to the Jenkins family which, incidentally, first settled on Bryher from Wales more than 300 years ago.

A rough track contours steeply up from the "island" past Bryher's second place of worship, the Baptist Chapel, into the

Town and to the post office. In the old days the postmaster or mistress used to benefit at the princely rate of ½d. a postcard, a penny a letter, and had the assistance of a celebrated old nag called Polly. Polly has long gone, and the mail has to be collected at the post office which, incidentally, is a mobile concern; whenever a new postmaster or mistress takes over the office moves with them. When I last passed the little granite building the window bore the following notice, vital to Bryher flower growers: "*Scillonian* leaving St. Mary's Monday 7.30, Tuesday 7.45, Wednesday 8.00, overnight loading."

Watch Hill, bouldered and gorse covered and rising sharply above the Town is crowned by a stone marker and readily beckons the visitor to its summit. Originally there was a coast-guard lookout hut on the top which also served as a mark for island fishermen. When it was removed the present marker was erected. From the peak of this hill a very fine view indeed can be gained of this quarter of Scilly. East across narrow New Grimsby Channel lies the extended northern shore of Tresco with the un-mistakable Cromwell's Castle clinging to the sea level side. In the background, showing through above Tresco, is the top of Round Island lighthouse and above the Grimsby waist St. Martins and St. Helen's. Swinging around in an anti-clockwise arc over the flower patches and the northern heathland of Bryher there is a superb panorama of the Norrad rocks, while further around is Samson, Agnes, the western rocks and St. Mary's in the back-ground. Even further around is the southern tip of Tresco, with its fir-fringed gardens, the channel dividing it from Bryher, the "island" and bay below, and New Grimsby Harbour across the strip of water.

A number of fields lie north of Watch Hill, but thereafter the landscape gives way to barren heathland, characteristic of the north of the island and which culminates in the great hammerhead of granite cliffs, Shipman Head. There is one of Bryher's little settlements tucked into the middle of the eastern flank of the island, a few houses and sheds called "Norr'ard". Just out from the beach of Norr'ard is Hangman's Island, a typically conical Scil-lonian rock pile rising sheer out of the waters of New Grimsby Channel. They say that the island got its grotesque name in the time of the Civil War when a number of recalcitrant Cavaliers were executed there by the Roundhead invaders, but there is reason to believe it dates back even further—to the early days of lawlessness in Scilly when it was common for pirates to be executed *en masse*.

A word must be said here about New Grimsby Channel a quite narrow strip of water, bordered on one side by the gentle slopes of Tresco and the other by the relatively precipitous side of eastern Bryher. This stretch of water, from the environs of Hangman's Island to the back of Tresco quay affords one of the best anchorages in Scilly. Unlike much of the neighbouring sand-barred waters in the south, it is quite deep; it is also effectively shielded from westerly and easterly winds. Thus many Bryher and Tresco boats ride at anchor in New Grimsby Channel while the seas to the north and west are at the mercy of the elements.

Much has been said and written about the northern extremity of Bryher, and indeed the magnificence of its cliffs cannot go unmentioned. Utterly exposed to the winds, the headland is as bare as any in Scilly. Nothing can be cultivated here, neither can a settlement be established as there is no shelter. So fierce are the elements that much of the soil of the heathland has been eroded and in many places the surface is a mere carpet of granite-shingle decomposition with the rock protruding through.

Shipman Head is undoubtedly one of the showpieces of Scilly and rivals Peninnis Head, St. Mary's in grandeur. A mighty crag of granite (the inner part is called House of the Head) it is actually an island separated from northern Bryher by a gulf. In rough weather the sea roars into the chasm—or Bight—sending spray yards into the air and drenching the higher heathland. The rocks of Shipman Head are much beloved by the seabirds. At all times they can be seen lining the many crevices of the pile and the surrounding air reverberates to their din.

Around from majestic Shipman Head, no wit less awesome, is Hell Bay. As the name suggests the western seas that pound into it are as violent as any in the islands. Even in calm weather there is a movement, and the sea is never quiet. The silky caress of water on beach as at the "island" is not for Hell Bay. The sea is always growling, and in rough weather, which is the rule rather than the exception for this quarter of Bryher, Hell Bay is like a Scillonian Biscay. At all times it throws up enough flotsam and jetsam to please the most avid of beachcombers: boxes, planks, lobster pots, oil drums, floats, there was even a ship's bell when I was last there.

The mood and terrain of the entire west shore, from Hell Bay down to Rushy Bay, is set by the former. The coast is as serrated as even the Agnes shore, while the powerful sea has made such obvious inroads that in some places the cliffs overhang sea-eaten caves. When one stands on the shore of Hell Bay or near Shipman Head with the wind whistling around one's ears and the sea in a frenzy, it is difficult to imagine that only ten minutes away the waters of the "island" pool and New Grimsby are almost calm.

From Hell Bay the shore stutters and stumbles southward. The landscape remains unchanged, little top soil and much bare rock, shingle and coarse heathland. Out to sea, black and unfriendly, are the Norrad Rocks—Scilly Rock, Black Rock, Illiswilgig (pronounced Illiswidjig). The shore from Hell Bay reaches Great High Rock, and then the rocks of Popplestones Brow—known to Bryher islanders as, simply, Popplestones. How it got its strange name is uncertain, but there is perhaps some link with Christopher Copplestone, a Devon squire who leased Bryher from the Duchy in 1578.

Further south lies the most westerly part of Bryher, the promontory of Gweal Hill, which with Popplestones encloses a small shingly bay. Gweal Hill is so named as it faces directly on to tiny Gweal island, one of the Norrad group, which is separated from Bryher by Gweal neck. Gweal Hill, one of Bryher's five hills—Timmy's, Heathy, Watch and Samson are the rest—is uninhabited, although there is a rusty old shed on the landward slope, while the remains of granite walls on the seaward side give an indication of former cultivation and a larger population. Now this eminence is given over to gorse and granite, as is most of this side of the island. It is too exposed for cultivation. In past days Bryher islanders used to put out from the shore below Gweal Hill to go to Gweal island to collect wiry grass to pack their barrels of potatoes for export.

Inland from Gweal Hill is a sea-level expanse of land and Bryher Pool—a small circle of very brackish water. Not surprisingly, the sea makes frequent incursions in this quarter and savaging the bank often floods the surrounding low ground as well as polluting the Pool. The Pool is well stocked with mullet which find their way in, remain for breeding purposes and leave again. A number of moody cows can usually be seen near the Pool, tethered presumably to prevent them from straying on to the beach and rocks. In the vicinity of the Pool there are some farm buildings and houses, Pool Farm, but farming in this part is a precarious business. Regularly the fields are under water, when spring tides are whipped inland by high seas, and cultivation is becoming increasingly hard.

Timmy's Hill separates Pool from the eastern side of the island and the harbour: the top of Watch Hill can always be seen, as can the island of Tresco across the water. On the southward slope of Timmy's Hill is the school, the pride of the Bryher men. And rightly so, for like their Agnes comrades who built their road, they constructed their own school. Originally schooling was carried out in the church vestry, while sometimes the children went daily across to Tresco school; later Major Dorrien-Smith provided for a Bryher school. In 1950 the island men agreed to erect a more modern building if the materials were provided. At low water on a spring tide over 7,000 concrete blocks were shipped across the channel from Tresco. Then sand, water and stones had to be carted from the shore. Cement was mixed by the hundredweight, foundations were laid, the building brought ashore section by section and within forty-eight hours the Bryher men had completed their new school.

The Ministry's dealings with Bryher over the school are amusing and perhaps illustrate how dangerous it is to approach Scillonian affairs with a mainland mind. An asphalt playground was a regulation "must" for a school said the white-collar administrators of Whitehall and ruled Bryher should be no exception. Protests were made that a fine natural playing ground of beaches, rocks and foreshore were already at the disposal of the children, but to no avail. It was not until the late Mr. George Tomlinson came to the island and sized up the situation first hand that the red tape ruling of London was waived! Bryher's tiny band of children (they number under ten!) have as fine a Primary Education as any in the country—as do the children on all the inhabited off islands of Scilly. The absurdly-small numbers spell a large degree of personal attention, in some cases almost amounting to private tuition.

South of Gweal Hill is Stinking Porth, and all around this area

great granite carns are bearded by grey and green lichen sometimes inches long. A small carn divides Stinking Porth from Great
Porth, or Par. On the bank bordering this beach are the remains of
the old gig shed from which the epic rescue of the *Deleware*
survivors was planned and put into operation. At high water on a
spring tide once the shed was flooded and the gig floated bodily
out through the shed doors. All round this shed the depredations
of the sea are obvious. Wholesale flooding is a relatively common
thing these days, and it was not so very long ago that the local
schoolmaster, complete with seaboots, was desperately caulking
up the doors of his house as the sea advanced.

Approaching the southern extremity of Bryher, Heathy Hill
is reached, with Stony Porth adjacent. As the name of the latter
suggests, the shore consists largely of stones and pebbles, all
rounded and smoothed by the western seas. The next bay in this
much indented western coastline is the already discussed Rushy
Bay, which gains its name from the fringes of rushes which
border the beach. Rushy is one of the most delightful spots on
Bryher. Although generally in keeping with the rugged, exposed
character of this flank of the island, Rushy can be calm and peaceful. The rushes of the bay hold a story. When Augustus first came
to Scilly in the 1830s he quickly appreciated the dangers inherent
in the march of coast erosion. So near the sandy shores of Tresco,
Bryher and St. Martin's he grew rushes, marram grass and even
the long-rooted mesembrianthemum which held and bound the
sand, in some measure compensating for the loss of eroded land.
Rushy Bay on Bryher provides a good example of the Lord
Proprietor's wisdom. The coast area of Bryher in this quarter has,
contrary to popular belief, actually increased over the years
through windblown sand anchored by rushes and marram grass
and nullifying the loss of coast by the western elements to the
north.

Rushy Bay lies to the seaward side of Samson Hill, the most
southerly eminence of Bryher. Just as Gweal Hill faces on to
Gweal island, so does Samson Hill face on to Samson island.
Samson Hill is perhaps the most attractive of Bryher hills. Coated
in the usual mixture of gorse and granite carns, at certain times in
the year it is carpeted in foxgloves, bluebells, broom, campion and
other delightful plants. Also Samson Hill boasts some fine barrows
of megalithic times, one in particular being outstanding. At the

foot of its southerly slopes are rows of flower patches. From the top of the hill, 138 feet above sea level, as good an aspect as that from Watch Hill can be gained, especially prominent being North Hill on Samson and the Norrad rocks, with steep-sided Castle Bryher particularly impressive.

Samson Hill occupies the south-east corner of the island and now the more sheltered south side of the island is reached. Across the water can be seen Tresco and its dazzling strand of Appletree Bay, with the Abbey Garden's trees atop. A few minutes' walk takes one along the shore of Southward Bay, and with the "island" rounded, Bryher island has been circumscribed in little more than half a day.

Like the inhabitants of Agnes, the Bryherite has the island life in the blood. The trappings of existence across the Roadstead at St. Mary's is not missed overmuch. Most houses have television; there is a reading room, built in 1936, with a billiards table; whist-drives are held fairly regularly and a communal plant provides electricity for four or five houses; Tresco is a few hundred yards across the water with its pub and its wider circle of social acquaintances. True islanders, every Bryher person, regardless of sex, knows how to handle a boat, whether it be propelled by outboard or by oar.

Although the Bryher man is generally content with his lot, whether it be fishing or growing flowers, the retired person, and above all the teenager finds life rather too limiting. Living in a small community and seeing the same faces every day is all very well and breeds a wonderful community spirit (as evidenced by the building of the school and the voluntary repair work to church and roads), but today's youngster thirsts after wider horizons and this problem could well provide the initial impetus to a trend towards depopulation which, I fear, must come one day.

Meanwhile life on Bryher is as lazy and sleepy as anywhere in the British Isles. The same pattern and routine is adhered to every day, the same people seen, the same acts unconsciously repeated. The pace quickens somewhat with the coming of the tourist season when Bryher people follow the general Scillonian pattern of "taking in" visitors. A number of them let out cottages and chalets. But nothing out of the ordinary ever seems to happen. One islander to whom I was talking a number of years ago spoke excitedly of the time when a Jenkins household caught fire; help was gained from Tresco from across the water to add to the Bryher firefighting force who had turned out *en bloc* to quell the inferno. The high spot saw the arrival of the St. Mary's fire brigade, headed by its unpaid fire officer, with a number of its members wearing very unregulation football kit and boots, having been summoned from the Garrison soccer pitch while an inter-island match was in progress.

But to my question: "What was the most memorable event in recent years?" my Bryher friend without hesitation replied, "The *Mando* wreck." As was noted earlier this Panamanian steamer foundered on the Golden Ball ledge one foggy night back in 1955, and the Bryher men played a major part in what was one of the last wrecks of any importance in Scilly. Every Bryher islander that night knew something was amiss for they could hear the repeated blasts of the ship's siren as the *Mando* felt her way north of the island. When the siren sounded continuously, they realized, as do all versed in the ways of the sea, that something was wrong. A rush was made for the gig, and the Bryher crew pulled their way through the treacherous rocks and thick fog out round the back of Bryher. Half-way between Shipman Head and the Golden Ball, they met the St. Mary's lifeboat *Cunard* which was returning from the *Mando* with all her crew and with two ship's lifeboats in tow. A message had already been passed to Bryher post office that help was needed to find the mouth of the New Grimsby Channel, obliterated in the dense fog. Two Bryher men hastened up to Shipman Head armed with flashlights and lanterns, and the rescuers and rescued nosed down the channel. The gig took the lifeboats to Bryher while the *Cunard* proceeded to St. Mary's with the rescued crew.

Such exciting incidents are chewed over for many a winter, and help to break up the set way of life which at times can become tedious.

Apart from the *Mando* wreck events, 1955 was the first year that Bryher was hit by election fever. Prior to that year Bryher always had two very cut and dried representatives for the island's two seats on the Isles of Scilly Council, but in 1955 four people contested the seats in the "municipal elections". Polling day dawned rough. When the St. Mary's official, plus special constable, arrived at Bryher, green seas were breaking over the "island" quay. The launch skipper informed them they would have to leave at 4 p.m. at the latest because of tides, otherwise they would have to stay the night. This presented a problem, as regulation polling hours stretched from 8 a.m. to 8 p.m. The four prospective candidates were consulted and it was agreed that polling time should be limited, if possible, to allow the boat to catch the tide back to St. Mary's.

By 3.30 every Bryher voter had polled, barring five—two of which were on the mainland on holiday and two in mainland hospitals. This left one person to be accounted for. He was a Jenkins living on Tresco, but still under the Bryher electoral umbrella. A phone call was made across the channel, the person concerned announced his apathy to the whole affair and the poll was complete. The door of Bryher reading room was locked and the four candidates and special constable looked on as the presiding officer turned counter to assess the votes. Then the hard-worked official, undertaking his third role, left the room, and as returning officer announced to five people, two children and a donkey that so-and-so had been duly elected—and made the boat on time.

The big question which hangs heavily over what may seem to an outsider an idyllic existence on Bryher is the future. The present population is under fifty; not very many years ago it easily topped the hundred and had a thriving public house, the Victory Inn, to boot. Imperceptibly families, alas, even the Jenkins, are drifting away to the more favourable circumstances of St. Mary's, two well-known and long-established Bryher families having moved there in recent years. There is also talk of a return to the old education system, whereby Bryher children are ferried across to Tresco school.

Most, if not all the inhabitants of Bryher are farmers. There are, in fact, eleven farms on the island, while there used to be over thirteen. As the area under flower cultivation does not exceed thirty acres, the average Bryher man has to make do with just seven or eight acres, if he is lucky. Most farms consist of three to four acres. These meagre small-holdings coupled with the fact that the islander is not benefiting from the tourist influx to the extent that his St. Mary's compatriot is could unite to turn the drift away from the island into a full-scale evacuation.

Bryher might be the "Pearl of Scilly", as Kay said in *Isles of*

Flowers—for us looking in—but its inhabitants have their obvious problems. However, I will only concede that the worst has happened when I walk along Rushy Bay or over Heathy Hill and in the course of my travels fail to meet a Jenkins!

IX

TROPICAL TRESCO, THE GARDEN OF SCILLY

Across New Grimsby Channel from Bryher lies the undoubted celebrity of Scilly, Tresco. Celebrated on account of its world-famous sub-tropical gardens which flourish in the south part of the island; celebrated because of its long and happy association with the Dorrien-Smith family who first leased the island from the Duchy in 1834 and still continue in that capacity. Throughout history Tresco seems to have been the "favoured" isle of Scilly.

In very early times it was chosen above all others as a retreat for Christian hermits; later the monks of Tavistock established their priory there, not, it must be noted, on the larger St. Mary's. In comparatively modern times Tresco was once again singled out by Augustus Smith, who on taking up the lease of Scilly, broke the tradition of a St. Mary's based authority, and decided Tresco should provide the site for his home. To Scillonians Tresco is still synonymous with authority even if it is these days through historical association rather than reality.

If I were asked to name the most striking factor about Tresco island I would be hard-pressed not to reply, once again, contrast. This word, so applicable to every quarter of Scilly, is as relevant to Tresco as Bryher, St. Mary's or Agnes. But whereas the biggest physical differences contained by these last-named islands are natural ones, those of wildness and bareness on the one hand and seclusion and tranquillity on the other, those on Tresco are largely artificial and to a degree not a difference born of nature. The north and west side of the island is bleak and wild, the south side very much the opposite because of plantations of fir trees which allow tropical plants and lush vegetation to flourish away from the depredations of the cruel Scillonian winds. The rapid transformation from the bare exposure of Castle Downs to the arbored seclusion of the Abbey Gardens, in a matter of a few minutes, is bewildering.

Tresco, however, is the most naturally sheltered of Scilly's islands. It is flanked by Bryher in the west, by St. Helen's, Tean, St. Martins and the eastern isles in the east. Augustus Smith realized, when taking up the lease, that despite these God-given advantages more shelter was needed if his passion for delicate sub-tropical plants was to be satisfied. So he planted belts of Cypress and tall Monterey pine from California. Today they dominate the southern part of Tresco, and make it easily the most distinguishable isle in the whole archipelago. From Hugh Town Tresco's garden end only is seen, the southern tip thickly wooded and vegetated, and it is often difficult to realize that beyond this sub-tropical part the island changes to an elemental bareness which rivals even the western parts of Agnes and the north of Bryher.

Tresco is the second largest island in Scilly, being just over half the size of St. Mary's. Containing about 200 people it has by far the largest off island population in Scilly. Yet even on Tresco the drift from the off islands is noticeable. A decade or so ago the population stood at well over 200. Numbers are boosted by the influx of seasonal workers, but when they leave things revert to normal.

Lieutenant-Commander T. M. Dorrien-Smith leases Tresco from the Duchy and a number of the island's inhabitants either work in the Abbey Gardens or the estate farm. The remainder, all his tenants, farm their few acres for the cultivation of flowers, are concerned with the Island Hotel situated at Old Grimsby harbour, or run the island's few shops.

There are three quays at Tresco. One at New Grimsby harbour, the island's main landing ground and the site of Tresco's capital settlement of New Grimsby, one at Old Grimsby on the opposite side of the waist, and one at Carn Near, the most southerly tip and nearest point to St. Mary's.

New Grimsby is a charming harbour. Fringing the sandy bay is a row of old world granite cottages with wall plants trailing to the ground. At certain times of the year the edge of this bay is a riot of colour with palm trees in the various gardens providing an exotic background. In the centre of this row of cottages used to be Tresco's post office, which in 1966 was moved lock, stock and barrel to a new site near the Abbey farm.

The main road either carries on around the margin of the bay down to the south-side of the island and the Abbey Gardens or turns left across the waist over the hill, through the charmingly named Dolphin Town, to Old Grimsby. The first building encountered is the inn, the only public house on the off islands. This is an attractive little place totally in keeping with the environment. Around its walls is a fine selection of pictures of many of the famous wrecks of Scilly. Most of the drinking islanders and many visitors spend their evenings there, as do many Bryher people, while on Saturdays a boatload of revellers often comes down from "dry" St. Martin's.

Above the inn on the hill overlooking New Grimsby harbour and Bryher in the background is one of the three stores on the island, run by the proprietor of the inn. Adjoining is the Tresco reading room, that communal building so peculiar to Scilly's off island communities. Here whist-drives take place throughout the year, with a special poultry drive at Christmas, and bi-weekly cinema shows.

Opposite the reading room are the premises of the district nurse with a remarkably unclinical-looking waiting room. Ministration to the Tresco sick takes place once a week on a Tuesday, when a St. Mary's doctor comes over by boat. The road meanders down the hill into Dolphin Town, called after the Lord Proprietor, Sir Francis Godolphin. On the left-hand side before entering the hamlet of a few houses is the parsonage, a recently-constructed building and erected largely on the charity of islanders and visitors who raised over 6,000 pounds. Dolphin Town is reminiscent of Holy Vale, St. Mary's. It is low-lying, right in the well of Tresco and secluded by trees. In Dolphin Town is the Tresco Parish Church, St. Nicholas, named after the patron saint of the island. Inside this tiny church one can get some true indication of the close links Tresco has with the Dorrien-Smith family. Windows have been donated by them, and there are a number of plaques commemorating members of the family, and recording to posterity how, within a week, no less than two sons were killed when serving their country during the Second World War. One such plaque says: "At evening time it shall be light; In memory of Robert Algernon Smith Dorrien this window is dedicated by Thomas Algernon and Edith Dorrien Smith."

The track winds from the church past the school green to the bay of Old Grimsby which contains two glorious curves of sand. On the green is Tresco school, which is attended by about thirty children. The Green provides a fine natural playground for the children, but because of its low-lying situation it is often flooded— a typically Scillonian state of affairs. The hamlet of Old Grimsby consists of ten or so houses, a stores, and at Norr'ard the fifty-bed hotel, the first and only one Tresco has ever had. Situated on the north-east corner of the bay, it commands a superb view— Old Grimsby harbour, the isles of Northwethel, St. Helen's, Tean, and the eastern isles. It also has a landing jetty, the private beach of Ravens Porth—and the strands of this particular area of Tresco are second to none in Scilly. The sand is almost pure white, so fine that it trickles through the fingers; the conchologist will find much of interest on Old Grimsby Beach, and especially so on the strand of Pentle Bay further round the southern shore. The bank of Old Grimsby beach is fringed by the characteristic Tresco marram grass, which anchors the sand.

The neck of land between New Grimsby and Old Grimsby (the original name was Grinsey) contains the vast percentage of the buildings of Tresco, and also a number of the islanders' flower patches. The waist marks the line between the island's secluded part and the wild section. North of the neck there is little else but heathland and granite. South are the palms, the firs, the aloes, the cacti of the Abbey Gardens.

Let us explore the northern part of the island, first taking note of the old Blockhouse which stands on the high ground of the southern corner of Old Grimsby harbour above the other beach, Green Porth, and facing across the bay to the hotel. The old Blockhouse is one of Tresco's three ancient monuments, King Charles' Castle and Cromwell's Castle being the others. A small, now granite shell, it contains a gun platform, which commanded the harbour, while the small garrison which manned the Block-house had their quarters in the rear. The date of construction is uncertain, although, as the adjacent Ministry of Works plaque says "There was a blockhouse in existence here in 1554". It is possible that the blockhouse opposed the Parliamentary landing in the Civil War.

From secluded Old Grimsby the coast climbs up over the gorse-covered and granite outcrop of Porth Mellon carn to the promon-tory of Merchant's Point, on whose slopes some tiny palm trees are in their infancy. Merchant's Point divides Old Grimsby har-bour from the more northern bay, Gimble Porth. From this carn the difference between the sheltered Old Grimsby location and the open north can be appreciated. In the south the water is often like silk, land-locked on all sides. North of Merchant's Point the northerly swell is always evident. There is a continual surge with the sea boiling white as it washes over the long and dangerous Golden Ball reef, which joins the Golden Ball rock with the north of St. Helen's isle. Gimble Porth, however, is one of the few sheltered parts of this northern promontory. Dense patches of rhododendrons crowd the banks of the bay and in season provide a fantastic contrast with the ultramarine of the sea. In the back-ground of this bay are plantations of *pinus insignis*, which go a long way to making Gimble Porth more secluded and providing a break so that the lush vegetation can grow.

Out of Gimble Porth the landscape turns barren and spare, and continues so round the whole headland almost to the back of the jetty in New Grimsby. Like on the adjacent headland of Bryher, there is very little soil in this quarter, which is known as Castle Down. Granite and heather have the tract to themselves, with rock in many places showing through the soil. Anything but a fertile area.

The northern shores of Tresco are very indented and hollowed out where the sea has made inroads—and in this rugged quarter is the famed Piper's Hole, a subterranean passage which goes about eighty yards into the cliff. At the entrance to the Hole is a jumble of huge boulders worn smooth by the constant action of the sea; the tunnel leads to a tiny underground lake, which can be crossed in a punt, although when the water level is high it is difficult to cross this Styx without hitting the head on the roof of the cave. On the other side of the lake, which is formed by fresh water coming through the cliff, is a beach, and thereafter Piper's Hole tapers to its end.

Near the Hole's entrance is a rusty old ring embedded in the grey granite, enough to send the imagination racing on lines of smuggling and the like. However, although it is possible in the heyday of Scillonian smuggling that contraband was stored in

Tresco Abbey Gardens

the Hole, away from the clutches of the Revenue men, and that it was used in Cavalier times as a storage place, the ring has a much more mundane story.

Until recently islanders used to station themselves near the entrance to the tunnel with their punt to show visitors around the Hole, ferry them Charon-style across the lake, and charge them 2s. a time. Business, it seems, was not brisk, and as one of these guides said, "I got browned off waiting all day for visitors to traipse out to the headland, so I packed it in." Nowadays those who wish to explore the mysteries of Piper's Hole have to go it alone. Incidentally the Hole is supposed to be haunted, inhabited by mermaids and joined by a submarine tunnel to its namesake at Peninnis, St. Mary's. . . . One legend of Piper's Hole concerns William Edgcumb who held Charles Castle for the Royalists after the Blockhouse at Old Grimsby had fallen. When all appeared lost, he blew up the castle and was thought dead, but he escaped to Piper's Hole. There he was found by the beautiful daughter of the Roundhead general—and they fell in love. She helped him to escape to St. Mary's, and then to France, and on the Restoration the lovers were married.

Around from Piper's Hole is the most northerly point of Tresco, Kettle Point. The coast is very serrated here. Across the channel to the west is the straggling promontory of Bryher, ending in the outcrop of Shipman Head, while just off the Tresco shore is the Kettle Rock, which even in calm weather is awash. The sea out here tends to be blueish, unlike the green of Old and New Grimsby harbours.

The cliff now turns south down the channel coast. Here and there are pits and holes which could either be megalithic barrows, ruined now by human or natural agents, or signs of tin mining dating from a former period (possibly a legacy of an abortive Godolphin venture). Some of them look as if they are subsidences over what used to be mine workings, or adits, but as geologists now wholly refute the notion that there ever was commercial tin mining in Scilly, it is difficult to attribute this origin to them.

Further along the granite-carned cliffs is the second of Tresco's ancient monuments, King Charles Castle, standing on high ground and commanding a superb view of New Grimsby Channel, Hangman's Island and Bryher across the way. Very little of the former building now remains, but the general layout

13

Round Island and the Golden Ball

can still be appreciated. Built in the early 1550s it was an artillery fort to command the approaches to New Grimsby Harbour. Although designed to give a wide arc of fire it was, like Harry's Walls on St. Mary's, badly sited for the guns, in this instance because of its elevation. Sir Francis Godolphin pointed out in 1600 that the castle could not prevent shipping from entering the harbour "for as it neither discovereth the whole harbour so through the imminent height thereof can make no good shot so steep downwards, and that which is worst, is of so weak form as it cannot be defended". It consisted of two storeys so that two tiers of guns—or more—could be brought into play, and in the Civil War period earthworks were thrown up on the landward side to protect it from invasion from this quarter.

Immediately below King Charles, near Pollock Rock and sited on a tiny isthmus protruding from the rocky foreshore just above the surface of the channel waters, is Tresco's third and last ancient monument, Cromwell's Castle, perhaps the best known monument in Scilly and easily recognizable from any angle. It is a circular granite gun tower which was built in 1651 after Admiral Blake and the Roundhead navy had subdued Scilly and in order to supersede nearby Charles Castle. There are still some markings visible where an external stairway afforded entrance to the first floor. Here were the garrison's living quarters and the magazine, while on the roof were mounted the guns. The present entrance dates from the mid eighteenth century, when a lower gun platform was added.

Cromwell's Castle (Cromwell is himself believed never to have visited Scilly) is in a remarkable state of preservation. At one stage the clay-soiled isthmus was being attacked by the sea, and the foundations of the tower began to suffer. It was feared, in fact, that the castle would be cut off from Tresco. To remedy this the south side of the isthmus has been faced with granite.

Cromwell's Castle is only a few minutes away from New Grimsby and when it is reached the northern bulge of Tresco has been completed. The gently sloping sides of this channel shore ending in Frenchman's Point is coated in bracken and heather and studded with granite outcrops. In the late months of the year the bracken takes on a remarkable reddish colour. The quay at New Grimsby, on which is built the quay shop run by Lieutenant-Commander Dorrien-Smith, was concerned in some publicity a number of years ago. The lessee has to provide for the upkeep of both roads and quay, indeed the general appearance of his island estate, and he decided not unreasonably that there should be a landing charge, 1s. per head (recently increased to 2s. per head) for every visitor who landed on the quay. To the eternal discredit of the St. Mary's boatmen, only minute amounts were forthcoming, despite the fact that thousands of trippers were landed at the jetty during the season. A dispute arose which won national newspaper coverage: the "pirates of Scilly", as they were called, versus a feudal despot of a Lord Proprietor—a Press natural! The boatmen threatened to by-pass the jetty and the toll by landing the visitors on New Grimsby beach under the very nose of the landlord and his quay. Fortunately matters sorted themselves out, visitors now hand over their landing fee, not the reluctant boatmen, and special collectors await the arrival of the St. Mary's launches, either at New Grimsby or Carn Near. People generally appreciate that Lieutenant-Commander Dorrien-Smith has to provide for the upkeep of his enchanting heritage, and that a landing fee is perforce necessary.

The lessee wields over Tresco similar, if somewhat diminished, autocratic powers as his forebear Augustus did over the whole of Scilly over a century ago. But his, like Augustus's, is a benevolent rule. He resolutely refuses to allow cars, camping and the like on the island, a stand which is widely appreciated. As on neighbouring Bryher, the favourite mode of transport is by tractor. Lieutenant-Commander Dorrien-Smith furthers the practice instituted by Augustus—the use of the pony and trap—and dignitaries and friends who stay at the Abbey for some shooting can be seen enjoying this traditional form of Tresco travel.[1] He also opposes the display of garish signs and notices, and apart from direction posts planted by the Ministry of Works in regard to the ancient monuments, there is hardly a sign to be seen. Tresco inhabitants are not allowed to keep dogs, although visitors may bring their animals on a lead.

The road from New Grimsby which leads to the Gardens passes through a silage plant on the southern side of New Grimsby harbour, and the surrounding buildings and sheds are part of

[1] The Queen, the Duke of Edinburgh, Prince Charles and Princess Anne toured the island in this fashion when they visited Scilly in August 1967.

the lessee's farm. These buildings have an interesting link with the 1914-18 war—when a railway all but came to tiny Tresco! The buildings were used by troops operating a sea plane base, and in order to carry materials more easily from the Carn Near landing ground, it was decided to construct a railway. Happily the cessation of hostilities prevented the plans from going through.

Continuing along the south-west shore of Tresco, over Plumb Hill (tiny Plumb island lies just offshore) the beautiful strand of Appletree Bay is reached. Bordered by the ever present marram grass, Appletree's sand is as fine as that on Old Grimsby beach on the other flank of the island, and the only factor which stands between the visitor and seaside perfection is the coolness of the water, a general Scillonian feature.

On the hill above Appletree tower the pines and shelter belts of the Abbey Gardens, first planted in the days of Augustus and providing effective protection for the plants and vegetation beyond. On the hillside above Appletree Point and reached from the Gardens through an avenue of pines is a rough granite obelisk dedicated to the instigator of the botanic wonders of the Garden, Augustus Smith himself. The inscription beneath the weathered monument reads: "In memory of Augustus Smith, thirty-nine years Lord Proprietor of these islands; died at Plymouth July 31, 1872. His remains lie at St. Buryan." Of all the monuments to the memory of Augustus, this is the most appropriately sited, close to his personal creation which so delights thousands of tourists—and on the soil of his beloved Tresco.

Let us leave the confines of the Gardens, more will be said of them later, and struggle through the grassy bank of Appletree on to the Abbey Green. This flat patch of heather-coated ground lies close to the entrance to the Gardens and a few minutes from the Carn Near landing quay. It is the island cricket pitch, soccer pitch (goalposts stand as a nostalgic reminder of Tresco's football days, but now the game has died out) and also the site of the annual Tresco fête.

South of the Green lies Appletree bank and the granite pile of Carn Near from which juts the quay (where landing can be a difficult business when there is a big sea running, as there is no shelter). Above this point once stood Oliver's battery, established by the Roundheads after taking Tresco, and sited for the bombard-

ment of St. Mary's and shipping in the Roadstead. There is little
trace of the battery today.

Looking south across the water is St. Mary's and Hugh Town,
while around from Carn Near with Mare Rock and Figtree Ledge
offshore is yet another Appletree-type strand. Again the mixture
is as before, fine white sand, and grassy banks. This beach is
divided from the next bay, Pentle, by the promontory of Skirt
Island and low-lying sand bars culminating in Tobaccoman's
Point. Pentle is regarded by many as being the finest beach in
Scilly. It is littered with an amazing variety of shells. The northern
point of this bay is Lizard Point, so named because it is on the
same latitude as the Lizard Peninsula in Cornwall.

A few more sandy indentations—Rushy Porth, Cradle Porth
and Cooks Porth—take one to Blockhouse Point and Old
Grimsby and the southern section of Tresco has been covered.
Inland lies Middle Downs and, of course, the Abbey Gardens.

Tresco is still very much Dorrien-Smith land. The very trees
spell out the occupation of the Smiths. To say the island lives under
the shadow of the Abbey would be suggesting something feudal
and oppressive and would be offensive, yet everyone, whether
they live on Tresco or visit it for a day, inevitably become aware
of the Abbey (the core of Tresco), the Dorrien-Smiths and the
traditional role the island has always played in Scillonian affairs.

But times are changed. An example of this was given a few
years ago when the Abbey cook, putting up for one of Tresco's
three seats on the Islands' Council, nearly toppled his employer
from the top spot. As one old Tresco resident said at the time:
"Old Augustus would have blown a gasket!"

The Abbey Gardens. The botanical gardens, which lie in the
southern sector of the island between Great Pool and Appletree
bank, is the *pièce de résistance* of Tresco. As the lone wooded area
in generally treeless Scilly they lay claim to special attention; as a
spectacle for the horticultural peasant they merit attention; as
gardens *per se* they invite the interest of even the most discerning
of botanists. The Gardens proper take in approximately twelve
acres, while the surrounding shelter belts to the north and west
enclose a further two or three acres.

When Augustus Smith arrived at Tresco in 1834 the physical
appearance of the island was similar to neighbouring Bryher, or

Agnes or even the uninhabited isles of Scilly: hardly a gorse covert broke the bare monotony of granite outcrop and heather and bracken run wild. The Hertfordshire squire selected a site near the crumbling ruins of the old Benedictine priory of St. Nicholas for his home. The wilderness of undergrowth was cleared, the present Abbey duly erected and Augustus set about the herculean task of clearing the whole hillside for the purpose of putting his Gardens plan into operation. This was soon done, and the plants which form the basis of the Gardens today were obtained from the Royal Botanic Gardens of Kew.

At this time Scilly's ship-building industry was flourishing and the resultant world-wide travels of island seamen in island-built vessels furthered the infant garden. They brought back rare seeds and exotic plants from various places in the southern hemisphere to add to the Lord Proprietor's steadily growing collection, and since those formative years Tresco Abbey Gardens has never looked back.

Augustus, employing the practical common sense which so characterized his administrative approach to the islands, realized the great need of his plants and shrubs for shelter: without it many of them, which hitherto had not even been attempted in the unfavourable conditions of mainland gardens, would have obviously been unable to thrive. So he planted shelter belts of pine from California which today, over a hundred years later, still dominate the island.

From time to time plants were added by the Dorrien-Smith successors of Augustus as a result of specially planned forays as far afield as South Africa, Australasia and the Chatham Islands: and as the Gardens flourished so its fame spread rapidly. Today they are the delight of botanists and gardeners the length and breadth of the country—even the world—and are appreciated by thousands of annual holidaymakers who, even if they lay no great claim to a specialist horticultural knowledge, can still recognize beauty when they see it.

Maintaining and improving Tresco Abbey Gardens has become a real trial and headache for Commander Dorrien-Smith (and his father before him) and the small army of willing gardeners. Taxation, two world wars and the rising cost of living in the islands played a part in making the running of the gardens virtually impossible without some sort of financial aid: for the

Gardens are a private concern. In 1949, much against the true inclinations of the Dorrien-Smiths, a small entrance charge had to be imposed, reluctantly, but it is indeed an insignificant inconvenience when weighed against so much beauty and originality.

The sandy soil of the garden end of Tresco is strangely fertile and responsive, and this allied to mildness of climate and the general absence of frost in Scilly has, over the years, been the decisive factor in the success of the gardens and the many rare plants it contains. However, the ever-present Scillonian winds are still the greatest enemy, despite the effective shields and breaks provided by the quick-growing Monterrey pine and the wind-hardy Cypress trees. At times when sustained gales savage Tresco and the wind reaches the eighty velocity mark, great holes are torn in the sturdy shelter belts with the resultant irreparable damage to the delicate plants and precious shrubs beyond. The salt borne on the wind is also damaging, and the effects of drought are yet another problem. Scilly's rainfall is low when compared with the mainland—32 inches per annum, and in dry summers many of the garden's valuable plants are lost.

Before the visitor pays his small fee to enter Tresco Abbey Gardens he should be warned against the danger of forming preconceived notions. If he has the conventional English lawn type of image in mind, then he will necessarily be disappointed. But if he goes in with an open mind, ready and willing to be captured heart and soul by what he sees, then he cannot possibly be dissatisfied. Tresco Abbey Gardens are exceptional, very different from any other garden on the mainland of Britain. They do not take on the ordered appearance which are characteristic hallmarks of run-of-the-mill, more mundane creations throughout the country. Many of its plants will only flourish in densely overgrown conditions, and because of this the gardens have a delightful irregularity, an uninhibited suggestion of Nature run wild which is far more arresting and refreshing than its many more tidy counterparts across the water.

All botanists and gardeners appreciate and fully understand the very individual problems tied up with the growing of plants in Tresco Abbey Gardens, but there are a small number of holiday-makers who do not. They unfortunately fail to realize the extent of the botanical feat that are the Abbey Gardens, and the pretentious criticisms are, needless to say, totally unwarranted and usually the products of arrogant ignorance. Recently I heard one such critic lamenting thus: "I could have seen as much at Kew round the corner instead of travelling over 200 miles to Scilly." Perhaps that is so, and I feel inclined to contest it, but he certainly would not have seen many of Tresco's rare plants at Kew. They simply will not grow there. In fact plants which will not "take" there are still being regularly sent to Lieutenant-Commander Dorrien-Smith for they will readily respond to the favourable circumstances of Tresco.

On entering the gardens from the Abbey Green an original *hors d'œuvre* is provided by the Valhalla, the resting place of the gods and goddesses, where a unique collection of ships' figureheads of vessels foundered in Scillonian waters have been assembled in an attractive veranda-type granite building approached across a lawn. These sea gods and goddesses, ashore after sailing the seven seas, are fine examples of wood carving, and hang in an unusual, yet appropriate environment. Littered around are great rough boulders, representing the rocks on which they met their fate; above them is a pebbled ceiling, the undulating bottom of the sea, while the sides of the walls are encrusted with large tropical shells, some of which were in the cargo of a foundered ship. There are twenty-nine figureheads, four Fiddleheads, eleven name and stern boards and other items in the collection which was first started over a hundred years ago by Augustus in connection with the launching of his gardens. The relics, brightly painted and surprisingly lifelike, cover a period of about a hundred years— from the end of the eighteenth century until the "take-over" of steam. Some of the figureheads have unfortunately suffered badly during the wrecking of the vessel they graced.

The Valhalla relics were restored and preserved by the Historic Buildings Council, and recently repaired by the National Maritime Museum of Greenwich. The old paint has been scraped off and restored as close to the original as possible.

Whenever I see these beautiful figureheads, especially one called the "Turk", my mind goes back to the romantic days of sail, to voyages round the Horn and to the southern hemisphere, when this proud figurehead forged through the seas of the world only to end up on the rocks of Scilly and Valhalla.

An unconventional garden such as Tresco's demands an equally unconventional approach: therefore it is as well to wander around it as the whim takes, and not to follow an ordered plan of campaign. The conducted tour, I think, is out—and so is a lay attempt to describe the content of the gardens in these pages. That would be presumptuous. A number of specialists have gone deeply into the subject anyway.

Suffice it to say that there are no less than 5,000 to 6,000 varieties of tree, shrub and plant ranging from species of Australian, New Zealand, Central American, and Chilean origin, to the Norfolk Islands, Yünnan, South Africa, Mexico, to Madeira, Japan, the Canaries, India and China. In one's ramble around the gardens one will perhaps come across an old worn notice to the Scillonian public erected by the prime mover of all the beauty, Augustus Smith. It reads: "All islanders are welcome to walk in these gardens, but are requested to keep to the main walks, not to go up to the house nearer than under the terrace in front, and to abstain from picking flowers and fruit, scribbling nonsense and committing such like small nuisances. Enter then, if it so pleases you, and welcome."

Only the most soulless can be displeased at what the gardens have to offer.

X

ST. MARTIN'S, THE "FRINGE" ISLE

St. Martin's is possibly the least appreciated and certainly the most underrated of all the islands in the Scilly group. One regularly hears criticisms from visitors, and even Scillonians that it is the least interesting, the least attactive of the islands—that, physically, it smacks of the mainland. Indeed it does not have the generally appealing façade of a Bryher or a Tresco. Perhaps the easterly situation of St. Martin's, the nearest inhabited isle to the mainland, has supplied it with a subconscious "on the fringe" separateness; moreover, it can barely be seen from Hugh Town, St. Mary's, is the island most remote from the capital of Scilly and also possesses the most introverted people in the islands. Whatever it is, and it is just something few critics can place, it exists, and is unjustified. St. Martin's may not be an island which provides the initial impact of an Agnes or a Bryher, but its appeal grows on one. It is not an island for undiscerning people; it has a more profound, a more subtle appeal.

St. Martin's is the third largest island in Scilly, possessing an acreage of 552. It is long, thin and bone-shaped and lies four miles across Crow Sound from St. Mary's quay. The island comes into view when the boat rounds Carn Morval Point, St. Mary's, when its entire southerly flank is exposed to view. Three settlements can be seen, one on the westerly end, another in the middle and a third on the eastern part.

The usual St. Martin's landing place is at the New Quay in Higher Town bay. It is called New Quay—although more usually Higher Town Quay or Par Quay—because a little further south is the original jetty now disused. The situation of Higher Town on the hill overlooking the "Par" is strikingly similar to that of the Town on Bryer. The quay juts out from the promontory of Cruthers Hill as does Bryher jetty from the "island" while the seaward slopes of Higher Town hill are rowed with box-like flower fields.

On all the off islands the quay is the important focal point and St. Martin's is no exception to the rule. Here the launches come in the season to collect the flower consignments, deliver the food-stuffs and mail and in summer discharge boatloads of visitors. There is an amusing story attached to St. Martin's Quay. Many years ago it was constructed by islanders, but as the island be-longs to the Duchy of Cornwall the landlords claim it, and, in fact, have undertaken recent renovations. However, one old islander indignantly muttered to me something to the effect that the original boulders used in the construction were taken by St. Martin's folk from below the high-tide mark: therefore immune from Duchy clutches! There is an old saying "easterly winds blow the sovereigns into Scilly", but the reverse happened recently when a gale from this quarter wrecked the quay, tossed boulders around like corks and flooded the flower fields above Higher Town beach.

The road winds up the hill into Higher Town where the greater majority of islanders live, where the Methodist and Anglican churches are located and where the inevitable reading room and post-office-cum-general stores are situated. On the centre of the village green is a little pile of granite called "The Rock" where St. Martin's men of old used to meet to discuss piloting affairs and exchange island gossip—and where today islanders keep a keen lookout for the approach of the Steamship Company launches coming "up channel" from St. Mary's.

The Methodist church is by "The Rock", while just further along the lane is the green-painted wooden post office. Not long ago I dropped in to deliver some cigarettes from the St. Mary's wholesaler. Like other off island post offices the main notice was that concerning the sailing times of the steamer from St. Mary's, but evidently election fever had gripped the island, for on the wall of the stores was the electoral register. On it were seventy-three names, eleven from Lower Town down at the other end of the island, sixteen at Middle Town, and the remainder in the immediate area of Higher Town. It is difficult to accurately assess the population of St. Martin's, for many of the teenagers are going away to or coming home from mainland schools, while some of the buildings are holiday cottages, owned by visitors.

However, the actual resident population probably just tops the hundred mark, a reduction from a decade ago (continuing the general depopulation trend of the off islands), when nearly 150 people lived on St. Martin's.

There is a fine view of this eastern sector of Scilly from the top of Higher Town hill. Below is the bay with as fine a curve of silver sand as anywhere in Scilly; indeed St. Martin's beaches are locally celebrated. Across the water to the east are the eastern isles, seeming close enough to touch—so different from Hugh Town, St. Mary's, when they are vaguely "over to east'ard". The individual isles almost fringe Higher Town bay, giving a secluded lagoon impression, while across Crow Sound is the eastern shore of St. Mary's.

When approaching St. Martin's by boat the main object that catches the eye above the elongated flank of the southerly shore must be a hideous red-and-white banded monstrosity which thrusts itself up rocket-like from the north-eastern high ground of the island. It has no connection with Cape Kennedy, however, and is, in fact, of no more import than a marker, like Agnes lighthouse, the Watch Hill mark on Bryher and Buzza Tower, St. Mary's. Called the Daymark, it was erected in 1683 as a guide to shipping by Mr. Thomas Elkins, who was the island steward of one of the early Godolphin Lord Proprietors. It still bears his initials T.E. and dominates some of the highest ground to be found anywhere in Scilly. It is an ugly and singularly unflattering reminder of a man who did much to repopulate the islands following the days of piracy and lawlessness. (Off this point the *Lafaro* foundered in 1902 after striking the Seven Stones. St. Martin's men launched the Higher Town gig to answer the heart-rending cries, but were driven back by house-high breakers. The next day three bodies were washed up on the beach.)

This north-eastern part of St. Martin's is cast in the same sparse mould of other off island areas: the same wildness, bareness of soil, the same close-clinging heather interspersed with shingle deposits. At times, however, the rough landscape is brightened by birdsfoot trefoil. The area is known as Chapel Downs, sometimes Daymark Downs, culminating in St. Martin's Head. The cliffs around this part are sheer, plunging down to the ever restless northern seas. Daymark Head at 160 feet above sea level, is second only to the 165 feet of Telegraph, St. Mary's, in elevation.

The coast from Daymark around to Higher Town bay, although not quite so indented as most Scillonian coastlines, still contains its faithfully recorded inlets, however small. There are Northward Bight, Southward Bight, a sort of St. Martin's version of St. Mary's. Izzacumpucca in Pope's Hole, Mullet Pool, Carnweathers, mentioned by Garstin in his Hard Lewis poem, Middle Bight and Brandy Point. The coast here faces on to the Eastern Isles, with Little English Island offshore, also Chimney Rocks with the treacherous Hard Lewis Rocks further out. Another bay, Perpitch (originally Porth Pitch and a favourite landing ground on the rocks when tides are against a conventional landing at the Par Quay) takes the shore to English Island Carn, opposite, naturally enough, English Island, and the sweep of Higher Town bay has been regained.

The back of St. Martin's from the Daymark and St. Martin's Head down to the western end is very bare, nothing more than bracken and granite. Not a house or building breaks up the rugged landscape, as islanders, used to living in a world of winds, have chosen the more hospitable southerly slopes for their homes. Going down the back end of St. Martin's the shore plunges from the granite mass of St. Martin's Head into the charmingly named Bread and Cheese Cove. In keeping with all the northerly shores of Scilly weed-covered rocks predominate with sand at a minimum. Even in fine weather the swell has stirred the sea into an unpleasant murmur. Offshore are the vicious Tearing Ledges, usually a mass of boiling white—dangerous ledges over which two unsuspecting Americans a number of years ago sailed their yacht— to the horror of St. Martin's people—and somehow lived to tell the tale.

This sector of St. Martin's, especially the part near St. Martin's Head, is much favoured by the sea gulls. They inhabit every crevice of the rock-fissured headland. Under the sheer overhanging cliffs of Bread and Cheese Cove and above the boulder-strewn high-tide mark, is a small area of typically white, powdery St. Martin's sand. The adjacent rock indentation is Stony Porth, similar in name and nature to its Bryher counterpart, and Burnt Hill. This eminence was again swept by fire in 1947 and signs of ancient walls characteristic of Iron Age cliff castles, were bared.

Further round from Burnt Hill is Bulls Porth, and nearby

Culver Hole, an eroded tunnel above which, until recently, the cliffs met to form a roof. The promontory of Burnt Hill ends in the inevitable outcrop adjacent to Murr Island, so called because once the rare Murr bird nested there. Near at hand lie the dangerous Santamana Ledges.

Still further bays or, in Scillonian parlance, pars, take the shore to the small promontory of Turfy Hill and to Wine Cove. At Wine Cove the general northern pattern of rocks gives way delightfully to a refreshing expanse of sand in one of the most impressive strands in the whole of the Isles of Scilly—St. Martin's Bay, my favourite beach. Few, if any, island northern shores have such a majestic sweep of powdery sand as the two bays, Great Bay and Little Bay, which go to make up the beach. This part of St. Martin's is as unspoilt as anywhere in Scilly. The curve of the bay is fringed with high marram grass while the slopes above, mischievously called "The Plains", boast nothing more animate than granite pile and bracken coat. Out to sea there is nothing, although on a clear day there is the faintest suggestion of Lands End and the cliffs of the mainland.

In the waters of St. Martin's bay are Great Merrick Ledge, Mackerel Rocks and Little Ledge of Mackerel Rocks, while adjoining the westerly curve of the beach is White, pronounced "Wit", Island. This is not an island at all at low water, as happens so frequently in the shallow-watered, sand-barred area of Scilly. A causeway of boulders joins the island to St. Martin's near a remarkable rock pile called Top Rock. The latter, which marks the western end of the beach, towers up steep-faced and scarred and its weird shape is said to date back to the eighteenth century when it was shattered by a thunder bolt.

A word must said *en passant* about White Island, which should not be confused with the smaller White Island off the back of Samson. The St. Martin's version is one of the largest uninhabited isles of the group, and at one time was a favourite centre for the burning of kelp. A few remains of some of the pits can be seen. White Island has two points of interest, some holes or tunnels called Chad Girt and Underland Girt. Neither of them go inland very far, Underland penetrating little more than sixty feet, yet a local legend tells of a dog vanishing and reappearing undaunted in Piper's Hole across at Tresco. . . . People should beware of visiting White Island because the tide "makes" deceptively quickly and there is always a danger of being cut off. The names of some rocks off White Island deserve a mention—the old favourite Shag Rock and the Baker and Brewer.

Round from White Island bar the northern isles and rocks of Old Grimsby Channel heave into view, Pernagie, Lion Rock, Black Rock, Plumb Island and the lighthouse-topped Round Island. Facing Pernagie is the St. Martin's area known as—Pernagie—with the adjoining bay of Persile or Persyle. One will not find either of these names on the map, only Porth Seal, which gives a clue to the corrupting abilities of the Scillonian. South of Persile is the delightful Tinklers Hill, delightful because it faces on to one of the most beautiful aspects in the entire archipelago. Offshore, divided by the narrow Sound, is the island of Tean, so much more familiar now than from Tresco's Old Grimsby across the channel. Alongside is Pednbrose, with St. Helen's in the background. The backcloth to this delightful setting, heightened by the blue of the channel waters, is the great white curve of Pentle Bay on Trescoe, and the pine belts.

On leaving Tinklers the uncultivated northern area is left behind and the track takes one into the quiet seclusion of one of the island's three settlements, Lower Town. Nestling into the southern slopes of Tinklers Hill with a row of flower patches between it and the waters of St. Martin's Flats, Lower Town is an enchanting hamlet.

I recently walked all round the northern shore of the island from Brandy Point down to Pernagie, and after rounding Tinklers decided to drop in on a friend in Lower Town. It was a March day when Scilly topped the national sunshine charts and when the level of the surrounding seas was as low as I had ever seen. It was low water on the lowest spring tide of the year, and St. Martin's Flats, a shallow one-mile expanse under normal circumstances, was an area chequer-boarded with sand bars. The colours will forever live in my memory. The sea was blue, violet and green in patches and where the sand bars showed through there was a rainbow suggestion of white, yellow, even pink. Many writers have gone into rhapsodies about the colours of the seas around this quarter of St. Martin's. Those of that particular day could not have been surpassed.

As plaice speared that very morning on the Flats sizzled in the pan, my Lower Town friend, a St. Martin's Goddard, told me that on a similar tide he once walked to Tresco, then on to Bryher, and could have made the return journey on foot had he not met a Bryher Jenkins on the beach and entered into a time-wasting conversation. He wore thigh-high waders, and made the spec- tacular crossing by walking straight out over the Flats to Guthers Island, in mid-channel, and then turning due west into Pentle Bay. This story gives one some idea of the shallowness of these Flats (could this sea-claimed area have been the Lost Land of Lyonesse?) and why boats have not enough water to land at the beach below Lower Town or even at the Old Quay. That was one of the main reasons for building the jetty at Higher Town where, at any rate, there is some semblance of water at low tide.

On that lovely day when I surveyed the breathtaking view I readily appreciated how all this area was once land joining St. Martin's, the eastern islands and the Old Grimsby Channel island group into one whole. In 1968 the St. Mary's Chaplain tried a crossing at low water from St. Martin's to St. Mary's. He had to swim the last few yards.

But he had proved his point, and the lay boatman navigating this area in these conditions is likely to get himself into trouble unless he is very careful.

Apart from farming their flower patches which hug the south shore in rows from Lower Town to Brandy Point (the average acreage of island holdings is ten to twelve) many St. Martin's men indulge in part-time fishing, sometimes sending their catches to Newlyn market. They pot, and fish for mackerel, but the presence of mullet on the westerly shores of the island turned their thoughts elsewhere. Two brothers one night landed no less than 700 in Lawrence's Bay, near the old quay. Apparently the Bryher mullet men had been closely watching the movements of a shoal for a number of days, and just as it looked as if their luck was in and the shoal was entering Bryher waters, a seal scattered them. They must have then made their way up New Grimsby Channel, around the Kettle and Tresco Head and down Old Grimsby Channel and that was where the St. Martin's men got in among them. The following day there was a phone call from Bryher to conduct a fishy post mortem. Ever since then a friendly rivalry has existed between the mullet fishermen of St. Martin's and Bryher.

The road (the S.M.1 as my friend humorously called it, and

humour plays a large part in the approach to island life) leads along the southerly shore to Town number two, Middle Town, a hamlet which comprises a few flower-packing sheds and cottages. Up the hill from Middle Town and down the other side is the island school, which provides for ten children and is set near the beach and bordered by the ever present flower fields.

The roads of St. Martin's deserve a mention, they have an Agnes look and indeed their circumstances of construction are very similar. Parts of them have been concreted by the islanders themselves who put aside a week a year for that purpose. At the end of 1969 the road improvement programme was completed with Higher Town and Lower Town being joined. What a splendid example of a community pulling together for the common good! These attempts to improve St. Martin's roads have no doubt been prompted by the presence of a fleet of tractors, vans and Land-Rovers which currently lurch and rumble around the island. Improbable as it may seem, there was a road accident on St. Martin's. Two men were involved in a collision on Par Hill when one was going to the quay and the other returning. Happily no one was hurt.

Until fairly recently driving tests were held on the island. One islander passed his test (who could fail, taking into account the total lack of traffic, signals, and crossing) and the very next week hired a car on the mainland when the Scilly cricket team went over on tour. When the match at Truro was due to start he, and indeed half the off island contingent who were his unfortunate passengers, had not turned up. An hour or so later a pathetic object limped into the ground, its front grotesquely stoven in. They had had a crash. No more tests are conducted on St. Martin's these days.

One other story, while on the subject of island vehicles, was it so long ago that I read in the local *Scillonian Magazine* that "the wedding party was conveyed to and from the church by Mr. So-and-So's van?"

Along from the school is Lawrence's Bay and the old jetty. A circuit of the island has now almost been completed. The eminence of Cruthers Hill stands in the way to Higher Town quay and the par.

Like many of its island colleagues the small St. Martin's community is suffering gradually and imperceptibly from the drift

14

St. Martin's Bay, with White Island off-shore

malady. However, most islanders are happy with their lot. They are men and women for the most part born and bred to off island life and are contented. Communal activities and reading room pursuits have largely died out in the face of television, which the majority of St. Martin's houses possess. It is an incongruous sight, the television aerials set against the backcloth of Daymark Downs.

Apart from farming, islanders take in visitors, a must to provide an all-the-year-round income, and this leaves little time for sports and recreation. Cricket used to flourish on one of the two St. Martin's pitches. One on the top, overlooking St. Martin's bay, had a concrete wicket, which today has been largely claimed by the encroaching gorse; the other on the Green beneath Higher Town and alongside the Par beach was, the last time I saw it, a fully fledged lake.

When I arrived at Par Quay from St. Mary's on that beautiful March day the tide was at its lowest ebb. At first the boat could not get alongside. She made several abortive attempts, going astern and then coming full ahead in order to drive in over the sandbars and shallows. The sandy bottom soon became churned up clouding the clear water, but we eventually got close enough to land. When I left later in the afternoon the tide had turned and was flowing with a vengeance. Just before the St. Mary's launch arrived the Steamship Company boat had been alongside taking aboard flower boxes. A veritable fleet of vans and tractors had appeared from nowhere, having trundled along the St. Martin's lane from Higher Town, Middle Town and all points west, through Pound Lane and Elbow Lane, past Barnacle Rock to put the precious cargo aboard.

The launch got stuck on the bar, hard and fast, and inter-island gossip was pleasantly exchanged by crew and the small knot of men on the jetty as they philosophically waited for the rising tide to lift her off. In similar low-tide conditions the late Willy Howard Jenkins, for many years boatman to the Dorrien-Smiths, countered the observation "not enough water" with the classic "Plenty of water about, but the bottom is too near the top!" A little later we, too, were away down channel with an astonishingly different aspect before our eyes. As the big spring tide neared its peak the network of bars were covered and all the rocks obliterated. No longer could one walk from English Island Carn to Little Gannilly in the eastern isles; no longer could

Guthers with its castellated rock pile be reached; an attempt to cross to Pentle Bay would have had to be put off for another few months. It was a totally changed aspect.

As we came in along the St. Mary's shore and skirted Bar Point I looked back at St. Martin's stretched out lazily in the afternoon sun and thought how absurdly ill-founded and superficial were those criticisms of the island. St. Martin's is different, yes, but all of Scilly's isles are different; uniformity is not a Scillonian characteristic. "Uninteresting" and "mainlandish" cannot be fairly linked with St. Martin's.

The words of a local island poet seemed particularly appropriate when applied to the island at that moment: "St. Martin's long flank dreams up the Sound".

XI

UNINHABITED ISLES

Samson. Everyone loves a desert island. There is something irresistible in its splendid isolation and its appeal to the primitive in man, especially so in these modern days of mechanization and conformism. Scilly is no different from any archipelago the world over, save for the fact that it is blessed with a hundred desert isles to satisfy the "return-to-nature" escapist.

But by tradition one island takes pride of place, and that is Samson, by far the largest of the uninhabited islands, situated south of Bryher and just under two miles across the Roadstead from St. Mary's. It must be stressed straightaway that the island is tiny lest the name Samson, with its biblical suggestion of size, misleads. Samson is made up of only eighty acres and a ramble around its coastline takes little more than half an hour!

Despite its lack of inches and relative proximity to St. Mary's, Bryher and Tresco, Samson compares favourably with any Juan Fernandez or storybook image of the perfect desert island. In the summer it is a confused jungle of briar, bramble and green bracken. At other times it is a vivid carpet of sea-campion, primrose, honeysuckle, bluebells, foxgloves, wild violets and pink sea-thrift. Their scent is heady and they go to make up a riot of colour. Neither building, road nor any semblance of man-made order taints the natural landscape which is given over wholly to thousands of sea-birds who perch in waves, on rock, cliffs and foreshore. The water surrounding Samson is the characteristic deep azure of island seas, and laps strands of fine shell-white sand.

Perhaps the one noticeable departure from the desert island ideal is Samson's treelessness. There are no swaying palms, no lush arboration on Samson, and from a distance the aspect is one of bareness, dispelled immediately however, on getting to close quarters. Many people remark on the lack of trees on Samson as if it is out of character with Scilly, but the fact remains the island is only remaining consistent to the general landscape pattern of the archipelago where trees are the exception rather than the rule.

Samson is straightforward. Just two hills, one 120 feet above sea-level and the other 140. Their names are typical examples of Scillonian logic. In a world where rock frequented by cormorants is called Shag Rock, where a round island is named Round Island and where a weathered rock is called Ragged Island, what could be more fitting and natural than the respective names of these hills based on geographical situation, North Hill and South Hill? These eminences are joined by a sandy, sea-level waist which gives the island the shape of a dumb-bell and which, like the Hugh Town isthmus of St. Mary's is no more than a hundred yards or so across.[1] Two squat hills, looking at a distance like the humps of a sea serpent, a narrow isthmus, the inevitable litter of granite boulders, a tangled undergrowth—there you have Samson—and not even a "noble savage" in sight! Sad to relate, however, there are many money-minded savages just waiting to get their not very noble hands on the island. In recent years a number of attempts have been made to secure permission to build a holiday camp on the island, or a luxury hotel or a caravan site. Happily the Duchy of Cornwall for whom Commander T. Dorrien-Smith holds Samson, realize the value to Scilly of a natural Samson and any such efforts which would inevitably result in the disfiguration of the island have been resolutely opposed. If Samson belonged to a landlord who, unlike the Duchy, did not have the true interests of Scilly at heart, one dreads to think what would happen to the little island.

Samson, like Agnes island with its distinctive lighthouse, is a familiar landmark in Scilly. Its twin peaks with the great granite pile of Castle Bryher showing through above the neck from its position at the back of Samson are unmistakable. Many of the unforgettable sunsets of Scilly occur with Samson providing a delightful foreground.

As is to be expected of a desert isle, Samson has no jetty. To land, the boats pass the miniscule Nut Rock, Stony Island and Green Island and head for the beach on the eastern side of the

[1] The figure-eight shape might have given Samson its name. It has been suggested it derives from the Norse Sammans-on which means the "joined together" island. A legacy of Viking Scilly?

island. When the tide is right at East Porth, as the bay is called, they ground in on the sand and it is an easy matter for people to jump straight ashore. At other times the oft-used Scillonian punt is brought into service to ferry passengers to the beach.

From the East Porth landing ground abreast of the waist of Samson, it can be easily seen that most of these islands to the north of Scilly were once joined. Samson Flats stretch from that island to Tresco, and at dead low water it is possible to wade, chest deep, from one to the other. In these tidal conditions the network of sand bars is bared and at times granite enclosures and tops of walls can be seen, proof of the encroachment of the sea over a once more extensive area.

Under the sandy top soil of Samson's isthmus is fertile clay which once, unbelievably, sustained a population of fifty. Postage stamp size Samson once had as many people as has Agnes today! There are still remains of cottages and walls to bear witness. But living was always of a subsistence standard and even more menial than on the other off islands. Samson islanders used to fish, make kelp, grow corn, corner the occasional piloting job (the westerly situated Agnes got the cream)—but the meagre proceeds from these never dispelled the danger of starvation which lurked continually overhead.

In the eighteenth century Samson was used by the St. Mary's Court of Twelve authority as a sort of Scillonian Devil's Island, or a penal colony for undesirables, and the basis of the small Samson settlement was formed by the banishment to Samson of two prominent St. Mary's families who had incurred disfavour. The story goes that the Webber and Woodcock families got on the wrong side of the Banfields and Mumfords who came to Scilly in the train of the Godolphins and rose to a position of authority in the Court of Twelve. They were ordered to leave their homes and move to Hugh Town, but being independent people they resolved to move lock, stock and barrel across the Roadstead to uninhabited Samson. This was how the island became populated. Gradually the numbers grew, although the standard of living remained abysmal, until at the turn of the nineteenth century fifty people crowded this tiny island.

The reduction of numbers and gradual depopulation of the island started, in a tragic way, in the Napoleonic Wars. One day a small French barque was seen becalmed, drifting with ragged sails out in Broad Sound. Samson islanders conceived the idea of taking her and benefiting by handing her over to the authorities. They rowed out in three boats, boarded her and soon overcame the Frenchman's crew of ten. They then took their prize into St. Mary's Pool and waited upon the commanding officer of the Garrison. On being informed that they would do better to sail the vessel to Devonport, the young men put the older inhabitants off on Samson, and set off for the mainland. But tragedy struck off Lands End. They ran on the Wolf Rock, which at that time was not marked by a warning light. The ship foundered in seconds, taking with her the ten Frenchmen and nineteen Samson men.

The locks of Samson had been shorn and the little island never recovered from this tragic draining of her man-power. Times got harder, the number of able-bodied men fewer, and when Augustus Smith took over the lease of Scilly in the 1830s circumstances were at a nadir, as indeed they were on all the off islands. The new Lord Proprietor in due course saw the hopelessness of a community fighting a losing battle with its environment. He resolved that the island should be depopulated, and the few remaining people (there were five families gaining a bread-line living off limpets and the like) were deported across the water to St. Mary's in the 1850s.

Samson was once again left to the rabbits which warrened the hill-slopes, the seagulls and the sea pinks. As time passed the little cottages nestling into the sides of the twin hillocks fell into decay; the walls made of stones from old gig sheds and built to enclose Augustus' deer herd fell into ruin; the few sheltered patches which were used for the cultivation of corn became overgrown and only piles of limpet shells told the melancholy story.

Soon few signs remained of a one-time hard-pressed settlement that was forever fighting eclipse.

Today there are some St. Mary's folk descended from the old Samson community, and one of the few signs of Samson's populated days are the ruins of a cottage half-way up the slope of South Hill. What remains of this little building is one of the most celebrated of Scilly's antiquities. In the latter years of the nineteenth century the famous romantic novelist Sir Walter Besant came to Scilly to do for Samson what Defoe did for Selkirk's Island. Samson was chosen as the backcloth for his novel

Armorel of Lyonesse and the home of the heroine, Armorel, was, and has been ever since, identified with this tumble-down cottage. Besant's love story has long been out of print, but its magic lives on, spurring thousands of visitors to flock to Samson every summer, just to see Armorel's cottage.

A word must be said of Besant's novel. Although dated by the somewhat stereotyped Victorian style, it is a superb work, and yet another piece of Scilly that lends itself well to the film screen, but as yet its potentiality has gone unrecognized. Briefly here is the plot. Armorel Rosevean is a beautiful, yet untutored teenage girl living on Samson. Two London holidaymakers, an artist and a journalist, get into difficulties in a boat and Armorel saves them from foundering on the Minalto rocks off the south of the island. The artist, Roland Lee, stays on at Samson with Armorel, her great-grandmother and relations for a fortnight and paints the girl. Before he leaves he imbues in the uncultured island girl a desire to see the world, to improve her education, to better herself. Sadly Armorel hears no more of Roland, but when she inherits a fortune from the will of her great-grandmother she leaves Scilly and travels the world. Eventually she arrives in London, an educated, elegant young woman. She has never forgotten Roland Lee, but when she finds him a fantastic change has come over the artist. Hard times have caused him to become an artistic hack who sells his pictures to a villain, who, in turn, resells them as his own. Now it is Armorel's turn to inspire Roland to find his feet and to regain his self respect. He does, denounces his oppressor, and Armorel and Roland return to Samson, the place where they had met so many years before, to settle down and live happily ever after as all lovers should.

Armorel of Lyonesse is a great love story and will never be forgotten in Scilly, even if the cottage which has come to be associated with the heroine crumbles into nothing. But enough of Armorel. Let us batter our way through the undergrowth to the peak of South Hill, or Holy Hill as it is called in Besant's romance, from where a sweeping view of Scilly is gained. Out to the west is the Bishop Rock lighthouse, from this angle utterly dissociated with the islands and seeming "half-way to America". Further around is Annet with the distinctive rock formation of the Haycocks. At the back of Annet only the barest of outline gives any warning of the dangerous Western Rocks. Continuing round is

Agnes and its dominant lighthouse and then St. Mary's. If the *Scillonian* has just arrived and the wind is in the right direction sounds of hustle and bustle drift across the waters of the Roadstead to Samson and contrast strongly with the solitude of this desert isle. When the steamer cannot dock at St. Mary's quay she anchors off Samson at Nut Rock.

The southern tip of Samson, much haunted by gulls, ends in South'ard Wells Point, while further out in the Roadstead lie Tar Barrel Rock and the Minaltos, Little and Great, and Great Minalto Ledges. The most easterly point of Samson is Shag Point with the adjacent two acres of White Island.

The flat waist of Samson immediately invites comparison with the neck of Hugh Town, but there is no reason to forecast invasion by the sea, or that North and South Hills will be separate islands; on that premise half of Scilly will soon be divided, then sub-divided.

On North Hill there are a few remains of burial chambers. One in particular, a great stone box with blocks of solid granite, was opened by Augustus Smith in the 1860s and in it were found some human bones. Anthony Armstrong wrote the following verse about it:

SAMSON RECLAIMED

A group of warriors stand
Guarding the dust in windy chambers
Immortal members
Of a long-lost land.
A kingly clan, towering, chanting
Above Samson's rock-strewn shore
Sinking slowly with the core
And on the wind, lost Lyonesse is singing.

The northern extremity of Samson is Bollard Point with the southern part of Bryher just across the water. Offshore lies Long Ledge and the curiously named Flea Rock, while off the north-east shore is Puffin Island. There are puffins to be seen in Scilly today although perhaps not on the same scale as in former days, when as we saw earlier island rental was estimated in puffins!

Samson island was first made popular by Besant's novel, a popularity that waxed while the book itself waned out of print. It is a favourite place of Mr. Harold Wilson when he comes to

Scilly and its quiet confines have never quite seen the like of the occasion when the Premier held a full-scale press conference there. The island was flooded with newspapermen and cameramen who fired questions of the gravest State importance to Mr. Wilson, while the waters of the bay swished gently on the sands and the bracken and heather formed an incongruous backcloth to the whole affair. Armorel would have been most surprised at this unwonted invasion of her island's privacy.

Samson until recently was the scene of the Carn Thomas school picnic. Boatloads of youngsters go there to ramble to their hearts' content along the shores searching for Portuguese men-of-war, beachcombing, picking winkles off the low-tide rocks to cook over driftwood fires, playing hide and seek among the undergrowth which envelops the slopes of the twin hills. And that is how Samson, or any other desert island should be treated.

There has been talk of bringing the island's thirty-odd cultivable acres under control for the growing of flowers, while one writer even suggested that anyone with the pioneering spirit should take the lease of Samson and would benefit from its fertile, albeit limited acres. Quite probably, but the Duchy and lessee Lieutenant-Commander T. Dorrien-Smith are absolutely right in their insistence to keep Samson untouched by humans, who have an unfortunate habit of ruining everything they touch. The Duchy's stand is generally supported by Scillonians and visitors who understand the dangers of over-commercialization confronting the islands.

Visit Samson by all means, a trip to Scilly would indeed be incomplete without a sortie to the shores of this tiny island. Even hold high-powered press conferences there, but unlike a certain lady marooned there for the night, remember the picking up time and return to St. Mary's, or Bryher or Tresco. Do not camp or caravan there; do not try to build or live there. Do not spoil Samson by harnessing it to human need, or rather, human greed.

The Eastern Isles. An archipelago within an archipelago, such are the Eastern Isles situated between St. Martin's and St. Mary's at the mouth of Crow Sound. If the main inhabited islands form a self-contained group then the even tinier circle of islets with their complementary plethora of rocks on the eastern flank of Scilly outdo them. Here the scale must be further reduced to one of yards and feet, for the ten islets of the eastern group are individually no more than five to seven acres, with the largest, Great Ganilly[1] possessing the gargantuan dimensions of twenty acres. Whoever named the Eastern Isles was prone to hyperbole. There are several "Greats", yet all the islands are minute.

The eastern group are the complete antithesis of their comrades across the Roadstead down beyond Agnes island. They are conventionally beautiful and generally peaceful. Whereas the western group are almost without exception virgin rock, the eastern isles are, as their name suggests, rather islets with grass and vegetation predominating. Consequently, in fine summer weather their brilliant colours contrast vividly with the surrounding sea to provide a beautiful setting. Some of them have sandy beaches, unheard of in the west, and their proximity to St. Martin's blesses them with a friendly, hospitable aura which the individualistic western rocks altogether lack.

Accepted attitudes to east and west are reversed in Scilly. The mystery traditionally associated with the former has become part of the western rocks, while those on the eastern flank, seemingly more of an integral part of Scilly and at low tide mostly joined by friendly strips of white sand, are far more sociable. I remember landing down on wild Gorregan one fine summer's morning. Despite the conditions there was a westerly swell and as always I experienced the loneliness and wildness so characteristic of the western rocks. In the afternoon I jumped ashore on Great Ganilly in the eastern islands and the contrast could not have been more marked. Just across the bar-bared water were the flower fields of St. Martin's nestling into the slopes of Higher Town Hill, and while Hugh Town could not be seen, the promontory of Bar Point, St. Mary's was comfortingly close. All around was verdure and colour.

The very names of the Eastern group are charming and suggestive of beauty of outline: Great and Little Ganilly, Great and Little Innisvouls, Great and Little Ganinick and Great and Little Arthur. How much more pleasant sounding are they than Hellweathers, Crebinicks and Gorregan.

The first of the group touched when crossing from St. Mary's are the Ganinicks. They comprise no more than twelve acres between them, but nevertheless, they are vegetated. At low

[1] "Ganilly" is a corruption of Cornish "Goonhilly", meaning heathland.

water it is possible to cross from one to the other by sand bar, a practice which can be pursued generally throughout the group. The Ganinicks can be landed on if a boatman is in agreement, as can most of the Eastern Isles, but these two have probably less to offer than their fellows.

East of the Ganinicks are the Arthurs, separated from Little Ganilly by Little Ganilly Neck. Little and Great Arthur are actually one island, but the strip joining them is so tenuous that they are classed as separate entities. All rather confusing, but nevertheless something which can be said for the whole group with their Littles and Greats and network of sand bars which one minute makes two islands one, the next the reverse.

Not very long ago Great Arthur was the largest of the group, an honour which now falls to Great Ganilly, but the constant action of wind and water has drastically reduced it. There are the remains of ancient barrows on the island and other signs of habitation. East of Arthur is Ragged Island whose name is self-explanatory.

Dominating the Eastern Islands is Great Ganilly, a sausage-shaped twenty acres, much loved by visitors. This island is quite extensively vegetated for its size and like Arthur still possesses signs of a former habitation. Great Ganilly is similar in shape to Samson, although smaller. It consists of two bulges joined by a narrow waist, a familiar insular shape in Scilly. The northern part of the island reaches the almost Everest height for this low-lying world of 110 feet above sea level. Although its perimeter is rocky, the "interior" is reasonably flat and tillable. The last time the island was inhabited was in the seventeenth and eighteenth centuries when kelp burners used to make it their base for gathering oreweed from the surrounding rocks and ledges. Great Ganilly can be landed on at most times and a view from the top of the Northern hill takes in all the surrounding islands.

North of Great Ganilly is yet another islet which can be attained at low water by a sand bar, Nornour, pronounced Nor-Nor. This islet can rightly claim to be the most famous of the whole group and the one possessing the most interesting history. Up until a few years ago, Nornour with its rocky fringe and small expanse of overgrown bramble and fern was little respected. The greatest thing it had ever done was to have given its name to a celebrated Steamship Company launch. Things are now very different following the discovery of the remains of ancient huts containing Bronze and Iron Age pottery and several Roman coins, brooches and figurines. The site was bordering the very beach and sea and as people would hardly build so close to the water, it is obvious that Nornour was once considerably larger. Archaeologists, the Ministry of Works and other bodies greeted the Nornour find with enthusiasm and digs led to the unearthing of much valuable data. And so Nornour now finds its miserable five acres very much on the Scillonian map.

South of Great Ganilly lie Great and Little Innisvouls, six and four acres respectively. They are divided from Menewethen by a neck of that name. It was on these bars and near the Mouls rock that the islanders of Tresco and St. Martin's used to haul their seines of old. The sea around Menewethen has a celebrated undertow, known in Scilly as the race of Menewethen. The rock is perhaps one of the Eastern Islands most impressive, thrusting up out of the sea in a particularly precipitous fashion. It is favoured by the sea birds and it is also rare not to see a seal around its base.

Further to the east and on the edge of the island group are the half-tide Hard Lewis Rocks, immortalized by Crosbie Garstin in the words: "Twice daily triumphant, twice daily outdone." But before one reaches Hard Lewis there is the conicle Hanjague, a pile strongly suggestive of the Norrad rocks. Hanjague is truly scarred and criss-crossed by the weather and rises abruptly out of the sea. It appears out of place in the friendly Eastern Isles, more fitted for companionship with Scilly Rock or Castle Bryher. It serves as an unmistakable landmark for those approaching Scilly, while there is much good mackerel fishing in the area.

The friendly Eastern Islands are surrounded by waters which at times can be tricky for the inexperienced sailor. There are a number of ledges and reefs lurking in the channels, notably Irishman's Ledge, Southward Ledge, Tonkins Ledge and yet another Shag Rock.

Recently I went potting off the Eastern Islands and the back of St. Mary's with a Hugh Town fisher friend, Mr. George Symons. It was a drowsy summer's morning with the promise of a hot day to come when we chugged out of a pond-like St. Mary's Pool and rounded Carn Morval point below the sixth tee of the golf links. St. Martin's looked asleep, stretched out in the blue water. Ahead shimmering in the heat haze were the Eastern

Islands, inviting and attractive. We passed the strangely forted-looking Guthers Island, passed safely over the Damasinnas Rocks (the "Sinners") and cutting inside Menawethan made for Watermill Bay at the back of St. Mary's, where we hauled two strings.

With pots overflowing the small blue craft and piled one on top of another in a pyramid of wickerwork, we turned and headed back to the Eastern group to shoot the pots afresh off Menawethan. It was a beautiful morning and the tiny islands sparkled like jewels in the so-blue sea. Even the usually impressive, rather than beautiful Hanjague looked friendly and not so austere in the morning sunlight, and perhaps it was a trick of the imagination that made it seem not so aloof from the group proper as it usually appeared.

Suddenly, without warning, a typical Scilly sea mist descended. Within minutes our neighbours Menawethan and the Innisvouls, only a stone's throw away, were no more and we were staring into cotton wool. When these quick mists clamp down to the west of Scilly, apprehension grips the amateur seaman like myself, but somehow in the friendly waters of the Eastern group there was little need to worry. St. Mary's was just across Crow Sound and we could hear the comforting lap of the water against the eastern rocks.

A hoot shook us out of our misty reverie, and there, looming ghost-like out of the fog, was the *Scillonian* feeling her way towards the entrance of Crow Sound and on to St. Mary's Pool. The tide was flowing and she was able to save time by taking the short cut instead of skirting the Garrison and entering St. Mary's Sound. One minute she was alongside causing us to wallow in her wake, the next she had disappeared, as mysteriously as she had come on the scene.

We moved on, threading through the Eastern Islands towards the back of St. Martin's and out to Broad Sound to shoot and haul more pots. Conditions were still "thick as a bag", but it did not matter: these were the innocuous waters of the Eastern flanks ... of Little Ganilly and Little Ganinick ... of Nornour and the Innisvouls.

The Norrad Rocks. True to the Scillonian phenomenon of difference are the Norrad Rocks which lie in clusters to the west of Bryher and Samson and in the north-west corner of the archipelago. They have a shape all of their own. Scarred and furrowed like all the granite bosses in Scillonian waters, the Norrads are notable for their boldness. For them there is none of the treacherous lurking near the surface of the water as favoured by their comrades in the west. They thrust up magnificently into the sky the most distinctive piles in Scilly. That does not mean to say that the area of the Norrad Rocks is free from reefs and ledges; no quarter of Scilly is. But they play a secondary role to the castellated carns of Castle Bryher, Mincarlo, Illiswilgig, Scilly Rock and the rest.

The most southerly of the Norrad Rocks are the two Minaltos, a favourite fishing ground for island potters. Close by lie the Castinicks, vicious reefs with the onomatopoeic name-sound of crashing surf, cymbals and storm music.

North of the Castinicks is the first of the Norrads proper, the black-faced Mincarlo. It is possible to land here, but only when a sea is not running. Perhaps one of the most noticeable characteristics of the Norrad Rocks are their blackness. By any standards granite is a grey, severe rock, but in the Norrads they take on a new austerity. They are black and with the restless sea of the north-west channel boiling around their bases, they look even more gaunt and forbidding than the western rocks.

Like sea-bird haunted Gorregan, Mincarlo is a favourite spot for the shag, and also like the western rock, Mincarlo boasts its own Biggal, a lesser rock lying south. East of Mincarlo ("min" or "men" in Cornish mean rock) lies Bream Ledge, and north is the greater bulk of the Norrad Rocks.

Perhaps the most inappropriate name for a Scilly rock is Maiden Bower. The suggestion of gentle outline and beauty is utterly belied by a cluster of granite carns which stolid and unmoved, have taken the battering of the cruel north-westers, one of Scilly's oldest enemies, and will survive many more. As if the appellation of Maiden Bower is not ludicrous enough, to the west lies an expanse of western rock-like reefs which bear the name Garden of Maiden Bower! Maiden Bower is the most westerly of the Norrad Rocks and its inhospitable garden is bordered on the east by Seal Rock. The "neck" routine of the western rocks is perpetuated here: Seal Rock is divided from the curiously and Celtic-sounding rock of Illiswilgig by Seal Rock Neck, and Castle Bryher Neck separates it from Castle Bryher.

Castle Bryher rises like a tower ninety feet out of the sea. Although Illiswilgig is as wild and gaunt as its name, Castle Bryher is the most striking of the group. Looking from St. Mary's on very clear days it can be seen providing an impressive backcloth to Samson. It is one of the most unmistakable landmarks in Scilly.

The outer and inner necks of Gerwick separate turretted Castle Bryher from Gerwick Rock, and the south-west shore of Bryher island is touched. Near here is Buzza Rock with Buzza Scud close by.

The line of rocks from Mincarlo, stretching through Illiswilgig, Castle Bryher to the Bryher shore form a rocky curtain across the sea to the west of that island. Only a knowledgeable boatman can take his craft in up the flank. When wanting to go around the back of Bryher the menacing Norrad Rocks are generally kept on the starboard quarter.

Past the appropriately named Black Rocks and abreast of the central bulge of Bryher is Gweal Island, its insular classification preventing it from being regarded as the largest of the group. Gweal, apart from giving its name to the adjacent high ground on the west of Bryher, is worth dwelling upon because of its connection with a fine ship which was wrecked on her eight uncultivated acres, on her maiden voyage. A local doggerel writer, Horatio Jenkins, crisply dismissed the disaster in the following four-line stanza:

> The *Award* from Liverpool did sail
> Bound for New Orleans:
> She struck upon the rocks of Gweal
> And went to Smithereens.

Gweal is separated from the Gweal Hill promontory of Bryher by, naturally, Gweal Neck!

North of Gweal is Scilly Rock, the last and best known of the Norrads. It is composed of two distinct piles. Both tower up impressively and are separated by the narrowest of channels. They say it is possible to take a boat through the gap, but the movement in the water makes it a foolhardy operation. The twin peaks of Scilly Rock bear curious names, North Cuckoo and South Cuckoo.

The Islets of Old Grimsby Channel. Blockhouse Point above Old

Samson from St. Mary's

Grimsby, Tresco, is as good a vantage point as any to see the last of the uninhabited island groups, that which includes the quite sizeable—for Scilly—isle of St. Helen's, and Tean, Round Island, Northwethel, Men-a-vaur and sundry other rocks. This little circle of islets and rocks lie like the pieces of a jigsaw puzzle in the channel between the north-east shore of Tresco and the north-west tip of St. Martin's. Until comparatively recently these isles were of little interest to the visitor, and for that matter, the islander, and this despite being more steeped in history than many of their larger neighbours. Pleasure boats tended to keep to set course patterns, to the Eastern Isles, to St. Martin's, to Agnes and the western rocks, to Tresco via New Grimsby Channel.

The recent building of a modern hotel on the shores of Old Grimsby has brought the focus of attention back to this old capital settlement of Tresco, and consequently the eastern channel and its islets find themselves more on the Scillonian map.

This part of Scilly, consistent with nearby St. Martin's Flats and the environs of the Eastern Isles, has, over the years, been much subjected to encroachment by sea. St. Helen's, Tean and their colleagues are shadows of what they used to be in extent and their surrounding waters are networked with sand bars at low water to prove it.

Dominating the group, which surprisingly has never been given a collective name, is St. Helen's, at fifty acres by far the largest in area, also the most elevated and the possessor of a quite remarkable history for such a tiny island. The size of South Hill, Samson, and covered by the traditional Scillonian mixture of rock and undergrowth, St. Helen's is believed to have been, as was noted in an earlier chapter, the home of the Welsh hermit Elid, who was later sanctified and who, legend tells us, converted the Viking King Olaf. In the Dark Ages the island was known as variously "Lide's Island", "Lyde's Isle", "The Isle of Seynt Elid" or "The Island of St. Elidius". St. Elidius, Mr. Sisam points out, was the one well-authenticated Scillonian saint. His feast date, August 8th, was in the medieval calendar of Tavistock Abbey and the hermit was buried on the island.

When the Tavistock monks came to the islands in the early twelfth century they almost certainly built a new church in place of the old chapelry on St. Elidius' island and dedicated it to the former hermit and looked after it. For many years Scillonians

15

The Eastern Isles

visited the church, but in the later days of the monks' occupation when lawlessness and piracy were rife, the little building
began to fall into decay and gradually the undergrowth took
possession.

It was after the departure of the Tavistock monks on the Dissolution that St. Elidius' isle became St. Helen's, and even to this
day there are still faint traces of the former church. In the last war
a fire on St. Helen's cleared much of the undergrowth and exposed
the remains of an oratory, a hut, a church and some walls—parts
of the legacy of the Celtic hermitage and the Tavistock monks.
The structures were all of granite.

Excavations were carried out in 1956 by Mrs. H. E. O'Neill as
a tribute to the late Mr. B. H. St. J. O'Neill who first started
exploration of the site in 1954 for the Ministry of Works. She
found the hut was twelve feet in diameter, at a height of four feet,
and that the oratory was fourteen feet long with thick walls.
Remains of an altar, courtyard and pottery were also found.
Today little of the Celtic hermitage of St. Helen's remains, but
there are other relics which bear witness to a later habitation on the
island. There are a number of walls, and what is left of a Pest
House, where sailor victims of the plague were quarantined. For
many years shipping used to anchor off St. Helen's, whose Pool,
protected by Tean and Northwethel, provided an ideal anchorage.
The Pest House was never actually used.

All these events, the early hermit activity and the later habitation, took place when St. Helen's was considerably larger, and
before the sea had made such devastating inroads. Nowadays St.
Helen's is a delightful back-to-nature isle, with fine rocky outcrops on its north side and with all signs of a former habitation
submerged under a welter of undergrowth.

Whether you stop off at St. Helen's or not, the passage up
channel provides a good view of the impressive rocks to the
northern mouth of which Men-a-vaur is outstanding. Men-a-
vaur competes with the likes of Hanjague, Castle Bryher and
Scilly Rock and for the islands' most imposing rock accolade.
Inevitably Men-a-vaur has been corrupted by some to "Man o'
War", surprisingly apt for not only is the sound similar but also
the mass does appear remarkably like the shape of a fighting ship.
Men-a-vaur is similar to Scilly Rock, three distinct piles being
separated by yawning chasms which look as if they can be navigated.

People are said to have threaded their way through, but when I see the ugly swell I always think of the fabled clashing rocks of Greek mythology, and shudder. Men-a-vaur, as unmistakable a landmark as Scilly and Hanjague, is sternly forbidding rather than attractive. Alongside it are the dangerous Golden Ball rocks joined to the north of St. Helen's by the Golden Ball Ledge of Mando notoriety.

If the northern shore of St. Helen's provides a good view of Men-a-vaur, then a walk around the north-east extremity will bring another imposing mass into sight—Round Island. The latter is well named. A circular conglomeration of black, austere granite surfaced by a layer of top soil, it rises severely 136 feet on all sides to a strange flat table top out of which Round Island lighthouse juts upwards. If it were not for the lighthouse and the admittedly imposing contours of the pile, Round Island would be of little interest for, in keeping with most of the rocks to the northern fringe of Scilly, it is ugly. The lighthouse, attended by a number of keepers' dwellings, makes its presence felt every ten seconds when its "bloodshot eye", as Geoffrey Fyson[1] called it, sweeps the islands; in foggy weather its lonely boom can be heard just like its compatriot's down to the west, the Bishop. In the steep-sided face of the island have been painstakingly hewn a succession of steps, to facilitate ascent by the resident keepers.

Off the southern tip of Round Island, where the sea is rarely still, lie the Camber Rocks. It was in the vicinity of these that a recent visitor thought her boatman looked pale and asked him whether he felt sick. The Scillonian eyed the questioner steadily for a few seconds, then speaking deliberately said, "Sick! When I gits sick you'll be dead in the bottom of the boat!"

South of St. Helen's, separated by Beef Neck, is Northwethel which lies adjacent to Tresco's Merchant Point. The ten acres of this island contain a remarkable number of burial barrows which, allied to decaying hedges and walls, bear witness to a once larger extent and, like on St. Helen's, a former habitation.

South-east of St. Helen's, across a stretch of water known as St. Helen's Gap, is Tean (with the dissyllabic pronunciation of Tee-un) the second largest isle of the group. Tean's forty acres looks something like a stranded starfish on the map, with straggly tentacles of land and rock waving out into the sea just off the west

[1] Poet and former headmaster of Carn Thomas School, St. Mary's.

shore of St. Martin's. Its irregular coastline contains a number of attractive bays and three sandy beaches. North of Tean, connected at low tide by a bar, is Pednbrose, while south is a tiny island called, simply, Old Man. Tean, like its neighbours St. Helen's and Northwethel, has suffered severely over the years from the encroachment of the sea. In the time of Woodley it consisted of seventy acres, today it is much less.

On Tean, formerly Sancta Theona, there are the remains of walls and hedges as on the adjacent isles, while offshore there are a number of submerged structures which were once part of the island before they succumbed to the inexorable progress of the sea. Among the remains on Tean are what is believed to be an oratory, some megalithic graves and a cemetery, which, when excavated in 1956 by students from Oxford, Cambridge and Edinburgh Universities, revealed skeletons dating from the fifth or sixth centuries. Tean was once the home of the Nance family, a well-known Scillonian name, who introduced kelp-burning to Scilly and chose tiny Tean as their base for the foul-smelling operation of burning oreweed.

The waters of this channel around St. Helen's, Tean and Northwethel are studded with rocks and reefs, the main ones being West Broad Ledge, Great Cheese Rock, Crump Island, and considering the number of sunken hedges the aptly named Hedge Rock. Further down towards the southern entrance to the channel are West Craggyellis and East Craggyellis rocks.

As I have said these group of islands are not as well known to visitors as the Eastern Isles or western rocks, yet this channel area to some extent in the friendly lee of St. Martin's and Tresco is one of the most attractive in Scilly in calm weather. On one side is the white sweep of Tresco's beaches from Old Grimsby to Skirt Island, while on the other there is the high point of Tinklers Hill, St. Martin's. When the tide is low the sand bars weave a pattern in the blue sea, and sheltered St. Helen's Pool is delightful. Men-a-vaur stands solemn guard at the northern entrance of the channel. When on St. Helen's or Tean it is impossible not to cast one's mind back and conjecture on the history of these tiny islands. Indeed, Tean has probably more signs of a continuous habitation than any other island in Scilly, ranging from the Bronze Age through to the eighteenth century. However, the individuality which the other Scillonian islands possess is not so marked in the case of the islets of this channel. Perhaps it has been submerged by the neighbouring larger islands of Tresco and St. Martin's.

The great days of St. Helen's, Tean and Northwethel are long gone. No longer do Scillonians flock to Elid's Isle for their spiritual needs; no longer are the skies around Tean darkened by the smoke of burning kelp; Northwethel sleeps with its dead. St. Helen's Pool, once a favourite anchorage, now lies empty. Just a few vessels in Old Grimsby harbour remind one of the days when the channel was the main shipping area of Scilly and bristled with rigging.

XII

THE DANGEROUS WATERS OF TOURISM

Holidaymakers have always been coming to the Isles of Scilly. They came, admittedly in negligible numbers, in the old days when the economic level of islanders was at its nadir and when virtually no provision was made for them and they kept on coming after Scilly had turned the corner and had embarked upon the halcyon era of flower culture. But there were still no signs that the trickling traffic would develop into anything more grand.

Today visitors no longer come in a thin stream, but flood in daily in their hundreds, literally, by both helicopter and steamers. In the summer the population of St. Mary's is doubled and the quaint streets of Hugh Town are congested with holidaymakers going to and from the quay. "Visitors" are not a mere complementary annual feature of island existence any longer: they are fully-fledged, red-blooded industry, certainly the biggest to have hit Scilly since the far off days when flower-growing rescued islanders from the threat of an economic relapse following the failure of ship-building.

From a financial point of view tourism has brought islanders a general and over-all benefit and with a stream of mainlanders moving to Scilly expressly to start guesthouses significantly underlining the boom in the industry, the horizon appears bright for Scillonians. Or does it?

The general level of prosperity which is evident on St. Mary's, even if it is less apparent on the off islands, masks the sort of dangers which invariably accompany tourist growth in a hitherto unexploited seaside resort; dangers which are causing some concern among those whose job it is to plan for the future well-being of both islands and islanders. If tourism threatens to revolutionize the approach to flower-growing in the islands, then Scilly is also faced with the prospect of being altered by the visitor traffic.

That vague evil, over-commercialization, is the major fear. The fate of countless resorts dotted around the perimeter of Britain which were ruined almost overnight by a welter of tourists and by the desire for quick money, must not be emulated by Scilly. And on face value it ought not to be. Being separated from Penzance by forty miles of water it has the quixotic advantage of inconvenient inaccessibility as compared with other Cornish resorts, while in addition its minuteness imposes severe physical limits on the intake of numbers. But these two factors are sadly in themselves not enough to avert the imminent dangers. More room for visitors could easily be created by increased building and development and if this happened too much the main appeal of the islands to the tourist, the natural state, would be threatened.

Apart from the problems of over-development the property speculator is nosing into this island set-up latent with possibilities, attracted by the artificially inflated values resultant on the unbalanced ratio of supply and demand.

Thus, briefly, are summed up the fears and dangers facing the islands. They have come to the cross roads, yet another, in their chequered history, although the crisis fast approaching is this time born of hearteningly healthy circumstances. This is indeed a vital time for Scilly and its inhabitants.

Happily the bodies that matter most, the ones that can prevent Scilly from going the wrong way, are all too aware of the situation, and in the joint hands of the Planning Authority, the Isles of Scilly Council, and the Duchy of Cornwall landlords, the destiny of the islands would seem well assured. The Duchy, especially, can put an effective brake on ill-judged development as they own the vast majority of land. Wise and benevolent landlordism can go a long way towards keeping intact Scilly's priceless asset of its natural state, and they can also scotch the soulless march of the property speculator who, in many cases, is little concerned with the welfare of Scilly.

The inestimable value to the islands of the Duchy as landlords can be well illustrated by the case of the Isles of Scilly Golf Club. Their nine-hole area belongs to the Duchy, who rent it out for the princely sum of 1s. per week! If the golf club's land was freehold property, or indeed, if it belonged to someone with less of the Duchy's excellent brand of generous landlordism, one shudders to think what could happen. In the mind's eye one can see blocks of flats despoiling the natural beauty of the coastline from Carn Morval to Bants Carn. If this sort of thing happened then Scilly would be on its way to becoming just another seaside resort and the tourist industry would be well down the slippery slope towards destroying the very things by which it was created.

In the Duchy there is something of a parallel with the "Friends of the Lakes", a charitable body formed to protect the Lake District from the same fate which could await an ill-guided Scilly. Yes, Scilly's own landlords, whose privileged "outside the law" position irritates so many islanders, are undoubtedly the archipelago's greatest ally, and if their past dealings with Scilly are a pointer, then the course towards a safe and prosperous future will be plotted.

Unfortunately, in the desire to keep Scilly unspoilt, the off islands of Agnes, Bryher and St. Martin's could well get the thin end of the wedge. They badly need a shot in the arm, and just because St. Mary's has already lost its Scillonian character because of too much building, it should not mean that the lesser islands should be the butts of a *laissez-faire* policy. Up to now they have had but a meagre nibble at the juicy tourist apple which has windfallen to St. Mary's and with flower farming uncertain their main hope lies on benefiting from the increasing numbers of tourists who prefer to stay on the off islands than on the more mainland-like environment of St. Mary's.

Perhaps the move which most significantly shows the council is aware of the situation was the engaging of Mr. G. A. Jellicoe, one of the country's top landscape architects. He prepared a "Landscape Charter for the Isles of Scilly", in which he planned the islands course ahead, suggesting both the areas and extent of development and the best ways of ensuring the islands have a safe future.

Assuming that the major points of the Charter are adopted by the council and that the Duchy and the authority subordinate their several little differences to the common aim of holding a course charted by such a celebrated landscape helmsman as Jellicoe, Scilly should be able to steer a safe way through the dangerous years that threaten, and give islanders a continuing standard of living which the tourist industry has of late brought them.

INDEX